America Online's
Creating Cool™
Web Pages

America Online's Creating Cool™ Web Pages

EDWARD WILLETT

IDG
BOOKS **IDG Books Worldwide, Inc.**
WORLDWIDE **An International Data Group Company**

Foster City, CA ♦ Chicago, IL ♦ Indianapolis, IN ♦ New York, NY

America Online's® Creating Cool™ Web Pages

Published by
IDG Books Worldwide, Inc.
An International Data Group Company
919 E. Hillsdale Blvd., Suite 400
Foster City, CA 94404
www.idgbooks.com (IDG Books Worldwide Web site)

Library of Congress Catalog Card No.: 97-078215

ISBN: 0-7645-3202-2

Printed in the United States of America

10 9 8 7 6 5 4 3 2 1

1B/RW/QX/ZY/FC

Distributed in the United States by IDG Books Worldwide, Inc.

Distributed by Macmillan Canada for Canada; by Transworld Publishers Limited in the United Kingdom; by IDG Norge Books for Norway; by IDG Sweden Books for Sweden; by Woodslane Pty. Ltd. for Australia; by Woodslane New Zealand Ltd. for New Zealand; by Addison Wesley Longman Singapore Pte Ltd. for Singapore, Malaysia, Thailand, and Indonesia; by Distribuidora Norma S.A.-Colombia for Colombia; by Intersoft for South Africa; by International Thomson Publishing for Germany, Austria, and Switzerland; by Toppan Company Ltd. for Japan; by Distribuidora Cuspide for Argentina; by Livraria Cultura for Brazil; by Ediciencia S.A. for Ecuador; by Addison-Wesley Publishing Company for Korea; by Ediciones ZETA S.C.R. Ltda. for Peru; by WS Computer Publishing Corporation, Inc., for the Philippines; by Unalis Corporation for Taiwan; by Contemporanea de Ediciones for Venezuela; by Computer Book & Magazine Store for Puerto Rico; by Express Computer Distributors for the Caribbean and West Indies. Authorized Sales Agent: Anthony Rudkin Associates for the Middle East and North Africa.

For general information on IDG Books Worldwide's books in the U.S., please call our Consumer Customer Service department at 800-762-2974. For reseller information, including discounts and premium sales, please call our Reseller Customer Service department at 800-434-3422.

For information on where to purchase IDG Books Worldwide's books outside the U.S., please contact our International Sales department at 650-655-3200 or fax 650-655-3297.

For information on foreign language translations, please contact our Foreign & Subsidiary Rights department at 650-655-3021 or fax 650-655-3281.

For sales inquiries and special prices for bulk quantities, please contact our Sales department at 650-655-3200 or write to the address above.

For information on using IDG Books Worldwide's books in the classroom or for ordering examination copies, please contact our Educational Sales department at 800-434-2086 or fax 317-596-5499.

For press review copies, author interviews, or other publicity information, please contact our Public Relations department at 650-655-3000 or fax 650-655-3299.

For authorization to photocopy items for corporate, personal, or educational use, please contact Copyright Clearance Center, 222 Rosewood Drive, Danvers, MA 01923, or fax 978-750-4470.

 is a trademark under exclusive license to IDG Books Worldwide, Inc., from International Data Group, Inc.

ABOUT IDG BOOKS WORLDWIDE

Welcome to the world of IDG Books Worldwide.

IDG Books Worldwide, Inc., is a subsidiary of International Data Group, the world's largest publisher of computer-related information and the leading global provider of information services on information technology. IDG was founded more than 25 years ago and now employs more than 8,500 people worldwide. IDG publishes more than 275 computer publications in over 75 countries (see listing below). More than 90 million people read one or more IDG publications each month.

Launched in 1990, IDG Books Worldwide is today the #1 publisher of best-selling computer books in the United States. We are proud to have received eight awards from the Computer Press Association in recognition of editorial excellence and three from *Computer Currents'* First Annual Readers' Choice Awards. Our best-selling ...For Dummies® series has more than 50 million copies in print with translations in 38 languages. IDG Books Worldwide, through a joint venture with IDG's Hi-Tech Beijing, became the first U.S. publisher to publish a computer book in the People's Republic of China. In record time, IDG Books Worldwide has become the first choice for millions of readers around the world who want to learn how to better manage their businesses.

Our mission is simple: Every one of our books is designed to bring extra value and skill-building instructions to the reader. Our books are written by experts who understand and care about our readers. The knowledge base of our editorial staff comes from years of experience in publishing, education, and journalism — experience we use to produce books for the '90s. In short, we care about books, so we attract the best people. We devote special attention to details such as audience, interior design, use of icons, and illustrations. And because we use an efficient process of authoring, editing, and desktop publishing our books electronically, we can spend more time ensuring superior content and spend less time on the technicalities of making books.

You can count on our commitment to deliver high-quality books at competitive prices on topics you want to read about. At IDG Books Worldwide, we continue in the IDG tradition of delivering quality for more than 25 years. You'll find no better book on a subject than one from IDG Books Worldwide.

John Kilcullen
CEO
IDG Books Worldwide, Inc.

Steven Berkowitz
President and Publisher
IDG Books Worldwide, Inc.

*Eighth Annual
Computer Press
Awards ≥1992*

*Ninth Annual
Computer Press
Awards ≥1993*

*Tenth Annual
Computer Press
Awards ≥1994*

*Eleventh Annual
Computer Press
Awards ≥1995*

IDG Books Worldwide, Inc., is a subsidiary of International Data Group, the world's largest publisher of computer-related information and the leading global provider of information services on information technology. International Data Group publishes over 275 computer publications in over 75 countries. More than 90 million people read one or more International Data Group publications each month. International Data Group's publications include: **ARGENTINA:** Buyer's Guide, Computerworld Argentina, PC World Argentina; **AUSTRALIA:** Australian Macworld, Australian PC World, Australian Reseller News, Computerworld, IT Casebook, Network World, Publish, Webmaster; **AUSTRIA:** Computerwelt Österreich, Networks Austria, PC Tip Austria; **BANGLADESH:** PC World Bangladesh; **BELARUS:** PC World Belarus; **BELGIUM:** Data News; **BRAZIL:** Annuário de Informática, Computerworld, Connections, Macworld, PC Player, PC World, Publish, Reseller News, Supergamepower; **BULGARIA:** Computerworld Bulgaria, Network World Bulgaria, PC & MacWorld Bulgaria; **CANADA:** CIO Canada, Client/Server World, ComputerWorld Canada, InfoWorld Canada, NetworkWorld Canada, WebWorld; **CHILE:** Computerworld Chile, PC World Chile; **COLOMBIA:** Computerworld Colombia, PC World Colombia; **COSTA RICA:** PC World Centro America; **THE CZECH AND SLOVAK REPUBLICS:** Computerworld Czechoslovakia, Macworld Czech Republic, PC World Czechoslovakia; **DENMARK:** Communications World Danmark, Computerworld Danmark, Macworld Danmark, PC World Danmark, Techworld Denmark; **DOMINICAN REPUBLIC:** PC World Republica Dominicana; **ECUADOR:** PC World Ecuador; **EGYPT:** Computerworld Middle East, PC World Middle East; **EL SALVADOR:** PC World Centro America; **FINLAND:** MikroPC, Tietoverkko, Tietoviikko; **FRANCE:** Distributique, Hebdo, Info PC, Le Monde Informatique, Macworld, Reseaux & Telecoms, WebMaster France; **GERMANY:** Computer Partner, Computerwoche, Computerwoche Extra, Computerwoche FOCUS, Global Online, Macwelt, PC Welt; **GREECE:** Amiga Computing, GamePro Greece, Multimedia World; **GUATEMALA:** PC World Centro America; **HONDURAS:** PC World Centro America; **HONG KONG:** Computerworld Hong Kong, PC World Hong Kong, Publish in Asia; **HUNGARY:** ABCD CD-ROM, Computerworld Szamitastechnika, Internetto online Magazine, PC World Hungary, PC-X Magazin Hungary; **ICELAND:** Tolvuheimur PC World Island; **INDIA:** Information Communications World, Information Systems Computerworld, PC World India, Publish in Asia; **INDONESIA:** InfoKomputer PC World, Komputek Computerworld, Publish in Asia; **IRELAND:** ComputerScope, PC Live!; **ISRAEL:** Macworld Israel, People & Computers/Computerworld; **ITALY:** Computerworld Italia, Macworld Italia, Networking Italia, PC World Italia; **JAPAN:** DTP World, Macworld Japan, Nikkei Personal Computing, OS/2 World Japan, SunWorld Japan, Windows NT World, Windows World Japan; **KENYA:** PC World East African; **KOREA:** Hi-Tech Information, Macworld Korea, PC World Korea; **MACEDONIA:** PC World Macedonia; **MALAYSIA:** Computerworld Malaysia, PC World Malaysia, Publish in Asia; **MALTA:** PC World Malta; **MEXICO:** Computerworld Mexico, PC World Mexico; **MYANMAR:** PC World Myanmar; **NETHERLANDS:** Computer! Totaal, LAN Internetworking Magazine, LAN World Buyers Guide, Macworld Netherlands, Net, WebWereld; **NEW ZEALAND:** Absolute Beginners Guide and Plain & Simple Series, Computer Buyer, Computer Industry Directory, Computerworld New Zealand, MTB, Network World, PC World New Zealand; **NICARAGUA:** PC World Centro America; **NORWAY:** Computerworld Norge, CW Rapport, Datamagasinet, Financial Rapport, Kursguide Norge, Macworld Norge, Multimediaworld Norge, PC World Ekspress Norge, PC World Nettverk, PC World Norge, PC World ProduktGuide Norge; **PAKISTAN:** Computerworld Pakistan; **PANAMA:** PC World Panama; **PEOPLE'S REPUBLIC OF CHINA:** China Computer Users, China Computerworld, China InfoWorld, China Telecom World Weekly, Computer & Communication, Electronic Design China, Electronics Today, Electronics Weekly, Game Software, PC World China, Popular Computer Week, Software Weekly, Software World, Telecom World; **PERU:** Computerworld Peru, PC World Profesional Peru, PC World SoHo Peru; **PHILIPPINES:** Click!, Computerworld Philippines, PC World Philippines, Publish in Asia; **POLAND:** Computerworld Poland, Computerworld Special Report Poland, Cyber, Macworld Poland, Networld Poland, PC World Komputer; **PORTUGAL:** Cerebro/PC World, Computerworld/Correio Informático, Dealer World Portugal, Mac*In/PC*In Portugal, Multimedia World; **PUERTO RICO:** PC World Puerto Rico; **ROMANIA:** Computerworld Romania, PC World Romania, Telecom Romania; **RUSSIA:** Computerworld Russia, Mir PK, Publish, Seti; **SINGAPORE:** Computerworld Singapore, PC World Singapore, Publish in Asia; **SLOVENIA:** Monitor; **SOUTH AFRICA:** Computing SA, Network World SA, Software World SA; **SPAIN:** Communicaciones World España, Computerworld España, Dealer World España, Macworld España, PC World España; **SRI LANKA:** Infolink PC World; **SWEDEN:** CAP&Design, Computer Sweden, Corporate Computing Sweden, it branschen, Macworld Sweden, MaxiData Sweden, MikroDatorn, Natverk & Kommunikation, PC World Sweden, PCaktiv, Windows World Sweden; **SWITZERLAND:** Computerworld Schweiz, Macworld Schweiz, PCtip; **TAIWAN:** Computerworld Taiwan, Macworld Taiwan, NEW ViSiON/Publish, PC World Taiwan, Windows World Taiwan; **THAILAND:** Publish in Asia, Thai Computerworld; **TURKEY:** Computerworld Turkiye, Macworld Turkiye, Network World Turkiye, PC World Turkiye; **UKRAINE:** Computerworld Kiev, Multimedia World Ukraine, PC World Ukraine; **UNITED KINGDOM:** Acorn User UK, Amiga Action UK, Amiga Computing UK, Apple Talk UK, Computing, Macworld, Parents and Computers UK, PC Advisor, PC Home, PSX Pro, The WEB; **UNITED STATES:** Cable in the Classroom, CIO Magazine, Computerworld, DOS World, Federal Computer Week, GamePro Magazine, InfoWorld, I-Way, Macworld, Network World, PC Games, PC World, Publish, Video Event, THE WEB Magazine, and WebMaster; online webzines: JavaWorld, NetscapeWorld, and SunWorld Online; **URUGUAY:** InfoWorld Uruguay; **VENEZUELA:** Computerworld Venezuela, PC World Venezuela; and **VIETNAM:** PC World Vietnam. 5/7/98

Credits

Acquisitions Editor
Andy Cummings

Development Editor
Katharine Dvorak

Technical Editors
Teri Deal
Brad Schepp

Copy Editor
Timothy Borek

Project Coordinator
Ritchie Durdin

**Graphics and
Production Specialists**
Stephanie Hollier
Jude Levinson
E. A. Pauw

Graphics Technicians
Linda Marousek
Hector Mendoza

Quality Control Specialists
Mick Arellano
Mark Schumann

Proofreader
David Wise

Indexer
James Minkin

About the Author

Edward Willett has used online services since the late 1980s and has been a member of AOL for years. A journalist by training, Ed was a newspaper reporter and editor for several years, and he currently writes a science column for several Canadian newspapers. Ed is also the author of several computer books (most recently co-authoring IDG Books Worldwide's *Internet Bible*) and science fiction and fantasy novels.

To Dan Wieb, my high school English teacher, for encouraging me to write. Just think how many writing books this would have filled!

Preface

The World Wide Web is aptly named. Like the web of a spider snares a fly, the World Wide Web has a way of snaring the imagination of those who enter it. Some are content with merely surfing through its twisting strands, but many people, on seeing the incredible variety of pages now linked to the Web, are immediately struck by one burning thought: "I gotta get me one of those!"

A lot of these people who have suddenly realized how empty life without a personal Web page can be are America Online (AOL) members. This is not surprising, as AOL is the largest online service in the world, with more than 12 million members, and was the first online service to offer members easy access to the Internet. AOL has also made it easy for its members to create their own Web pages by providing each screen name with 2MB of storage space, and most important, by creating an easy, wizard-based program for creating Web pages called Personal Publisher.

America Online's Creating Cool Web Pages is really two books in one. It not only teaches you the ins and outs of using Personal Publisher 3, the most full-featured, easy-to-use version of AOL's Web design program yet, but it also covers the basic principles of Web page design so that the pages you create will be purposeful, pleasing, and popular with friends, family, and strangers alike.

The World Wide Web is an amazing medium. It is young (conceived less than ten years ago), yet growing by phenomenal leaps and bounds every day. It's a place where anyone with something to say can say it, where individual creativity can flourish, where people from around the world with similar interests can form virtual "cyberhoods" woven together by the insubstantial links between their Web pages.

As an AOL member, you can become one of the hundreds of thousands of people all over the planet who are helping to mold the infant Web into . . . *something*. No one knows what the Web will become, and that's why it's so exciting to be a part of it now, when each new contribution to its links helps to shape its intriguing future. The possibilities are mind-boggling — the potential, enormous. Give your imagination free reign, and with the help of AOL and Personal Publisher 3, spin your own multicolored strand into the fabric of the World Wide Web.

About the Book

I've tried to make *America Online's Creating Cool Web Pages* both informative and interesting, with lots of practical, hands-on examples of how to use Personal Publisher, lots of pointers to additional resources on creating Web pages, and lots of examples of interesting pages from all over the Web.

I start at the very beginning (a very good place to start) with an introduction to the World Wide Web (Chapter 1, "Oh What a Tangled Web We Weave"), and then plunge right into using Personal Publisher 3, though not without a quick look back at Personal Publisher 2 and how Personal Publisher 3 has added to its functionality. If you're in a real hurry, you can create a quick Web page in Chapter 3, "Create a Personal Web Page in Five Minutes." If you have more time, you may want to explore Personal Publisher's possibilities in detail in the ensuing chapters.

You learn how to write and edit text for your Web page, insert your own graphics, add links to pictures and text, add lists, and link to sound and video files. You even learn how to make other types of files, such as word processor files, available for downloading.

Once you get a good handle on Personal Publisher, I focus in detail on how to create some of the specific types of pages that are among the most popular: personal pages (all about you!), pages for small business, and kids' pages, providing a ten-point quality-control checklist for each. But don't feel limited to one of these types of pages; anything can be the basis of a Web page, as I prove with a whirlwind tour of some of the many unique pages people have posted to the Web (Chapter 14, "A Page for Every Passion").

Finally, you look at what to do after your Web page is up: how to keep it fresh, how to keep it evolving, and how to promote it so other people pay it a visit. I also point you to other books and online resources that you can draw on when you're ready to try more complicated Web designs than you can achieve with Personal Publisher.

What You Need to Use This Book

You need just three things to get the most out of *America Online's Creating Cool Web Pages*:

An AOL Account

Chances are you already have this, as you've just bought a book about creating cool Web pages, but if you don't, you can sign up for AOL online at http://www.aol.com.

America Online 4.0

This is the most recent version of the AOL interface, and Personal Publisher 3 won't work without it. If you're still using AOL 3.0, you need to upgrade.

Personal Publisher 3

You can download Personal Publisher 3 for free from AOL. Go to keyword **PP3** and follow the instructions for downloading. It should take less than 10 minutes with a 28.8 Kbps or better modem. It installs automatically, and you can begin using it at once with no need to restart AOL 4.0.

About You

I wrote *America Online's Creating Cool Web Pages* for any AOL member who wants to have his or her own Web page for any reason—personal, business, whatever—but who doesn't quite know how to begin. If the thought of learning HTML intimidates you (or, more likely, simply bores you), or if you've held off on creating a Web page because you just didn't want to spend the hours and hours you've been told it will take, then this book is for you. Creating a good-looking, fully functional Web page has never been easier than AOL has made it with Personal Publisher 3. There's absolutely no reason why anyone with an AOL membership who wants to have a Web page shouldn't have one, and this book can help.

Even people who have already created Web pages using Personal Publisher 2 or some other tool can benefit from this book. The sections on good Web page design are applicable to everyone, whether they're creating their first Web page or their one hundred first.

About Me

Basically I'm just like you. I was fascinated by the Web from the moment I saw it and had my first home page up and running just as soon as it was possible. Since then I've expanded and improved my site several times, using a variety of tools, from raw HTML to top-end Web-page design software. All I can say is that I wish Personal Publisher had been around when I struggled through that first home page years ago!

I've used online services since the late 1980s and have been a member of AOL for years. I use the Web, too, constantly, as a source of information for my many forms of writing. I'm a journalist by training (I was a newspaper reporter and editor for several years) and currently write a science column for several Canadian newspapers, as well as computer books and science fiction and fantasy novels. In other words, I'm a writer, and as a writer, I believe the Web is far more important as a means of communication than as an entertainment medium. I believe in the importance of content — of substance over style — something I've tried to emphasize throughout this book.

I'm also a professional singer and actor, so I'm not going to denigrate the importance of entertainment! Multimedia, animation, fancy graphics — they, too, play an important role in this new medium. The trick, as in performing a humorous play about a serious subject (or vice versa) — or in walking a tightrope, for that matter — is to find the correct balance.

How This Book Is Organized

America Online's Creating Cool Web Pages is organized into the following 16 chapters and two appendixes:

Chapter 1: Oh, What a Tangled Web We Weave

You have questions, I have answers. I explain what the World Wide Web is, what it's good for, how it's different from AOL, how you access it, and why you might want your own Web page.

Chapter 2: What's New in Personal Publisher 3

Personal Publisher 3 is the most advanced version of AOL's Personal Publisher Web design software yet. In this chapter you look at some of the improvements over Personal Publisher 2.

Chapter 3: Create a Personal Web Page in Five Minutes

If you just can't wait any longer, this chapter runs you quickly through the step-by-step process of creating a personal Web page in Personal Publisher. It may take a little longer than 5 minutes — but not much!

Chapter 4: A Template for All Seasons

Personal Publisher is based on *templates* — completed Web pages into which you can plug your own graphics and text, replacing what's already there. In this chapter you look at some of the templates Personal Publisher provides.

Chapter 5: Advanced Options

If you want more control over your Web page design than Personal Publisher seems to provide at first glance, you can have it by calling on the Advanced Options. With these controls activated, you can create a customized color scheme, add links to anything you want, format your graphics — even rotate or flip them — and adjust indents and alignment.

Chapter 6: Managing Your Pages

Once your Web page is finished, you need to publish it to the Web. Learn how to save, publish, and unpublish pages in this chapter, plus how to edit completed pages and link several pages together into a unified Web site.

Chapter 7: Web Publishing Resources on AOL

There's a lot of support for Personal Publisher on AOL, whether you're looking for answers to questions about the program or suggested ways to improve Web pages created using it. I also point you in the direction of several sources of graphics and other Web page elements available on AOL.

Chapter 8: Text and Hypertext

You begin your look at the basic elements of every Web page with the one I consider most important: text. Text, not graphics, ultimately communicates your message, so you should spend just as much time getting it right as you do making graphics eye-catching and trendy. As well, this chapter looks at the idea of hypertext — the capability that can link any page to any other page that makes the Web a web, so it's important to choose those links carefully!

Chapter 9: Graphics

There are whole books devoted to the topic of Web graphics, but here's a single chapter that covers some of the most important considerations: how to balance the need for graphics (because text by itself, however vital its message, is boring) with the need to have a page that loads in a reasonable amount of time, where to find graphics for your page, and the importance of obeying copyright laws.

Chapter 10: Multimedia —
The Extra Dimension

When are sound files, video files and animated GIFs a plus, and when are they just a drag on your page's loading time? This chapter looks at how and when to use multimedia elements — and when to avoid them.

Chapter 11: Creating Cool Personal
Web Pages

Most people's first Web page is about the topic they know best: themselves. Making that topic interesting to other people is the challenge of creating a Personal Home Page. This chapter gives you a ten-point checklist to consider, and points you in the direction of some interesting personal home pages on the Web, so you can see what others have done.

Chapter 12: Creating Cool Small-Business Pages

Maybe you never thought of putting a page about your home (or small) business on the Web—but maybe you should. This chapter explores some of the ways businesses are using the Web, and provides a ten-point checklist to help you decide what your business Web site should contain. Finally it points you to some examples of business pages on the Web, so you can see how others have done it.

Chapter 13: Creating Cool Kids' Pages

If you want kids to visit your page, you have to work twice as hard to make it interesting. If you're a kid yourself, you may even have an edge over adults, because you already know what kids like yourself find interesting. Whatever your age, you can benefit from the ten-point checklist on creating a kids' page and the criteria used by the American Library Association to decide which kids' pages qualify as "great sites." Then take a look at some examples of great sites to get some ideas for your own.

Chapter 14: A Page for Every Passion

The World Wide Web is also the Wide Open Web (which, you'll notice, forms the appropriate acronym *WOW*—think it'll catch on?). Anything you're interested in can be the basis for a fascinating Web page that will illuminate others and could lead you to people who share your passions. Follow the ten-point checklist that applies to every Web page, then follow the Web to a selection of interesting sites on topics ranging from collecting playing cards to werewolves.

Chapter 15: Your Online Hometown

America Online is based on the concept of community, and with Personal Publisher 3, AOL hopes its members will begin to form more and more "cyberhoods"—virtual communities of shared interests—on the Web. But in order to build a cyberhood, you need to be able to make connections with other Web-page creators. In this chapter you look at searching the Web for pages similar to your own, using AOL's NetFind and other Internet search engines, and at some ways to promote your page and draw interested visitors to it.

Chapter 16: Keeping Your Page Fresh

There's nothing worse than a stale Web page! In this chapter you learn how and why to keep your page fresh and alive. You learn about the revolutionary Theory of Web Evolution, and track down and eliminate the dread "Not Found" message before one of your visitors is snared by it.

Appendix A: Learning More About Web Page Design

Aha, Web designing has you hooked, doesn't it? Don't worry; it happens to a lot of us. When you're ready to move on from Personal Publisher 3, this appendix can help by pointing you to books, AOL resources, and Web resources for more information on all elements of Web design, from the simple to the complex.

Appendix B: Gallery of Cool Web Pages from AOL Members

Glossary

How to Reach Me

Want to contact me? You can send e-mail to ewillett@sk.sympatico.ca, or visit my home page on the Web at http://www.sk.sympatico.ca/ ewillett.

The Web awaits your contribution. Let's get started.

Acknowledgments

Many thanks to my editors: Andy Cummings, for giving me the opportunity to do this book and working hard to make it happen, and Katharine Dvorak, for calmly keeping afloat in the sea of e-mails and helping shape this book into its finished form. Thanks also to Brad Schepp and J. P. Tierney at AOL for all their help, and very warm thanks to all the talented designers who allowed me to include their Web pages in my book.

Contents at a Glance

Table of Contents

Oh, What a Tangled Web We Weave

In This Chapter

What is the World Wide Web?

How do I access the Web?

Why would I want my own Web page, anyway?

You can't look at an advertisement, pick up a book or CD-ROM, or go to a movie these days without seeing it: a string of words separated by periods and slashes, starting with three little letters: *www*. Those three little letters are supposed to tell you that the advertiser, publisher, music company, or studio is hip, happening, with it, and wired. Those three little letters are pointing you to an address on the *World Wide Web*, a "place" where visitors can get more information about that particular product via their own computer, assuming their computer is hooked up to a modem and they have access to the Internet. Well, guess what? You, too, can join the hip, happening, with-it, and wired set by creating your own page on the World Wide Web, using the easiest method going: America Online's Personal Publisher 3, which makes Web page design as easy as plugging your own text and pictures into an existing template. But before we get to that, perhaps a little background is in order.

What Is the World Wide Web?

The World Wide Web enables someone using a computer hooked up to the network (you, for instance) to get his or her hands on information contained on another computer hooked up to the network, anywhere in the world—without necessarily having to know where that second computer is (see Figure 1-1).

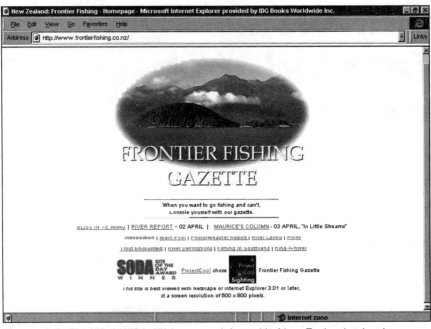

Figure 1-1: This World Wide Web page originated in New Zealand — but it doesn't make any difference to my computer. Copyright Marc Cohen, NZ Country Matters, LTD.

The network in question is the Internet. The World Wide Web has become so front-and-center in any discussion of the Internet that many people think the two terms are synonymous — but they're not. The Internet predates the World Wide Web by decades.

An extremely short history of the Internet

The Internet grew out of ARPANET (ARPA stands for *Advanced Research Projects Agency*), a U.S. military project of the late 1960s. ARPANET linked defense companies and universities that were doing military-related research. Nonmilitary corporate and university sites soon came online. Other countries created similar networks, networks linked to networks, and so grew the Internet, an amorphous network of thousands of interlinked computers.

Its decentralized structure is a result of its birth as a military project. The idea of the original ARPANET was to create a network that could survive a nuclear war. Thanks to the way information is passed around on the Internet (parts of a message may follow a variety of paths to arrive at their destination), the loss of a computer here or a phone line there causes no disruption; information simply routes around it.

Until 1993 the Internet was used almost exclusively by computer scientists and university professors and students (there are probably quite a few of them who wish that was still the case!). But the cozy primordial soup of the Internet eventually gave rise to a whole new form of online life — the World Wide Web.

The birth of the World Wide Web

The World Wide Web began in March, 1989, at the European Laboratory for Particle Physics (CERN), located near Geneva, Switzerland, and France. At CERN physicists from all over the world collaborate on complex physics, engineering, and information-handling projects (see Figure 1-2).

Figure 1-2: The home page of CERN (http://www.cern.com), birthplace of the World Wide Web.

Because the physicists involved in these projects are often scattered all over the world (and there's a huge turnover of the ones who are there), the physicists at CERN needed a good way to get up to speed quickly on projects when they arrived and to leave a lasting contribution behind before departing.

The system they came up with was the World Wide Web (a name chosen by one of the original programmers, Tim Berners-Lee, over other contenders such as "Information Mesh," "Mine of Information," and "Information Mine"). It was built around *hypertext*; words and phrases in one document could be linked to other, related documents, so that a scientist reading about a particular high-energy physics project, for example, could easily call up any related notes, diagrams, or mathematical data that might also be stored on one of the networked computers (see Figure 1-3).

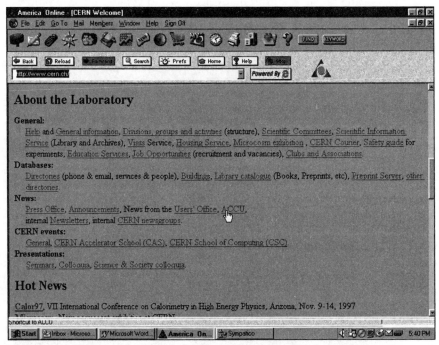

Figure 1-3: Clicking the highlighted text on this page will take you to another page with more information about that topic. That's hypertext!

If use of the system had been limited to people actually at CERN, probably nobody outside of CERN would ever have heard of it. But to make it easier for scientists all over the world to work on their CERN projects, it was connected to the Internet — and began to grow. Rapidly.

There were two good reasons for that. One reason is that CERN made the source code for the software behind the new system publicly available, and encouraged others in both the academic and commercial fields to emulate it. The second reason is that one of the basic principles of the Web's design was that users should be able to add new material to it.

That they have done, with a vengeance. Today millions of people surf the Web every day, and of those, hundreds of thousands have linked documents, called *Web pages*, of their own creation to it. And among those Web pages are thousands created by America Online users with Personal Publisher.

These Web pages are a far cry from the straight-text documents available when the Web was created. Today's Web pages include color, pictures, animation, sound, interactive games, video, and even virtual-reality simulation. In fact, just about anything you can think of can be added to a World Wide Web page. Which brings us to . . .

What good is the Web?

The uses of the World Wide Web are limited only by your own imagination.

Okay, okay, I know: while that may be true, it's also such a wishy-washy statement as to be useless. Which is why, in this book, I focus on the following four things for which you might want to use the World Wide Web:

➡ **Personal home pages.** Isn't it about time the world knew what a special person you are? Tell them about it! A personal home page can include a biography, photographs of you and your family, information about your hobbies or other interests, your up-to-the-minute resume (useful for pointing prospective employers to), and links to some of your favorite places on the World Wide Web. My Web page, for example (see Figure 1-4), includes samples of my weekly newspaper science column, some of my short fiction, photographs from various musicals and operas I've been in, two resumes (one for my writing career and one for my performing career), and pages of links to sites I've found of interest, complete with a comment about each one.

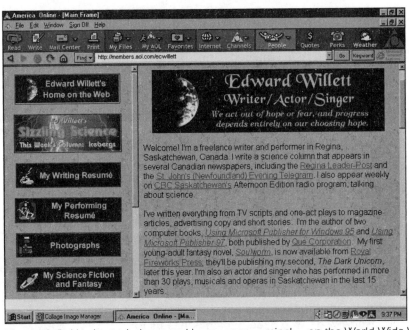

Figure 1-4: Here's a typical personal home page — mine! — on the World Wide Web.

➡ **Kids' pages.** Kids' pages can be created *for* kids — by parents or by teachers, for example. Or they can be created *by* kids, especially with the help of Personal Publisher 3. In the former case, it takes clever writing and page design to hold kids' interest. In the latter case, the World Wide Web provides a new outlet for childhood creativity. Some kids are even putting up Web pages as part of school projects (see Figure 1-5), and, through the Web, making connections with other children around the world.

➡ **Home business pages.** Home businesses are the wave of the future — and the present. More and more people are setting up home businesses: some because they're tired of looking for a job and decide to create their own, some because they're seeking a second income, and some just because they want to be their own bosses. Whatever the reason you set up your home business, you face the same problem small businesses have always faced: letting people know about what you have to offer. A page on the World Wide Web won't replace traditional advertising methods, but it can put you in contact with customers all over the world who otherwise might never have known you existed. You can even sell your products online (see Figure 1-6).

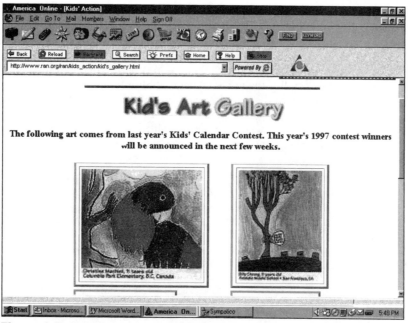

Figure 1-5: Children love exploring, and adding to, the World Wide Web.

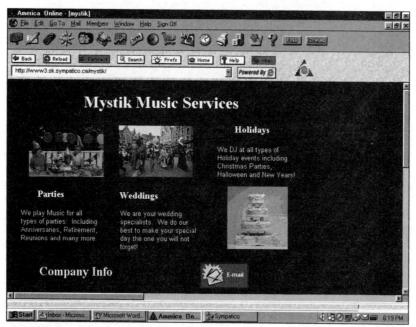

Figure 1-6: A page on the World Wide Web is like a virtual storefront for your home-based business.

➡️ **Special-interest pages.** These aren't Web pages put up by the "special interests" politicians who always claim are behind other politicians' campaigns (but never, somehow, their own!). By *special interest*, I mean those things that fascinate you. Maybe you're an expert in Xijing pottery (the coolest teapots you can imagine) or you're dying to share your enthusiasm for the vocal stylings of Slim Whitman with the world. Or maybe you're the founder and chair of the Society for the Preservation of Daisy-Wheel Printers. Whatever your special interest, a World Wide Web page is a great way not only to share your knowledge with others but also to find other people who have the same passions (see Figure 1-7).

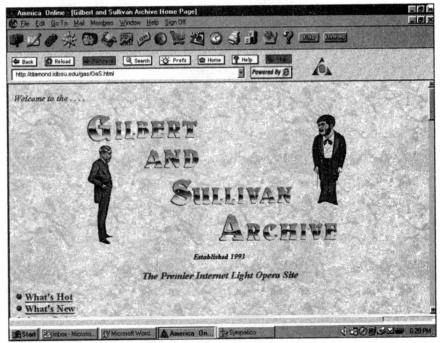

Figure 1-7: People devote pages to almost anything you can imagine, and more than a few things you can't, on the World Wide Web.

What Is America Online?

In the beginning, back when Internet access was something only the government and universities had and the World Wide Web had yet to be invented, there was, nevertheless, an online community, tenuously connected by 300 bps modems. The early pioneers into cyberspace were early subscribers to *online services*, companies that operated independent networks that provided news, e-mail, discussion groups, files for downloading, and other such online services to its subscribers.

America Online (AOL), founded in 1985 and headquartered in Dulles, Virginia, was one of those services and one of the first online services to provide easy Internet access. Since then it has become more and more popular, until today, with more than 12 million members worldwide, it's the planet's largest online service provider.

How Is the Web Different from AOL?

The World Wide Web and America Online (AOL) both make vast amounts of information, including text, graphics, computer programs, and more, readily available to millions of people. So what's the difference?

One word: *organization*. America Online is a commercial service with a corporate structure and a plethora of staff members, everyone from graphic designers to programmers, whose goal is to channel information to subscribers in an organized fashion. They even call the categories into which they organize information *channels* (see Figure 1-8). Also, America Online serves as an editor: it selects the information that is available on America Online and maintains some control over its quality and presentation.

Figure 1-8: AOL's channels: a level of organization you're not going to find on the World Wide Web.

The World Wide Web, by contrast, isn't as structured. No one's in charge. In most cases, nobody is vetting the information that is available at the click of a mouse button. And just about anyone who has access to the Web also has the capability to add to it — with nobody telling him or her whether something is appropriate or just a waste of data storage.

You could think of America Online as a clean, neat, well-lighted city (such things must exist somewhere!), and the World Wide Web as the tangled, disorderly wilderness surrounding it. You can live happily in the city without ever venturing beyond its limits, and many do, but you're missing out on the beauty and excitement found in the wilds.

Of course, it's also worth noting that you're missing out on a lot of nasty stuff. Like any wilderness, the World Wide Web has its share of slimy things hiding under rocks (pornographers, racists, and terrorists, to name a few), whereas in the city of AOL, such things are generally exterminated. But unless you actually make a point of turning over rocks and searching for those slimy things, you're unlikely to stumble across them.

America Online makes it simple to jump to Web sites that interest you. You can easily find yourself on a Web page without even realizing you've left AOL. Which brings us to the next obvious question . . .

How Do I Access the World Wide Web?

To view World Wide Web pages, you have to have a piece of software called a *browser*. No need to go looking for one, though; AOL has one of the best, Microsoft's Internet Explorer, built right in.

To call up a page on the World Wide Web, you first have to know the address of the Web page, also known as the *Uniform Resource Locator* (URL). World Wide Web addresses all begin with `http://`, followed by a string of words and punctuation of varying length. Generally, the `http://` is followed by `www`, a period, then a *domain name*. The address of America Online's World Wide Web site, for example, is `www.aol.com` (see Figure 1-9).

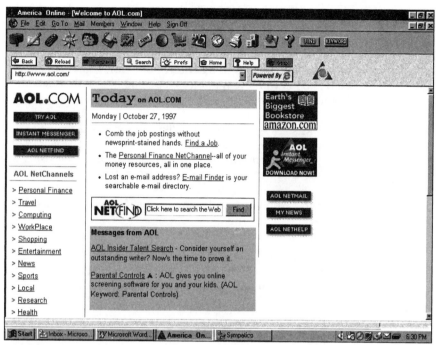

Figure 1-9: AOL isn't the same thing as the World Wide Web, but it has its own site on the Web.

Web page? Web site? What's the difference?

You'll notice throughout this book that I sometimes refer to a Web page; sometimes I refer to a Web site. The difference is simple: a Web *page* is a single HTML document on the Web. A Web *site*, on the other hand, is a collection of several HTML documents, usually linked together and accesible from a primary, or "home" page.

When you visit a Web site, you usually start at this home page, but every Web page in a Web site has its own address and can be accesssed independently of the other pages in the site — if you know that address!

With Personal Publisher 3, you can create a single Web page or a series of linked pages that together form a Web site.

The domain name basically tells the browser on which of the many computers connected to the World Wide Web the information is located. If you just want to see the index, or "home" page of that Web site, that's all you need. Sometimes, though, the URL is much longer; in that case, the rest of it usually consists of a series of directories and subdirectories, and sometimes ends with the name of a specific file on that distant computer which you want to view.

Locating URLs for Web sites you'd like to visit is made easier by software called *search engines*, which scour the Web for sites which contain specific words or phrases you provide. For more information on using search engines, see Chapter 15, "Your Online Hometown."

Accessing the Web via AOL is simple; just follow these steps:

1. **Log on to America Online.**

2. **Type the URL into the space provided in the toolbar, where it currently says, "Type Keyword or Web Address here and click Go." If you do not have a specific URL in mind, click the Internet icon (the globe) on the toolbar.**

3. **Click Go.**

Voila! You're on the World Wide Web.

Once you've explored the Web a bit and have seen pages other people have created, the chances are, you'll find yourself itching to have your own Web page. When I first got on the Web a couple of years ago, it took me all of about a day to feel the urge to create my own page. You may be more resistant — it may take you two.

AOL knows you're itching to make your presence known in cyberspace, and so it's provided a way to scratch that itch. Every AOL subscriber has two megabytes of storage space set aside where they can set up their own contribution to the World Wide Web — and with Personal Publisher 3, AOL has made it easier than ever to create sharp-looking pages that tell the whole online world that you're a happening dude (or dudette). Currently, you must be using AOL 4.0 to access Personal Publisher 3.

Yes, you too can create cool Web pages on AOL. All you need is an AOL membership — and this book.

Have both of them? Good! Then let's get cracking.

Summary

The World Wide Web is an amazing phenomenon. Although it's only a few years old, it now boasts millions of users who surf its hundreds of thousands of sites for information and entertainment. America Online makes it easy for its members to explore the Web — and, with the development of Personal Publisher 3, easy for members just like you to create their own Web pages.

What's New in Personal Publisher 3

2

In This Chapter

A word about Personal Publisher 2

All the new bells and whistles in Personal Publisher 3

As I mention in the previous chapter, I'd barely started surfing the World Wide Web before I had a hankering to create my own Web page. It's a hankering shared by hundreds of thousands of America Online members, and as AOL began opening up the Web to its users, they made their hankerings known. AOL responded with its first easy-to-use Web-page-publishing tool, Personal Publisher 1. Eventually, that evolved into Personal Publisher 2, which had many more capabilities than Personal Publisher 1 while keeping the same ease of use. Now comes Personal Publisher 3, which has even more capabilities than the two versions before it. In this chapter I take a quick look at Personal Publisher 2 before giving you a brief overview of what's new in Personal Publisher 3. (For a more detailed look at the new features, obviously, you have to read the rest of the book!)

A Word about Personal Publisher 2

AOL realized early on that its members wanted to be able to create nice-looking, useful Web pages that they could share with friends and family (and others who shared their interests) without knowing anything about Web publishing and without spending more than a few minutes. It seemed to AOL that the best way to do that was with a "wizard"-based publishing tool.

Wizards are the computer programs that take you through what might otherwise be a complicated process — say, installing a game or plugging in a new video card — step by easy step. Most computer users are familiar with them and used to working with them. When you installed AOL itself, for instance, a wizard guided you through the process, telling you to input information at certain points, to click OK, giving you options, and eventually telling you that the program was successfully installed.

By applying the wizard concept to Web publishing, AOL made it possible for any user, no matter how much of a novice, to make a nice-looking, basic Web page.

Personal Publisher 2 is simplicity itself. From the very first screen (see Figure 2-1), it keeps the process as simple as pointing, clicking, and typing—tasks even a beginning computer user has to already be familiar with by the time they've logged on to AOL!

Figure 2-1: Personal Publisher 2 welcomes you with the friendly suggestion to "Create a Page."

You can literally create a Web page in 60 seconds (albeit not one with very much content). First, you're invited to choose a template: personal, business, or greeting, depending on the purpose of your page (see Figure 2-2).

Next, you're invited to enter a title for your page (the default title of *Your Screen Name's Home Page* means you don't even have to go to that much effort if you don't want to) and a headline, which will show up in bold type at the top of your page (see Figure 2-3).

Background color or images and text color are only a click away on the next screen (see Figure 2-4).

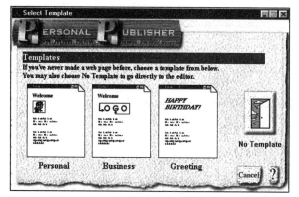

Figure 2-2: Personal Publisher 2 offers three templates — and the daring "No Template" for those who know a little HTML.

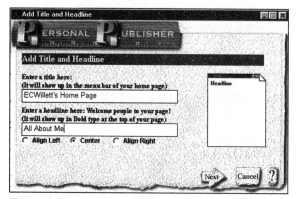

Figure 2-3: Next, Personal Publisher 2 prompts you to enter a title and a headline for your Web page.

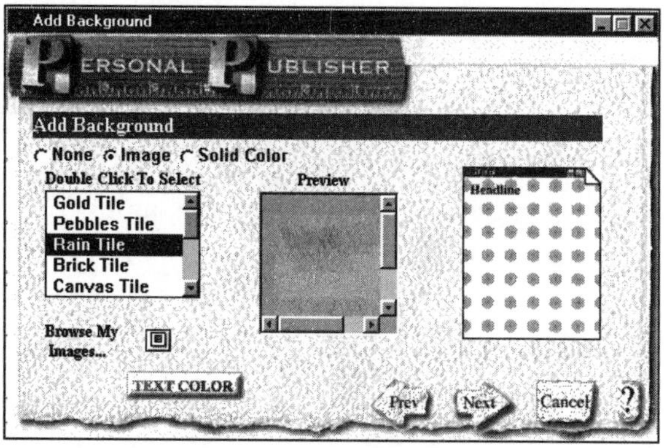

Figure 2-4: Use one of the backgrounds provided or apply your own, and set the colors of your text.

Add an image, either one AOL offers or one of your own (see Figure 2-5) . . .

Figure 2-5: Maybe in the early days you could get by with just text, but now everyone expects you to have pictures on your Web page!

. . . provide information about your location and hobbies (see Figure 2-6) . . .

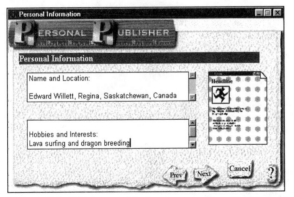

Figure 2-6: Tell the world about yourself — or, if you prefer, make something up.

. . . write out the story of your life — or whatever else you'd like to say — and add links to some of your favorite places (see Figure 2-7).

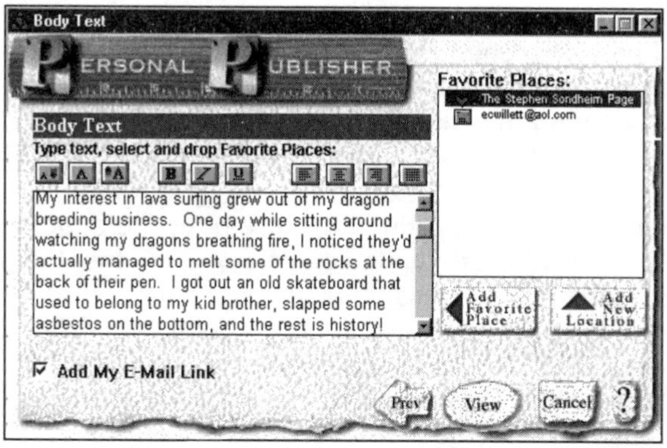

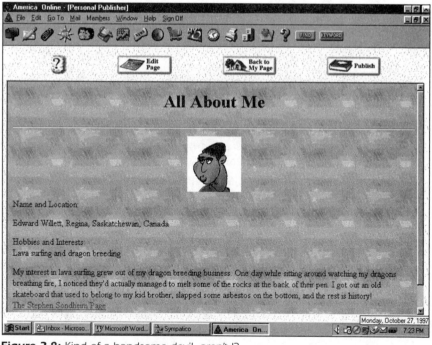

Figure 2-7: Okay, I made up the lava-surfing bit. But my real life is so boring.

Click View, and there you have it! Your very own (albeit very basic) Web page (see Figure 2-8). Click Publish, and away it goes to the Web for the enjoyment of anyone who happens to come across it.

Figure 2-8: Kind of a handsome devil, aren't I?

You can also click Edit to change any of the information you put on the page and/or add new elements: additional pictures, headlines, and so on. This makes it easy to review and update your page on a regular basis. (For more information on the importance of keeping your Web page up to date, and ways to do so, see Chapter 16, "Keeping Your Page Fresh.")

Personal Publisher 2's strengths include its ease of use, the fact that pages can be published to the Web with a single click, and the fact that it provides basic artwork. But for all its success, Personal Publisher 2 also has its drawbacks: making it easy to use also limited what it could do. Also, you must be logged on to AOL to use it, and it doesn't provide a simple way to manage a multitude of Web pages (it doesn't take long for users to feel the limitations of having just one page!).

To coincide (more or less) with the rollout of its new interface, AOL 4.0, AOL decided it was time to improve Personal Publisher, too.

What's New in Personal Publisher 3

In enhancing Personal Publisher, AOL made several important changes. The most important enhancement is the creation of many more templates, for everything from a home page for your pet to resume pages, photo albums, and sports pages. Also, Personal Publisher 3 can

➡ **read HTML.** *Hypertext Markup Language* (HTML) is the language that Web pages are *really* written in, even if they're created with a wizard-based system like Personal Publisher. Personal Publisher 3 can read HTML, unlike Personal Publisher 2, which means members can use it to edit Web pages created by other HTML editors or to use other editors to edit Web pages created using Personal Publisher 3.

➡ **be used offline.** You can create Web pages using Personal Publisher 3 without having to be logged on to AOL — handy if, for example, you want to work on your Web page while awaiting an important phone call and don't have a separate phone line for your modem.

➡ **be used from multiple machines.** Personal Publisher 3 doesn't care if you're at home or at your office; you can still edit your Web pages.

➡ **make it easier to manage multiple pages.** Personal Publisher 3 lists all your HTML files, whether they're still on your hard drive or already published to AOL, and lets you easily edit them, publish them to the Web, or unpublish them. In addition, Personal Publisher 3 offers several new basic and advanced features. (Users can choose whether to follow a basic or advanced path through the wizard.)

Basic features

Personal Publisher 3's new basic features include

➡ **color schematic.** Members can choose from several predesigned combinations of text colors, background colors, and images to ensure a pleasing design.

➡ **rich text.** All text can be formatted in a variety of ways: it can be bolded, italicized, underlined, resized, and more.

➡ **checkbox functionality.** This means that members can easily add e-mail links, logos, guestbooks, and other such fancy features simply by clicking on a check box.

Advanced features

New advanced features in Personal Publisher 3 include

➡ **text and image links.** Text and image links enable you to easily add links to specific words or phrases, or images or parts of images. You can link different parts of the same image to different places.

➡ **image manipulation.** Got a great picture you want to add to your site, but it's entirely the wrong size? Now you can resize, reshape, and otherwise manipulate images until they look just the way you want them.

➡ **bulleted lists and dividers.** Nothing dresses up a list of links (or favorite books, or anything else) like bullets. (Notice what I'm using to set off this list of features?) Now you can use them on your Web page.

➡ **intrasite linking.** If you have lots of pages on the Web, you can link them all to one master page, making it easy for visitors to navigate amongst your fascinating creations, and creating a full-fledged Web site of your own.

How to Access Personal Publisher 3

To access Personal Publisher 3, you have to be running the latest version of America Online's interface, AOL 4.0. Then, follow these steps to access Personal Publisher:

1. Log on to AOL.

2. Click the Internet button in the main toolbar.

3. Choose Internet Connection from the menu that appears. This opens the Internet Connection window shown in Figure 2-9.

Figure 2-9: The Internet Connection window is your gateway to the Internet from America Online — and your gateway to Personal Publisher 3.

4. From the Internet Connection window, click Internet Extras. This opens the window shown in Figure 2-10.

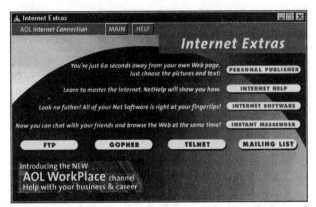

Figure 2-10: Internet Extras includes Internet Help, access to FTP and Gopher, and access to Personal Publisher 3.

5. From the Internet Extras window, click Personal Publisher.

6. You'll be offered the opportunity to download Personal Publisher, a process that takes about eight minutes with a 28.8 Kbps modem. Accept, and Personal Publisher will be automatically installed. You don't have to restart your computer.

7.   Once Personal Publisher 3 is installed, you'll see the welcome screen shown in Figure 2-11 — and are ready to begin designing your own Web page!

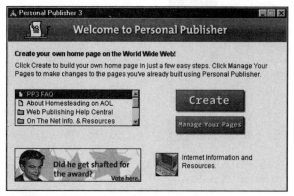

Figure 2-11: The Personal Publisher Welcome screen appears after you've installed PP3.

Summary

Personal Publisher 1 started it; Personal Publisher 2 extended it; now Personal Publisher 3 makes it easier than ever for AOL members to create their own Web pages — and making those Web pages look better than ever.

In the next chapter, you actually create a basic Web page using Personal Publisher 3 — and discover how successfully it has combined Personal Publisher 2's ease of use with a whole range of new capabilities.

Create a Personal Web Page in Five Minutes

3

In This Chapter

Create your first Web page before finishing this book

Ten steps to Web page glory

If you follow the steps in this chapter, you'll find that, using Personal Publisher 3, you can create a handsome Web page in practically no time at all—which is why this is Chapter 3, not Chapter 1. Chapter 1 is the chapter people typically leaf through when deciding whether to buy a book, and I'm afraid that, having discovered how easy Personal Publisher 3 makes Web page creation, you'd have decided that you didn't need to read the rest of this book! However, as this is Chapter 3, you've probably bought the book—which is good, because later chapters offer lots of great information to help you make your Web pages shine. Still, there's no denying Personal Publisher 3 makes creating Web pages easier than ever. Follow along, and you'll see what I mean.

Step 1: Access Personal Publisher

Before you can begin using Personal Publisher, you first have to access it. To do so, follow these steps:

1.   Log on to AOL.
2.   Click the Internet button in the main toolbar.

3. Choose Internet Connection from the resulting menu.

4. From the Internet Connection window, click Internet Extras.

5. From the Internet Extras window, click Personal Publisher.

Step 2: Choose a Template

Next, you have to choose a *template*, which may be thought of as a kind of blueprint for your Web Page. Personal Publisher 3 offers several templates from which to choose (see Figure 3-1), designed to draw users into online communities. From time to time, AOL adds new templates to those available, so eventually, as the number of available templates increases, music lovers may be able to find a music lover's template; writers, a writer's home page template; and so on. By choosing a template that matches your interests, you'll also be joining an online community of other people with similar interests who have also made use of that template, a process AOL calls *homesteading*. For more information on homesteading, see Chapter 15, "Your Online Hometown."

To choose a template, follow these steps:

1. In the initial Personal Publisher screen, click Create. This opens the window shown in Figure 3-1.

2. Highlight the name of the template you're interested in from the list provided.

3. To see what the template looks like, click Preview.

4. When you're happy with your choice of template and ready to proceed, click Begin.

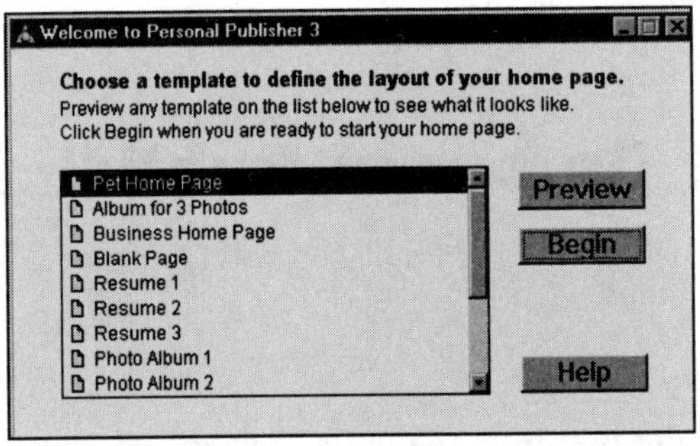

Figure 3-1: Choose your weapon — er, template.

Once you've chosen a template that pleases you, click Begin. A brief message appears telling you that Personal Publisher is saving that template to your computer.

 The exact number and order of the steps that follow varies, depending on which template you choose. The steps that follow use the Pet Home Page template, and are typical of most of the templates offered. For more detailed information on using templates, see Chapter 4, "A Template for All Seasons."

Step 3: Title Your Page

The first thing Personal Publisher asks you to enter into your Web page is a title, as shown in Figure 3-2.

Figure 3-2: This is where you really begin creating your own Web page.

Some templates suggest a title for you. If the template you're using offers you a title, decide whether you want to use it. If you do, simply click Next to proceed to the next step.

If you'd prefer to enter your own title, decide what you want it to be. Choose it carefully. Not only will the title be displayed at the top of your Web page, it's also what will show up in other people's lists of Favorite Places, should they add your Web page (which, considering what a brilliant Web page you're going to create, they will).

 Depending on what template you've chosen, a title may be suggested for you. You can either keep that title or edit it.

Enter your title into the space provided, labeled "Type your title here." When you're happy with your title, click Next.

If you can't think of a good title just yet, don't worry about it. Just leave the suggested title or leave the title space blank and go on to the next step. Chances are, a title will come to you as you continue to create your Web page, and you can always get back to the title screen by clicking the Back button at the bottom of each screen.

Step 4: Choose a Background Style

If you've poked around the Web much at all, you've seen every combination of text color, link color, and background color you can imagine. Personal Publisher 3 offers several background style choices from which to choose (see Figure 3-3).

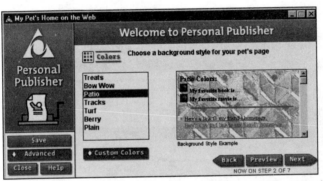

Figure 3-3: There's more than one way to color a Web page. I chose the Patio background for my Pet Home Page.

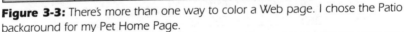

To choose a background style for your Web page, follow these steps:

1. **In the Colors screen, highlight the name of the background style you want to use from the list on the left. For example, I chose "Patio."**

   A preview of the background style appears in the scroll box on the right.

2. **When you've found a background style you like, click Next.**

Each color scheme offers a different combination of colors for the background, regular text, links, followed links, lines, and bullets. Just highlight the name of the color scheme in the box at left to see a sample in the box at right. When you find the one you want, click Next.

Personal Publisher 3's Advanced Options give you more control over your Background Style. For more information, see Chapter 5, "Advanced Options."

Step 5: Enter Text

As far as I'm concerned (maybe because I'm a writer), the most important element of your Web page is what you say on your page. In other words, the text. Pictures are like the appetizers on a restaurant's menu, while text is the entrée. The appetizers add flavor and excitement, but the entrées keep people coming back.

The sort of text you'll be asked to add varies from template to template. In some, you'll be asked to enter text several times. In this particular template —the Pet Home Page template —you're asked to "Introduce your pet and describe his/her best qualities," as shown in Figure 3-4.

Figure 3-4: Type your text into the window provided, and then format it using the buttons in the toolbar at the top.

To enter text, follow these steps:

1. Highlight any placeholder text that appears in the text window.

2. Begin typing your text (for example, "Rover is a loving, if none-too-bright, companion."). It will replace the highlighted placeholder text.

3. Once you've typed your text, you can edit it using the buttons in the toolbar at the top of the text window. At left in the toolbar are three buttons that set the size. Clicking the one on the left reduces the size of the text one notch; the button in the middle makes the text the standard text size for text on the Web; and the one on the right increases the size of the text one notch.

Text in Web pages isn't like text in a word processor; you can't display it in an almost infinite variety of sizes. Instead, Web text must be displayed in one of several preset sizes. The buttons described in the previous paragraph move the text to either the next-largest or next-smallest preset size.

4. Set the text's alignment with the three buttons at the center of the toolbar. Click the left button to align the text with the left side of the Web page; click the middle button to center it on the page; and click the right button to align it with the right side of the Web page.

5. If you wish, you can make text bold or italicized (or both). Highlight the text you want to change, and click the button marked *B* to make the text bold, or the button with the slanting letter *I* on it to place the text in italics.

6. You can also change text's color. Highlight the text whose color you want to change, and then click the rightmost button. A color menu will appear. Select the color you want to apply to the text, and then click OK.

7. When you're happy with your text and its appearance, click Next.

For a more in-depth discussion of adding text to your Web page, see Chapter 8, "Text and Hypertext."

Step 6: Add a Picture

Once upon a time in the dark ages of the Web (say, five years ago), Web pages were mostly text. But faster modems and better Web browsers have resulted in an explosion of images on the Web. Graphics are now part of the Web's appeal, and they're also part of all Personal Publisher 3 templates (see Figure 3-5).

See Chapter 9, "Graphics," for more information about working with digital pictures.

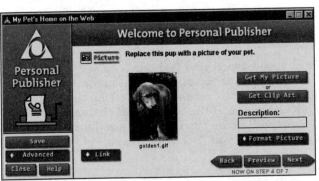

Figure 3-5: Add a fun photo (or two) to your fabulous Web site with the click of a button (or maybe two).

Personal Publisher 3 makes adding pictures to your Web page a snap. Each template comes with a sample picture (or pictures) already in place. You can choose to use that picture, add a picture you've saved on your computer, or choose a picture from the clip art provided with Personal Publisher.

To add a picture from your computer, follow these steps:

1. Click Get My Picture. This opens a standard Windows directory.

2. Locate the folder that contains the picture you want to use and click Open Gallery. This opens a window like the one shown in Figure 3-6.

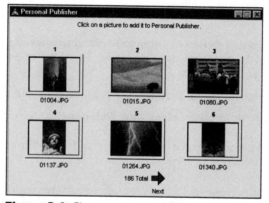

Figure 3-6: Pictures you've already saved on your computer can easily be added to your Web page.

3. You'll see a series of thumbnail-sized previews of your saved pictures; single-click the one you want to use.

4. Your selected picture automatically replaces the placeholder picture in the template. Type a description of the picture in the space provided.

5. Click Next to continue creating your Web page.

You can also add clip art to your page. To do so, follow these steps:

1. From the Picture window shown in Figure 3-5, click Get Clip Art. This brings up the window shown in Figure 3-7.

Figure 3-7: Each template comes with a variety of appropriate clip art. Choose what you want from the thumbnail images here.

2. Again, you'll see a series of thumbnail-sized previews. Click the one you want to use, and then click Get This One to add it to your Web page.

3. Type a description of the picture in the space provided.

4. Click Next to continue creating your Web page.

 Wherever the picture came from, be sure to enter a description in the space provided before clicking Next to move to the next step.

Personal Publisher 3's Advanced Options let you rotate, resize, crop, and adjust the brightness and contrast of pictures you place on your Web pages. For more information, see Chapter 5, "Advanced Options."

For more information on where you can obtain cool pictures for your Web pages, and how to use them effectively, see Chapter 7, "Web Publishing Resources on AOL," and Chapter 9, "Graphics."

Step 7: Add a List

Some templates include lists of items, each highlighted by a bullet, which you can edit to suit yourself (see Figure 3-8).

A word about copyright

Digital images are everywhere, but they're not all freely available for you to use on your Web page. Something too many Web surfers forget is that many pictures belong to someone — and that someone has to give you permission to use them. It's called *copyright*, and using copyrighted material without the permission of the copyright owner is against the law.

Sometimes it's hard to tell if material on the Internet is copyrighted. The best way to be sure is simply to ask. If you see an image on someone else's Web site that you'd like to use for your own purposes, e-mail the Webmaster of that site and ask if the image is copyrighted; if it is, ask who owns the copyright; and (if copyright belongs to the Webmaster or whoever owns the site) ask if you may have permission to use it. Explain clearly why you want it; if you're just saving it on your computer, there's probably no problem, but if you want to reproduce it in a calendar you're going to sell for $20 each, the copyright owner may want a piece of the profits.

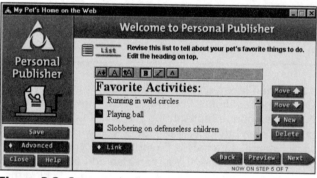

Figure 3-8: Create and edit a list here.

Click New to add a new item to the list; the bullet automatically will be added. To remove an item already on the list (such as one of those provided in the template), highlight the item and click Delete. To move an item up or down the list, highlight it and click one of the Move buttons.

As with any other text, you can change the look of your list by using the formatting buttons above it.

When your list is complete, click Next.

Step 8: Add Favorite Places

Something else you've probably noticed about Web pages is that many of them contain a list of links to their creator's favorite Web sites. If you've been an AOL member for a while, you have a similar list stored under Favorite Places. Personal Publisher makes it easy for you to turn your Favorite Places into links on your Web page, so your visitors can also enjoy them (see Figure 3-9).

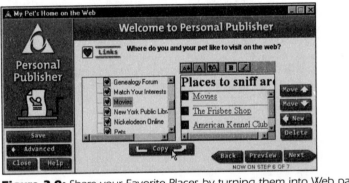

Figure 3-9: Share your Favorite Places by turning them into Web page links!

Highlight a Favorite Place you'd like to turn into a link on your Web page, and click Copy. The highlighted Favorite Place shows up in the box at right as a link in a list. Continue highlighting Favorite Places and clicking Include until the list contains all the Favorite Places you want listed on your Web page. If you accidentally include a Favorite Place you don't want on the list, just highlight it and click Delete. You can also add an entirely new link by clicking New, and arrange the order of your links by clicking the Move buttons.

Format the list using the buttons for adjusting text size and style, and when you're satisfied, click Next.

Step 9: Add Extras

You're almost done! Now is your opportunity to add those little extras to your Web page that, while not absolutely necessary, add a little spice, like an extra dash of salt in your bouillabaisse (see Figure 3-10).

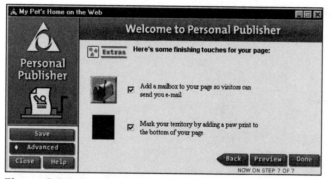

Figure 3-10: Time to add that little something extra that makes a Web page stand out in a crowd

Personal Publisher 3 offers you a variety of "extras" you can add to your Web page just by checking the box by each item. These vary from template to template. For the Pet Home Page template, you have the following choices:

➥ **E-mail link**. An e-mail link on your Web page makes it easy for visitors to e-mail you with criticism, praise, or questions. This extra is offered for all templates.

➥ **Paw print**. Add a paw print graphic to the bottom of your page to "mark your territory."

Step 10: Save and Publish

When you've added all the extras you want, click Done. You'll be prompted for a filename. The default filename is `index.html`, but you can change the name as long as it ends with `.html`. Enter one and click OK. This saves your page to your hard drive.

Congratulations! You've created a Web page, which Personal Publisher displays (see Figure 3-11).

Assuming everything is okay, click Publish to place your Web page on AOL and make it available to anyone with a browser. You'll be prompted for a filename; provide one, click Publish, and voila! Your page is on the Internet.

Figure 3-11: There it is! Just five minutes (more or less) since you began, and you already have your very own Web page.

See Chapter 6, "Managing Your Pages," for more information about publishing your page on AOL.

Summary

Personal Publisher 3 makes creating Web pages a snap, as you've seen. However, the Web page I created for this chapter is basic. Personal Publisher 3 also makes creating more complex Web pages easy — you just have to click a few more buttons than you did this time around. In the next couple of chapters, you take a closer look at Personal Publisher's templates and at some of the advanced options you can use to make your Web site even more exciting for visitors from all over the cyberworld.

A Template for All Seasons

4

In This Chapter

What are templates?

Previewing templates

A sampling of some Personal Publisher templates

When you start Personal Publisher and click Create Page, the first thing you're asked to do is choose a template. Picking the right template for your Web page is as important as picking the right blueprint for a prefabricated house; the template largely determines what the finished product will look like. Sure, you can make some changes, but if you make the right choice to begin with, you won't have to make as many. That means less work, and getting your Web page up and running more quickly.

What Is a Template?

I've already compared a template to a blueprint, and that's a pretty good analogy. Blueprints for buildings give you some idea of what the finished product will look like and show you where important structural elements such as walls, windows, doors, and floors will go. Personal Publisher templates give you a good idea of what your finished Web page will look like, and show you where important structural elements such as text, pictures, and lists will go.

Fortunately, changing template elements and moving them from place to place is a lot easier than changing blueprints. Moving a wall on a blueprint could make the final building subject to unfortunate occurrences, such as falling down. The worst thing that can happen when you move something around on a Web page is that the Web page will turn out ugly. Another useful way to think about the various elements of the templates (text, pictures, and so on) is as placeholders, which you replace with your own selections.

Technically, there's nothing complicated about Personal Publisher's templates; they're just Web pages that you download to your computer and then edit. You can actually use Personal Publisher to edit any Web page created with Personal Publisher 3 or any other Web publishing tool (see Chapter 6, "Managing Your Pages," for more information on editing Web pages). What makes these Web pages *templates* is that AOL designed them to be easily edited by Personal Publisher, and added them to the list of templates that appears when you click Create Page on the opening screen of Personal Publisher (see Figure 4-1).

AOL designed these templates with the concept of *homesteading* in mind. Many of the templates included with Personal Publisher fit directly into the Hometown AOL "communities," such as music or politics, the idea being that when you use a Personal Publisher template, you're joining a community of other people who have used the same template, and thus share your interest in the topic for which the template is designed. For more information on Hometown AOL and the concept of homesteading, see Chapter 16, "Keeping Your Page Fresh."

> **Welcome to Personal Publisher 3** ▢▢▢
>
> **Choose a template to define the layout of your home page.**
> Preview any template on the list below to see what it looks like.
> Click Begin when you are ready to start your home page.
>
> | Pet Home Page | **Preview** |
> | Album for 3 Photos | |
> | Business Home Page | **Begin** |
> | Blank Page | |
> | Resume 1 | |
> | Resume 2 | |
> | Resume 3 | |
> | Photo Album 1 | **Help** |
> | Photo Album 2 | |

Figure 4-1: Many of AOL's Personal Publisher templates are designed to let you integrate your Web page into a larger community of similar Web pages.

Previewing Templates

If all you had to go on were the names AOL gave the various templates, you might not pick out the one that best suited your needs. Fortunately,

you can take a sneak peek at any of these templates by highlighting one that interests you and then clicking Preview (see Figure 4-2).

Figure 4-2: Use the Preview button to see what your selected template looks like.

 Sometimes it's hard to get a good look at a template in AOL's default window. To expand the window and get a better idea of what the page looks like in your AOL Web browser, click the full-screen button (the middle one of three) in the upper-right corner of the window.

Touring the Templates

Each template contains a different set of elements and will give you different choices as you make changes to it with Personal Publisher. To give you an idea of some of the kinds of templates available and how they use the various elements, take a look at some of those that AOL has posted for your use (with the caveat that templates come and go, so not all of these may be available — if they are, they may not look exactly the same).

Pet Home Page

A home page for your favorite pet? Why not? After all, as any pet owner can tell you, pets are people, too — why shouldn't they have their own home pages on the World Wide Web?

It may never be voted Coolest Site on the Web, but other pet owners may get a kick out of it — and so will everyone who knows you and the animal that shares your life!

The Pet Home Page template starts with a title and includes two text sections, with accompanying pictures, as shown in Figure 4-3.

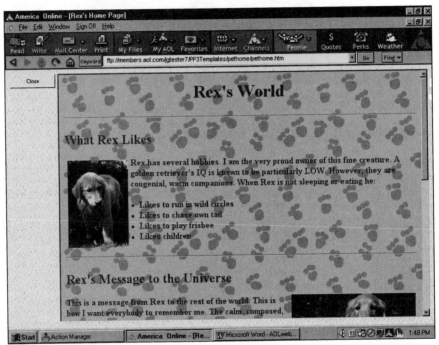

Figure 4-3: Share whatever information you feel is most important about your pet in the text areas of the Pet Home Page.

Beneath the title, Text and Pictures is an area devoted to your pet's favorite AOL and Internet links. Extras that you can add to the Pet Home Page template include an e-mail link (presumably to you, unless your pet has his or her own e-mail address!) and a paw-print graphic to "mark your territory" — an opportunity to take credit for the work you've done on your pet's home page. (See Figure 4-4.)

For more information on adding links to your Web pages, see Chapter 5, "Advanced Options," and Chapter 8, "Text and Hypertext."

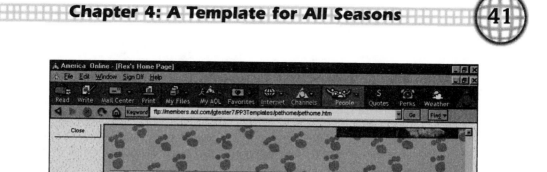

Figure 4-4: Links to other sites and to your e-mail address round out the Pet Home Page.

Don't let template titles tie you down

Each template has a specific name, of course, and the content that's already present relates to that name. But don't let that stop you from using that template for other purposes. The Pet Home Page template, for example, also happens to be a perfectly good template for a personal home page. After all, it could just as easily have pictures of you and your family and list your activities and favorite links as your pet's.

In other words, if you're planning to create a Web page for which there doesn't seem to be a template, look again — but instead of looking at content, look at design. Any template can be adapted to another purpose simply by replacing the pictures, text, and links with your own.

As we continue this tour of the templates, I make suggestions for each template's other possible uses.

Business Home Page

There are probably more personal pages devoted to individuals (or, as you just saw, pets) on the Web than anything else, but running a close second would be pages devoted to business. A business home page is an inexpensive form of advertising compared to, say, newspapers (and especially compared to television), and has the added benefit of extending the reach of your advertising from the local market to, potentially, anyone in the world.

AOL's Business Home Page template gives you the outline of a basic business home page (see Figure 4-5).

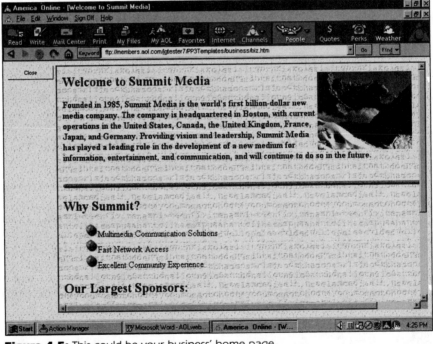

Figure 4-5: This could be your business' home page.

The Business Home Page template has a welcoming message describing the business at the top, along with the company logo. Below that is a list of important points about the business that need to be communicated, followed by links to related companies. At the bottom (out of sight in the figure) are an e-mail link and a visitor counter that lets you track the number of *hits* on the page — giving you some idea of how effective a communication tool the page really is.

Again, this template could be adapted to several other uses. For example:

➥ The home page of a community organization — a service club, perhaps, or an amateur theater group. A group photo could replace the logo, and a list of upcoming events could replace the list of important points about the business.

➥ The home page of a school, or of one class within the school: "Mrs. Edding's Grade 4s," for example. A photo of the class or Mrs. Edding could replace the logo, and the list could be of class activities.

➥ The home page of a church, with a photo of the church instead of a logo, and service times and upcoming sermon topics in place of the list of important points.

I'm sure you can come up with many similar examples yourself.

 For more information on creating a Web page for your business, see Chapter 12, "Creating Cool Small-Business Pages."

Resumes

In these days of downsizing, rightsizing, and, indeed, every-which-way-but-upsizing, it's a good idea to keep your resume up to date and have plenty of copies ready to hand out at a moment's notice. But what if you're schmoozing someone who's really interested in your training and background, but you don't have a resume handy?

Simple. Post your resume on the Web. Then, instead of handing out an actual copy, you can simply hand out a business card with the URL of your resume printed on it. And because it's so easy to update a Web page with Personal Publisher, you can ensure that your online resume is always up to date.

There's more than one way to create a resume. AOL's Personal Publisher templates offer several.

Resume 1, for example, looks like the template shown in Figure 4-6.

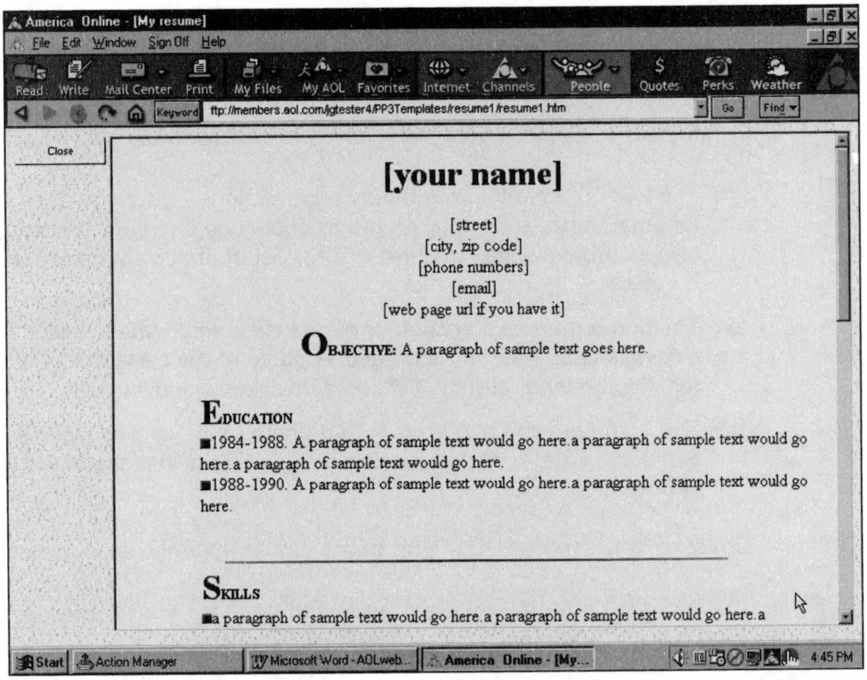

Figure 4-6: Proclaim your proficiencies to the world with an online resume.

This template provides you with a place for your name, address (both postal and e-mail), career objective, and then the sections Education, Skills, Experience, and the catchall "Other Information," ending with "References available upon request." It has a staid, conservative look, appropriate to a lawyer, perhaps, or maybe a professor of English.

A resume doesn't have to look like this, of course. The Resume 2 template offers a bit more dash, in the form of a photo (although probably not one like that AOL has chosen to insert!). See Figure 4-7 for an example of the Resume 2 template.

NOTE See Chapter 9, "Graphics," for more information about how to insert a picture into your Web page.

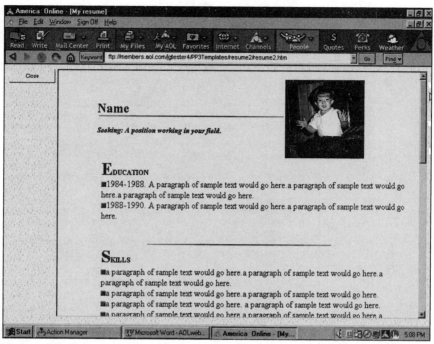

Figure 4-7: This template lets you add a photograph of yourself to your resume, although you may want to consider something from a little later on in your career than this one.

Too shy to include a photograph of yourself? Then use clip art instead. Pick an image that's related to your field of work. The author of the Resume 3 template, shown in Figure 4-8, is apparently a computer programmer — or maybe a Web page designer.

What are other uses for resume pages? How about a Web-based yearbook for a high-school graduating class? You could create a page for each student, including a picture, a list of accomplishments, and the kind of humorous statement for which yearbooks are notorious.

Political campaigners could use these templates to create profiles of the candidates their party is running for office; coaches could use them to create profiles of each player on their teams: online baseball cards, if you like.

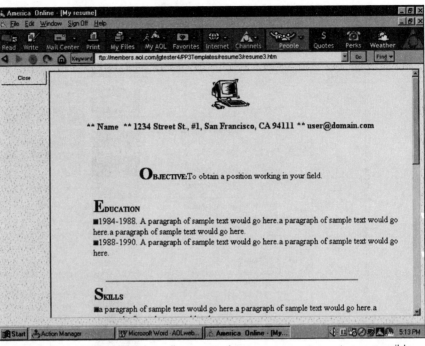

Figure 4-8: A bit of appropriate clip art can dress up your resume, too — possibly more than a mug shot of yourself (especially if the only photo you have handy is the one from your passport).

Whenever you want to provide online information about an individual, the resume templates are good starting points.

Photo albums

Most people who surf the Web enjoy looking at pictures — probably more than they enjoy reading text (although, as a writer, it pains me to admit it). But the only thing more fun that looking at other people's pictures is posting a few of your favorites so other people can look at yours.

Collections of photos appear on just about every Web site, whether it's devoted to a zoo, the wonders of Tahiti, or the wonders of the local Lions Club. AOL posts several templates for creating photo pages, one of which, Photo Album 3, I show you in Figure 4-11.

Photo Album 1, shown in Figure 4-9, includes a heading, a space for one photo, a caption, text, and a list of links.

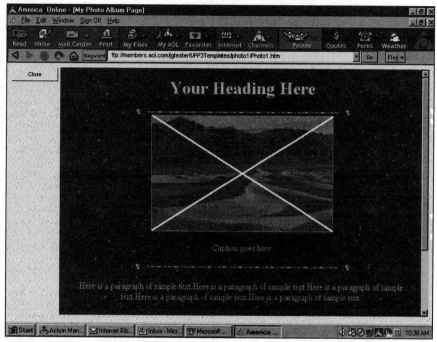

Figure 4-9: The Photo Album 1 template is a good basic template for showing off a single photo.

Photo Album 2 (see Figure 4-10) includes space for two photos with captions, and a list of links, but doesn't include text. But hey, since a picture is worth a thousand words, you probably don't need a lot of text, anyway.

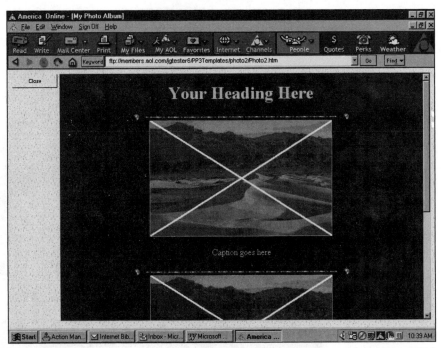

Figure 4-10: If you'd like more than one picture on your page and less text, use this template.

Photo Album 3 (see Figure 4-11) includes space for three photos — one large, and two smaller ones underneath it. Are you beginning to see a pattern here?

Finally, Photo Album 4 has (big surprise!) room for four photos. (Otherwise it looks just like Photo Album 2, shown in Figure 4-10.)

Your "photo album" doesn't have to contain photographs; you could also use it as an online art gallery, highlighting your daughter's finger-painting masterpieces or your own watercolors. Professional artists can use these templates to create online portfolios to which they can direct potential purchasers or employers.

For more information on adding pictures to Web pages with Personal Publisher, see Chapter 9, "Graphics."

Team Sports

A lot of people love sports, and everyone, it seems, has a favorite team. Often it's one of the teams from the city in which they live, or another one that's close by, but not often. There are plenty of Toronto Maple Leaf hockey fans living in, say, Vancouver, home of the Canucks.

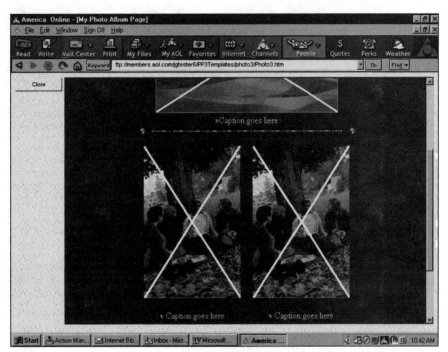

Figure 4-11: Do you have one photo you want to feature and two smaller ones you'd like to show off, as well? Then try this template.

A Web site devoted to your favorite team proclaims where your loyalties lie to the whole world, no matter where you live, and allows you to connect with other fans of the same team, who'll appreciate whatever wonderful pictures, facts, and memories you're able to provide.

The Team Sport 1 template shown in Figure 4-12 will give you a good start on presenting your passion to the rest of the planet.

This template is more complex than most of the others, and is a good example of the sort of thing that can be done with Personal Publisher 3. It features both an attractive banner across the top and an interesting border down the left side, several photos (there's a third one at the bottom), eye-catching bulleted lists of facts and figures, lots of text, a list of links, and an e-mail link.

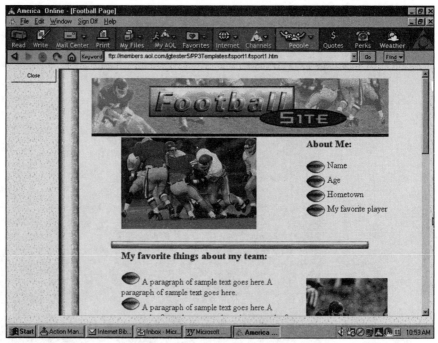

Figure 4-12: This attractive template is set up to let you brag about your favorite football team — but it could just as easily be used to brag about a hockey team, a soccer team, a baseball team, or your favorite NASCAR driver.

Think what you could do with this template even if you don't have the slightest interest in sports! It would be just as effective for presenting an overview of your favorite symphony orchestra, musical, movie, author, or just about any other interest you might have.

Other templates

The templates mentioned so far just scratch the surface of what is or soon may be available from AOL. At the time this book was written, other templates under development included Military, Women, Teens, GenX, Genealogy, Love and Romance, Love and Marriage, Friends, Selling Your Home, Baseball, Automobiles, Asian Food, Jazz, Travel, TV, Film, Politics, Science, and Work Place. By the time you read this, many more may have appeared.

Blank page

I left this template for last, because it's not really a template at all—it's exactly what it says it is: a blank Web page that leaves you free to indulge in your own creative impulses, free from the design ideas of whoever created the templates.

Some people will bypass the templates entirely and start straight in on a blank page. For others, facing a blank page is either frightening, because they don't know what to do, or frustrating, because they know what they want to do, but they don't have time to do it from scratch.

If you're new to designing Web pages or desktop publishing, I suggest you begin by experimenting with AOL's many templates. You may find that the pages you create using templates suit your needs admirably—but if, at some point, they don't, you can start with a blank page and create your Web site from scratch with confidence.

Summary

Templates are blueprints for well-designed, good-looking Web pages. You can use them for their suggested purposes, or you can turn them into something else entirely and just use the design. In other words, use the provided templates for ideas and to save layout time, but don't be limited by them. They should be springboards to vault you to your own creative heights, not straitjackets for your imagination.

Advanced Options

In This Chapter

Moving beyond the basics

Customizing the background style

Adding links to text and graphics

Formatting pictures and other graphics

If you followed all the steps in Chapter 3, "Create a Personal Web Page in Five Minutes," you may have noticed other options that I didn't go into — buttons I didn't tell you to click. Those buttons lead to the advanced features of Personal Publisher 3. Sooner or later, you're going to want to click them because they let you move beyond just replacing the placeholders in the templates with your own text and graphics, and they let you start customizing your page.

Beyond the Basics

To access the advanced features of Personal Publisher 3, you first have to access Personal Publisher. To refresh your memory, here are the steps:

1. Log on to America Online.
2. Click the Internet button in the main toolbar.
3. Choose Internet Connection from the menu that appears.
4. From the Internet Connection window, click Internet Extras.
5. From the Internet Extras window, click Personal Publisher.

With Personal Publisher started, follow these steps to access the advanced features:

1. **Click Create.**

2. **From the Welcome to Personal Publisher 3 window, choose a template, and click Begin.**

3. **Once the template has loaded and the first My Page window has appeared, click Advanced. This opens the Advanced Features window shown in Figure 5-1.**

```
PP3: Advanced Features                              [X]

Advanced Features
By choosing to display advanced features you can access
these additional features. Click Help for more information.

◆ Hyperlinks for Text and Pictures
◆ Custom Background Styles and Colors
◆ Formatting and Resizing for Pictures

Advanced features appear on dark blue buttons. Only
some screens have advanced features.
─────────────────────────────────────────────
              ☑ Display Advanced Features
─────────────────────────────────────────────

         OK      Cancel      Help
```

Figure 5-1: If you want to create a more sophisticated Web site, Personal Publisher 3's advanced features are for you.

You can activate the following three advanced features:

• **Hyperlinks for Text and Pictures.** This feature enables you to select phrases and images you want to link to other Web pages, anywhere on the Internet. You can also use hyperlinks to link to other pages that are part of your own Web site.

• **Customize Background Styles and Colors.** This option enables you to choose colors for the text and backgrounds on your Web pages other than those in the preset color schemes.

• **Formatting and Resizing for Pictures.** Selecting this feature enables you to vary the style and size of text and the sizes of pictures to better suit your design needs.

4. **Check the box labeled Display Advanced Features to activate the advanced features.**

5. **Click OK to return to the Web page creation wizard.**

Advanced features will appear as buttons that are a darker blue than the ordinary Personal Publisher buttons.

Customizing Your Colors

The first opportunity you have to use the Advanced Options is in the selection of colors for your Web page, typically the second step of the Personal Publisher wizard. To customize your colors, follow these steps:

1. Click Custom Colors to bring up the Custom Colors screen shown in Figure 5-2.

Figure 5-2: You're not limited to the color schemes Personal Publisher provides. You can change the text and background colors to suit your tastes.

2. The preview window on the right shows you the current colors for text, links, and followed links. You can't change the colors for links and followed links here, but to change the color of your ordinary text, click the Text button. This brings up the Color palette shown in Figure 5-3.

3. Click the color you want and then click OK. The new text color will be displayed in the Background Style Example window at right.

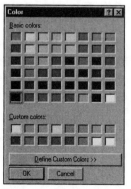

Figure 5-3: Choose a color for your Web page's text from the Color palette.

4. If you don't see exactly the color you want, click Define Custom Colors to expand the Color palette (see Figure 5-4).

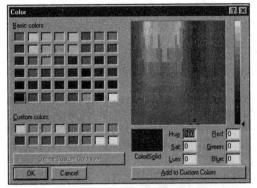

Figure 5-4: If the colors Personal Publisher provides aren't good enough for you, you can always design your own.

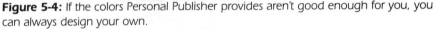

5. If you happen to know the exact figures for Hue, Sat, and Lum (hue, saturation, and luminance), or Red, Green, and Blue for the color you want to use, type those numbers directly into the spaces provided.

6. If you don't know those figures, use the color matrix and the brightness slider beside it to design your color. Move the crosshairs around on the matrix to the color you want, and adjust the brightness using the slider. The Color/Solid box displays the color for you.

7. When you're happy with the color you've designed, click Add to Custom Colors. Your color will appear in the Custom colors area of the palette.

8. Click the new color, and then click OK. The color of the text in the preview window will change to the new color.

9. To change the background color, click Background Color instead of Text Color, and follow steps 3 through 8 again.

10. Give your new style a name in the "Name this style" blank, and click OK. Your new style will now appear in the list of background styles available for use with this template.

Some of the Personal Publisher templates use pictures "tiled" together to create a background. Picture-based backgrounds like that aren't affected by changing the background color.

Adding Links

Hyperlinks are a basic part of the World Wide Web. The ability to link any word or phrase to any other page on the Web via a simple address, or *Uniform Resource Locator* (URL), is what makes surfing the Net so much fun. It also adds immeasurably to the interest your Web page will hold for visitors. If your passion is the Titanic, for instance (either the ship or the movie), you don't have to put all the information you've discovered on the Internet on your page; you can just provide links to sites where that information is already presented. Some popular pages consist of almost nothing but links — the search engine Yahoo! comes to mind.

You can add a link to a picture, to text, or to the elements of a list.

Adding links to graphics

You've probably visited many Web sites where links are embedded in pictures. On a Web site run by a zoo, for instance, you might find yourself looking at a map, with images of various animals indicating where they're kept in the zoo. Clicking any animal takes you to an area of the Web site that tells you all about that particular species.

You can achieve the same kind of effect with Personal Publisher 3, by either making an entire picture "hot," so that clicking anywhere in it takes the visitor to another site, or by making different parts of the picture link to different sites.

To add one or more links to a picture, follow these steps:

1. From any Personal Publisher window that allows you to add a picture to your Web page, click Link. This brings up the screen shown in Figure 5-5.

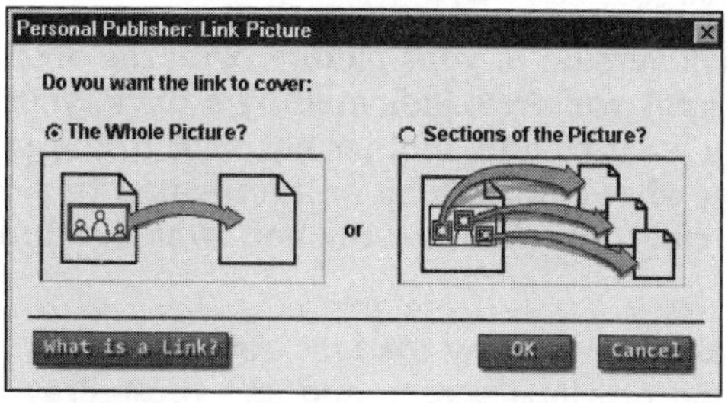

Figure 5-5: You can link an entire image or selected parts of it to any other site on the Internet.

2. Decide whether you want the link to cover the whole picture or just sections of the picture. Click OK.

3. If you choose to have the link cover the whole picture, you'll see the screen shown in Figure 5-7. Proceed to Step 4. If you choose to have the link cover just sections of the picture, you'll first see the screen shown in Figure 5-6.

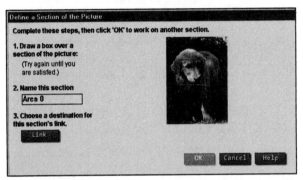

Figure 5-6: Create "hot spots" on a picture using these controls.

To create a hot spot within a picture, follow these steps:

1. Draw a box around the part of the picture you want the link to cover.

2. Give that part of the picture its own name; type it in the blank provided.

3. Click Link to move to the next step.

4. Now it's up to you to decide where you want the link to point (see Figure 5-7). Select the type of link you want using the pull-down menu.

5. Once you're satisfied, click OK.

6. You'll see a small version of your picture, with the area covered by the last hot spot you drew indicated by a thick, yellow rectangle. If you want to add another hot spot to the same picture, creating what is known as an *imagemap* (a picture with multiple links), click Add Another Section, which returns you to step 1.

7. To change the area covered by the last hot spot, click Edit, which returns you to the previous screen and lets you redraw the last hot spot.

8. To change the link to which a hot spot points, click Edit. Again, you'll return to the previous screen, where you'll see that the Link

button has become an Unlink button. Click Unlink to remove the current Link to the selected hot spot; the Unlink button changes back to a Link button, which you can then click to add a link as before.

9. To remove a hot spot entirely, click Delete.

10. Repeat steps 1 through 6 until you've added all the hot spots you want to the picture, and then click Done.

Figure 5-7: Whether you're placing a link in a picture, in text, or in a list, you use these controls to specify where the link points.

Choose from the following several categories of links:

➡ **AOL's Hot Links.** This brings up a list of sites AOL recommends as hot places on the Web (see Figure 5-8).

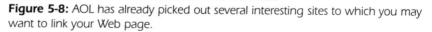

Figure 5-8: AOL has already picked out several interesting sites to which you may want to link your Web page.

➡ **Your Favorite Places.** These links point to sites you've saved in your Favorite Places folder (see Figure 5-9). They could be Web sites or AOL sites (in which case they may only be available to AOL members who are browsing your site).

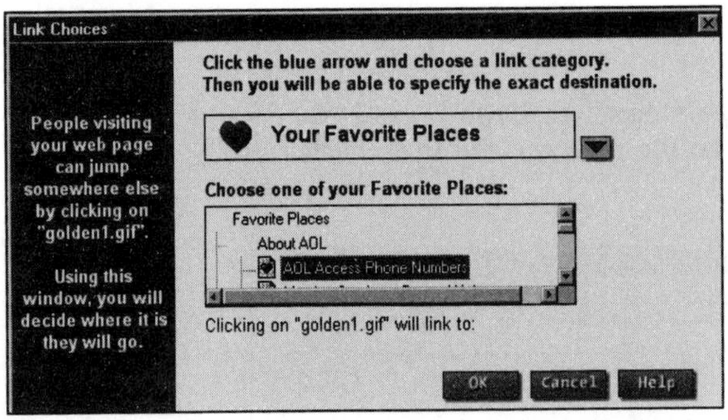

Link Choices

Click the blue arrow and choose a link category.
Then you will be able to specify the exact destination.

People visiting your web page can jump somewhere else by clicking on "golden1.gif".

Using this window, you will decide where it is they will go.

♥ **Your Favorite Places** ▼

Choose one of your Favorite Places:

> Favorite Places
> > About AOL
> > AOL Access Phone Numbers

Clicking on "golden1.gif" will link to:

OK   Cancel   Help

Figure 5-9: Make your Favorite Places someone else's favorite places, too, by linking your Web page to them!

➡ **Type any URL.** If you know the URL of the Web page or other Internet resource to which you want your link to point, you can type it in directly by choosing this option (see Figure 5-10).

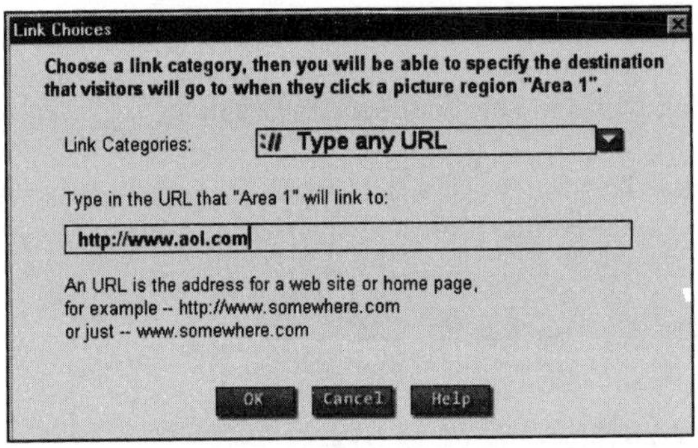

Link Choices

Choose a link category, then you will be able to specify the destination that visitors will go to when they click a picture region "Area 1".

Link Categories: `://  Type any URL` ▼

Type in the URL that "Area 1" will link to:

`http://www.aol.com`

An URL is the address for a web site or home page,
for example -- http://www.somewhere.com
or just -- www.somewhere.com

OK   Cancel   Help

Figure 5-10: Type any URL into the blank provided to link your page to that page. (The URL shown is a particularly good URL — it's for AOL's home page.)

➡ **Your Other Web Pages.** If you have other pages in your Web site, a menu listing all the pages you've created is presented for you to choose from (see Figure 5-11).

Figure 5-11: You'll probably want lots of links among the various pages on your Web site. Add them from here.

➡ **Within This Page.** Sometimes you just want to send someone to another part of the same page — a particular section of text or a specific picture. The menu you get when you choose this option lists all the other elements on the page on which you're currently working (see Figure 5-12).

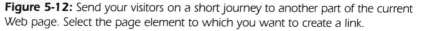

Figure 5-12: Send your visitors on a short journey to another part of the current Web page. Select the page element to which you want to create a link.

➡ **Send E-mail.** It's always nice to get feedback from visitors. Provide a one-click e-mail link to enable anyone who's been inspired by his or her visit to your page to write you a note (see Figure 5-13).

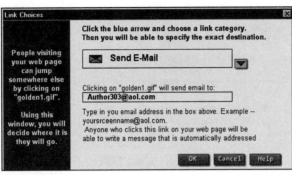

Figure 5-13: Leave your e-mail address in the blank to let visitors to your page send you a message.

Adding links to text and lists

The Link button also appears on any Personal Publisher screen from which you enter text. To add a link to a word or phrase, follow these steps:

1. Highlight the text to which you want to add a link.

2. Click the Link button. That will take you to the Link menu described above.

3. Choose the type of link you want from the menu.

4. When you're satisfied, click Link. You can add a link to any item in a list the same way.

Once you've added a link and clicked OK, the Link button changes to an Unlink button (see Figure 5-14). If you decide you've made a mistake, click it to remove the link you just added.

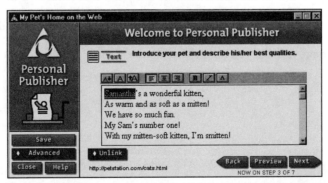

Figure 5-14: Once you've added a link to text, the Link button changes to an Unlink button. Note that the item the text is linked to is displayed below the button.

Formatting Your Graphics

Another advanced option becomes available whenever you insert a photograph or clip art. Click Format Picture, and you'll see options for positioning your picture just where you want it (see Figure 5-15).

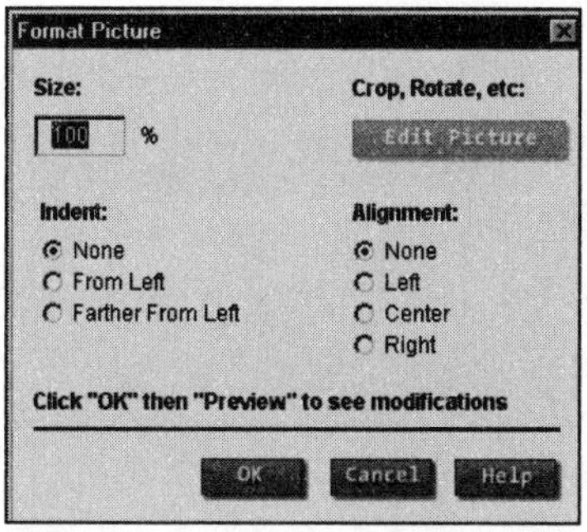

Figure 5-15: Fine-tune the size and placement of graphics with these controls.

Here you have three adjustments you can make to your graphic: Size, Indent, and Alignment.

To adjust the size of a graphic, follow these steps:

1. **Click Format Picture.**

2. **Decide how much smaller or larger you want to make the graphic.**

3. **In the Size box, enter the number that corresponds to what percentage of the original size the new size will be. In other words, if you want it to be half as big as it is now, enter 50 percent; if you want it to be twice as big, enter 200 percent. Remember that the reduction or expansion applies to both height and width, so at 150 percent a picture that was originally 100 pixels by 100 pixels would be 150 pixels by 150 pixels, while at 50 percent it would only be 50 pixels by 50 pixels.**

4. **Click OK.**

5. **To see the effect of the change, click Preview.**

Changing the size of a graphic is illustrated in Figures 5-16 and 5-17.

Indent and Alignment work together to determine the placement of the picture on your Web page. Indent determines how far from the edge of the page the graphic is placed, while Alignment determines its relationship to both page edges.

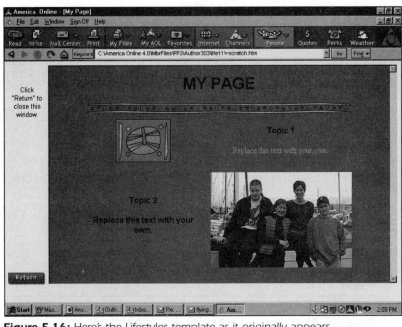

Figure 5-16: Here's the Lifestyles template as it originally appears . . .

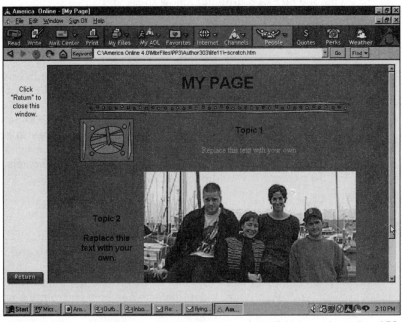

Figure 5-17: . . . and here's what it looks like with the picture enlarged to 150 percent of its original size.

To set your Indent and Alignment, follow these steps:

1. **Click Format Picture.**

2. **Under Indent, select the None, From Left, or Farther From Left radio buttons to determine how far in from the side of the page the graphic will appear. If Alignment is set to None or Left, Indent will indent the graphic from the left side of the page; if Alignment is set to Right, however, Indent indents the graphic from the right side of the page.**

3. **Under Alignment, select None, Left, Center, or Right to determine whether the graphic will be placed as far left as possible, as far right as possible, or in the middle.**

4. **Click OK.**

5. **To see the effect of the change, click Preview.**

Figures 5-18, 5-19, 5-20, and 5-21 provide some examples of how Indent and Alignment work together.

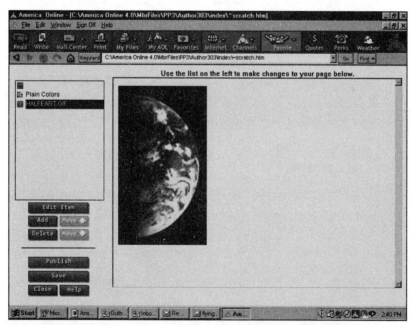

Figure 5-18: If Indent is set to None and Alignment is set to None or Left, the picture will be flush with the left side of the Web page.

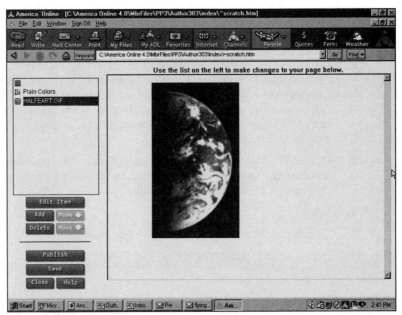

Figure 5-19: If Indent is set to From Left and Alignment is set to None or Left, the picture will appear slightly closer to the center of the Web page. Changing Indent to Farther From Left will move the picture even closer to the middle, as in this image.

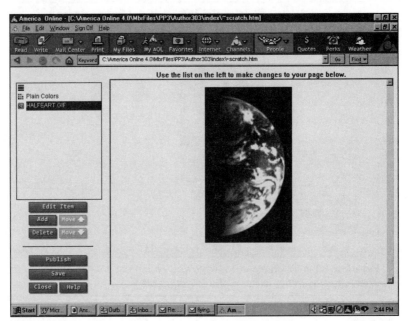

Figure 5-20: If you set Alignment to Center, the picture will be centered between the two sides of the page, no matter how Indent is set.

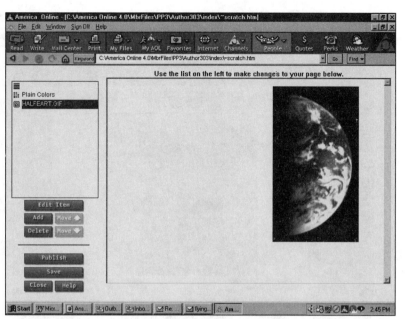

Figure 5-21: If you set Alignment to Right, Indent begins working in reverse. In this instance, Alignment is set to Right and Indent is set to From Left, but the effect is actually to indent the picture from the right side.

By combining Indent and Alignment effects, you can place any graphic in one of five distinct locations across the width of your page.

If you return to the screen shown in Figure 5-15, you'll see there's one more picture-formatting option available: Crop, Rotate, etc. Click the Edit Picture button to bring up the controls shown at the top of Figure 5-22.

Figure 5-22: There's no excuse for a bad-looking picture on your Web page, if you make careful use of these additional formatting controls.

Now you have several other formatting options. From left to right across the top of the screen, they are as follows:

Rotate. Each click of this button rotates the picture 90 degrees to the left.

Vertical Flip. This turns your picture backwards. Think of your picture like a photographic slide. This button is like flipping the slide so that the left and right sides are exchanged and you're looking through the opposite side.

Horizontal Flip. This turns the picture backwards and upside down: it's like flipping a slide over with your fingers so the top becomes the bottom and, again, you're looking through the opposite side.

Scale. Choose the percentage of original size you want the picture to be from the pop-up menu, or click Other and type a percentage. The current percentage always appears on the button in red; in this case, the image is at 75 percent of its original size.

Crop. Sometimes a picture looks better if you only use part of it. Click this button once to activate the cropping tool; use it to draw a box around the portion of the picture you want to keep (notice that the size of the area you're cropping, in pixels, is given to you as you draw the box). Click the button again to cut the cropped section out of the main picture and display it on its own for further editing.

Contrast. These two buttons work like the contrast controls on your monitor. Click the button with the plus sign (+) on it to increase the difference between the darks and lights in your image. If an image looks washed out, increasing the contrast can help. Click the button with the minus sign (–) on it to decrease the difference between darks and lights; in some pictures, this may make more subtle detail and colors visible.

Brightness. These buttons also work just like the corresponding control on your TV. Turn brightness up (by clicking the button with the sun icon), and the picture becomes lighter. Turn brightness down (by clicking the button with the crescent moon or eclipse icon) and the picture becomes darker.

Invert Picture. Click this button to replace lights with darks and colors with their complimentary colors — in other words, to create a photographic negative of your original image.

Convert Picture to Grey Scale. Click this button to turn a color picture into a black-and-white one by removing all color information and showing only darks and lights.

If you'd like to hide the editing tools and just admire your picture, click the control in the upper left corner that looks like a triangle over a dash. Click it again to restore the editing controls.

If you make a change you regret, you can always restore your image to the way it originally appeared by clicking Revert. Once you've formatted your picture the way you like it, click Done on this screen and OK on the first Format Picture screen to continue creating your Web page.

So you've finished formatting your picture, and you're so proud of it you just have to show it to someone else. Personal Publisher 3 makes doing that easy. From the Edit Picture screen, just click Insert in E-mail. AOL's usual e-mail creation screen will appear, with the picture you were just editing already inserted into the message space (see Figure 5-23). It's a great way to create e-mail Christmas cards or share pictures of the kids with Grandma.

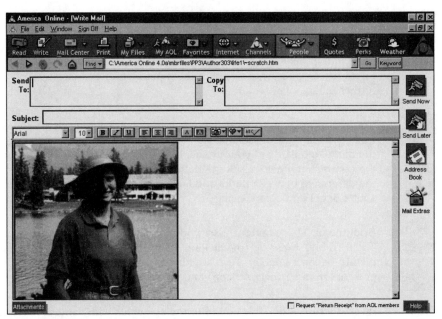

Figure 5-23: You can insert a picture you've edited into an e-mail message, as well as into your Web site.

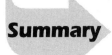

Summary

By using Personal Publisher 3's Advanced Options judiciously, you can make your Web site more your own — and make it more interesting for your visitors. With eye-catching new colors, cleverly formatted graphics, and links to interesting sites all over the Web, your site will soon be making its own appearance in the Favorite Places files of others.

Managing Your Pages

6

In This Chapter

Saving, publishing, and unpublishing pages

Editing pages

Using pages created without Personal Publisher 3

O kay, so you've created your Web page. Now you can relax, right? Well, maybe — if nothing in your life ever changes. But the odds are, it won't be long before something on that page isn't quite right. Maybe you created a business page, and your business has added a new product. Maybe you created a personal page, and you just got married. Maybe you put your resume online, and you just won Employee of the Year. Maybe you created a pet home page, and your dog had puppies. Change is inevitable, and that applies to your Web pages, too. Otherwise they run the risk of becoming like those sad pages every surfer has hit, full of broken links and still talking about things that happened two years ago in the future tense. Fortunately, Personal Publisher 3 makes managing and editing your Web pages easy.

Saving, Publishing, and Unpublishing

Before you can place your page on the World Wide Web, you need to save it to your computer. The Save button, under the Personal Publisher logo, is available each step of the page-building process, so you can save your page at any time (see Figure 6-1).

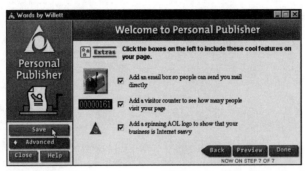

Figure 6-1: You can save your Web page at any time by clicking the Save button, but you'll definitely want to save it if you've reached the final step — adding Extras — and haven't clicked it yet.

When you click Save, you'll see the dialog box shown in Figure 6-2, which asks you for a name for your page. If you've created a *home page*—the page you want visitors to see first—stick with the default `index.htm`. If you're working on a multipage site, you can call the page whatever you want, as long as you make a note of the name and use it for any links to that page from other pages within the site. Your page will be saved in your hard drive's AOL folder, and can be accessed any time by opening Personal Publisher and choosing Manage Your Pages.

The default name for a single Web page is `index.htm`. That's because, when a browser accesses a Web address and the page name isn't specified, `index` is the name the browser seeks. By using `index` as your page name, you can therefore use a shorter URL: `http://members.aol.com/ecwillett`, for example, instead of `http://members.aol.com/ecwillett/firstpage.htm`. If you have a multipage site, you should name the home page `index.htm`. You can then name the other pages anything you want, and link them to the index page.

Figure 6-2: For a single-page Web site, stick with the default name, `index.htm`.

Once you've saved your completed page, you can publish it. "Publishing" means that the page is placed on the Web in a format that Web browsers can read.

When you've completed the last step of the Personal Publisher page creation process, and have saved your page to your hard drive, click Done. This opens the window shown in Figure 6-3. Here you can preview your page, edit it (more on that a little later in the chapter), and publish it.

Figure 6-3: Check over your page here, and when you're happy with it, click Publish.

Clicking Publish brings up the dialog box shown in Figure 6-4.

Again, you're asked what you want to name the page: the name you've already given it appears by default, but if for some reason you want to change it (perhaps you have two pages named index.htm in two different folders on you hard drive, and you have to rename one before you place it on the Web), this is the place to do it.

You're also given information about its size and how many graphics files the page uses, and asked if you want to "Include a menu of all my pages on this page."

Checking this box adds one more item: a text section listing the names of all the pages you've published, with each name linked to the page it describes. It's a quick way to make navigating your site easy for your visitors.

When you've made your decisions, click Publish

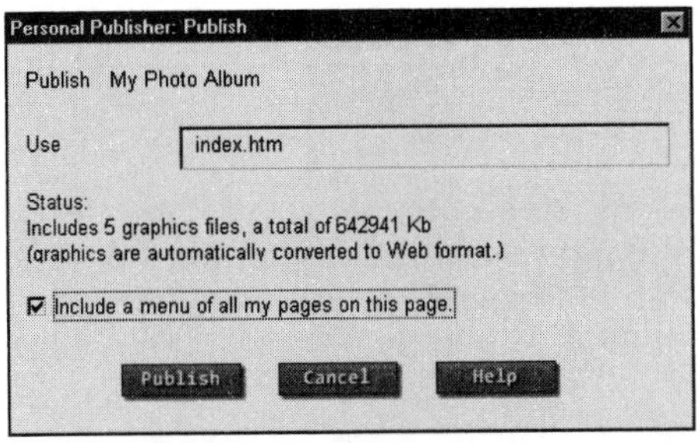

Personal Publisher: Publish ☒

Publish My Photo Album

Use | index.htm

Status:
Includes 5 graphics files, a total of 642941 Kb
(graphics are automatically converted to Web format.)

☑ Include a menu of all my pages on this page.

[Publish] [Cancel] [Help]

Figure 6-4: Name your page (the name you use will become part of the URL), and decide if you want a menu to your other pages automatically added to it.

When you click Publish again, your page is added to the World Wide Web. You get a final message (see Figure 6-5) telling you what the URL is and asking if you want to add your newly created page to your own list of Favorite Places. (And if it's not one of your favorite places, why on earth did you create it?) See Chapter 15, "Your Hometown," for information on publicizing your URL.

Personal Publisher: Success! ☒

The file My Photo Album is now published on the web at
'http://members.aol.com/Author303/Photo1/index.htm.

Do you want to add this file to your Favorite Places?

[Add] [Don't Add] [Help]

Figure 6-5: There's your URL at the top of this dialog box. Now any Internet user in the world can visit your page, if he or she knows the address.

Editing Your Web Pages

If you look back at Figure 6-3, you'll see you have another button you can choose in addition to Publish: Edit. If you're having second thoughts about your design, or if you've just been struck with a brilliant notion that you think will make your Web page even better, Edit lets you make changes.

To Edit your page before Publishing it, follow these steps:

1. From the screen shown in Figure 6-3, click Edit. This calls up an-introductory page that tells you what you'll find on the ensuing screen, which is exactly what I'm about to tell you, too!

2. Click OK, and you'll proceed to the Edit screen itself, shown in Figure 6-6.

Figure 6-6: Use these controls to edit and relocate each of the elements you've placed on your Web page.

3. Personal Publisher displays a preview of your Web page in the main part of the Edit screen. At left, it lists all the elements on that particular page: pictures, text, lists, Favorite Places, and Extras. Within the list, highlight the element you want to move or edit by clicking it once.

4. If you want to move the element closer to the top of the Web page, click the top Move button; if you want to move it closer to the bottom of the Web page, click the bottom Move button. Each click up moves it above the preceding element in the list (and above that element in the preview, too); each click down moves it below the following element.

5. To edit the element, click Edit Item. Doing this brings up the screen you used to add that particular element during the initial page creation process (minus the Personal Publisher logo), as shown in Figure 6-7. Make whatever changes you wish, and then click OK to return to the editing controls.

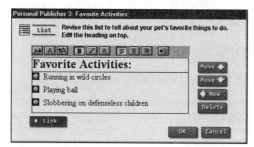

Figure 6-7: Editing an item brings up the same controls you used to create the item in the first place.

6. To add a new element, click Add. You are then given an opportunity to add one of the types of basic elements Personal Publisher uses to assemble Web pages: a picture, an empty list, an empty list of favorite places, or text (see Figure 6-8). Highlight the one you want and click OK to bring up the same controls you used to insert those types of elements during the step-by-step process.

7. To delete an element, click Delete.

8. Once you've made all the changes you want, click Save to save the revised Web page to your hard drive.

9. Finally, click Publish to send the revised Web page to your personal space on AOL.

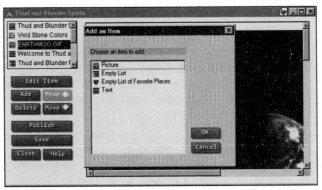

Figure 6-8: You can add additional elements to your Web page here.

Managing Your Web Pages

Personal Publisher provides lots of tools to help you manage your pages after they've been saved or published. You can rename them, remove them from the World Wide Web, and edit them.

To manage your pages, follow these steps:

1. Go to the Personal Publisher area.

2. From the initial screen, click Manage Your Pages (see Figure 6-9). The Manage Your Pages screen appears, as shown in Figure 6-10.

Figure 6-9: Personal Publisher lets you manage your pages, as well as create them . . .

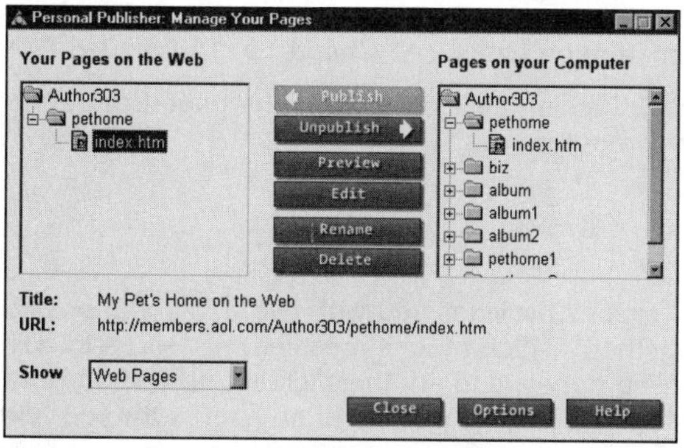

Figure 6-10: . . . using the tools on this screen.

The pages you've published to the Web are listed on the left; the pages you've created and saved on your computer but haven't yet published are listed on the right.

3. To remove a page from the Web and return it to your computer (which you must do to edit it), highlight the page you wish to remove.

4. Click Unpublish.

5. To place a page that's on your computer onto the Web, highlight the page you wish to include.

6. Click Publish.

You can also publish, unpublish, and delete pictures by using the little pull-down menu in the lower left corner of the Manage Your Pages dialog box. By default, you only see Web pages, but you can also choose to only see images. Or you can choose Any Files, which shows you both Web pages and images, and anything else you might have posted (such as sound or video files; see Chapter 10, "Multimedia — The Extra Dimension").

You can also choose from the following other buttons:

➡ **Preview.** As you've already seen, Preview enables you to look at an unpublished page before placing it on Web.

➡ **Edit.** This button takes you to the Edit Page area described in the previous section of this chapter.

➡ **Rename.** You can rename any of your Web pages. Remember, if you rename a page, you must change any links you've put on any other pages that point to that page by its original name. (For more information on Links, see Chapter 5, "Advanced Options.")

➡ **Delete.** Clicking Delete removes the page from either the Web or your computer.

Options

Clicking Options provides you with two additional possibilities: "Link your pages together," which makes it easier for visitors to navigate among multiple Web pages, and another, "Direct uploading/downloading," which you can use to easily share files of any sort with your virtual visitors (see Figure 6-11):

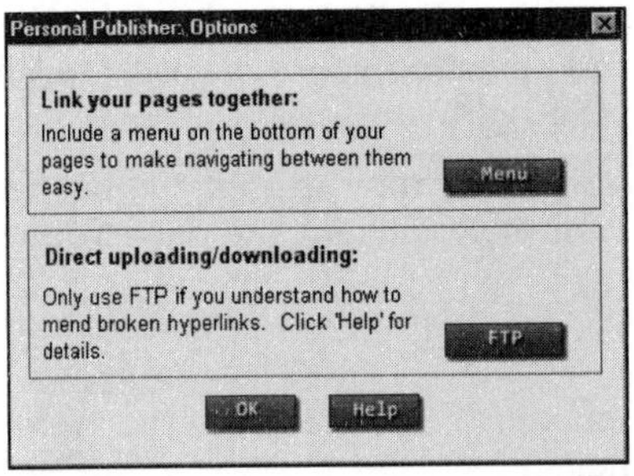

Figure 6-11: Personal Publisher offers a number of options you can use to make your Web site more functional for yourself and for your virtual visitors.

Link your pages together

If you're creating more than one Web page, chances are you want to make it easy for visitors to navigate among them. To do so, let Personal Publisher create a text-based navigation menu on the bottom of your page.

To link your Web pages together, follow these steps:

1. When you first Publish the page, click the checkbox labeled "Include a menu of all my pages on this page" (see Figure 6-4).

2. From the Manage Your Pages dialog box (see Figure 6-10), click Options to open the dialog box in Figure 6-11.

3. Click Menu to open the dialog box shown in Figure 6-12.

```
Personal Publisher: Link Your Pages Together                              [X]

                              Decide which pages to include in the menu.
                              Provide a short description for each page.
        Link your pages        ☑ "Words by Willett" biz1/index.htm
        together by putting     ☑ "My Pet's Home on the Web" pethome/index.htm
        a menu on each page.    ☑ "My Photo Album" album2/page3.htm
        Visitors can use the
        menu to jump between
        your published pages.

        The preview below
        shows how the menu
        will look at the bottom
        of the selected pages.   Type a short description: [ Words by Willett        ]

                                 Reposition in Menu?   [◄ Move]      [Move ►]

            My Pet's Home on the Web || Words by Willett || My Photo Album

    Menu Preview (links not active)
                                            [  OK  ]  [ Cancel ]  [ Help ]
```

Figure 6-12: Help visitors get the most out of your Web site by adding links to all your pages at the bottom of each one you create.

4. A box at right lists all your published pages. Click the checkboxes to mark the pages you want to include in the menu. The Menu Preview at the bottom of the page shows you what the menu will look like.

5. To rearrange the order in which your pages appear in the link menu, highlight the one you want to move, and then use the Move keys to move it to the left or right of its current position.

6. To have a name different from the actual page name appear on the menu, enter text in the "Type a short description" box.

7. Once you're happy with your menu, click OK.

Direct Uploading/Downloading

If you would like visitors to be able to upload or download files from your Web site, click the FTP button in the Options dialog box. FTP stands for *File Transfer Protocol*.

FTP is not just a good way to move files around the Internet: it's also a good way for you to make files available to others and for others to send you files. You can save a file of any sort in your personal storage space on AOL and create a link to it from your Web page. All your visitors have to do is click the link, and the file is automatically downloaded to their computer.

FTP files, like your Web page, are stored in the 2 megabytes (MB) of Internet-accessible disk space AOL provides for each screen name on the members.aol.com computers. AOL calls this disk space "My Place." Since there are a maximum of five screen names per account, each account is limited to a total of about 10MB.

When you click the FTP button from the Options dialog box, you first see an introductory screen. Click Go to My Place to open the dialog box shown in Figure 6-13.

Figure 6-13: This window gives you control over your personal storage space on AOL. Notice that each Web page you've created using Personal Publisher has its own folder.

To make a file available for visitors to your Web site to download, open one of the file folders, and then click Upload. Then follow these steps:

1. **In the dialog box that opens (see Figure 6-14), enter the name you want the file to have and whether the file is ASCII or binary. (ASCII is the code computers use for straight text. ASCII files can generally be recognized because they end in** .txt. **Anything**

else, including most word processor files, or straight text mixed with pictures, are binary files.) Click Continue.

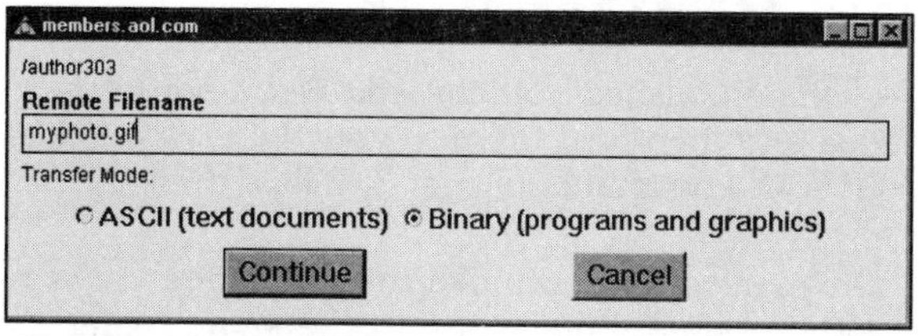

Figure 6-14: Upload files — such as a photo of yourself! — to your FTP space from this window.

 Be sure the names you give files you're uploading to your FTP space are acceptable. Valid names can include letters and numbers and underscores; they can also contain hyphens and periods, but they cannot begin with a hyphen or period. Also, they cannot contain a space.

2. An Upload File window will open (see Figure 6-15). Click Select File to browse your computer for the file you want.

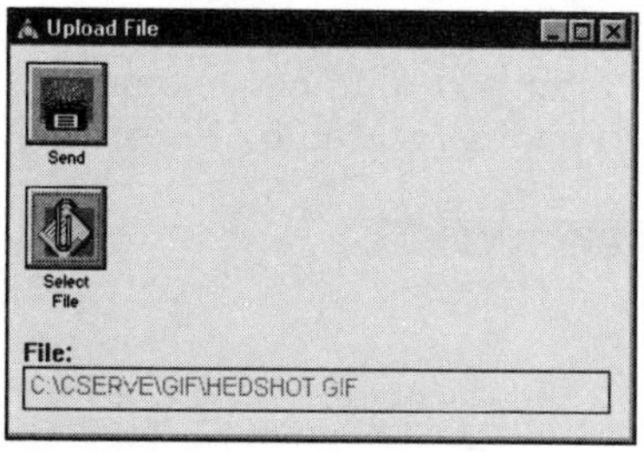

Figure 6-15: Locate the file you want to place in FTP space from here.

3. Once you've chosen the file you want to upload, click Send, and your file will be uploaded.

Once you've uploaded a file to your FTP space, you can return to the editing tools and add a link to that file from any page on your Web site by choosing "Type any URL" from the Link menu. The URL will be similar to your own Web site, except instead of being `http://members.aol.com/screename`, it will be `ftp://members.aol.com/screename/folder/filename`.

For example, the photo I just placed in my FTP space would have the URL `ftp://members.aol.com/Author303/biz1/myphoto.gif`.

Managing Other Web Pages with Personal Publisher 3

Using Personal Publisher, you can edit Web pages created with other applications and then post them to your AOL Web space. To manage other Web pages with Personal Publisher 3, follow these steps:

1. On your computer, move the Web page you want to manage with Personal Publisher into the same folder as the Web pages you've created with Personal Publisher. The path is typically something like `C://America Online 4.0/mbrfiles/PP3/Your Screen Name/`.

2. Go to the Personal Publisher area.

3. Click Manage Your Pages. The Web pages you moved there will now appear with the pages you created using Personal Publisher 3 and saved to your hard drive.

4. Use the Publish, Unpublish, Rename, Delete, and Edit buttons just as you would with Personal Publisher-created Web pages. The highlighted Web page shown in Figure 6-16, for example, was originally created using Microsoft Word, but now you can use Personal Publisher to move items up and down within it, change graphics, alter text, add new elements, and everything else you can do to pages created by Personal Publisher.

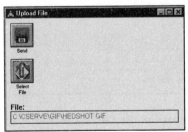

Figure 6-16: Personal Publisher can be used to edit any Web page, regardless of the program or application used to create it.

 Remember that you must also publish any images or other files associated with a Web page for it to display the way it should. Personal Publisher does that automatically with the pages it creates, but if you use Personal Publisher's page management tools to move a non-Personal Publisher Web page to your AOL Web site, you must also move any related files manually.

Summary

Personal Publisher 3 is more than just a powerful tool for creating Web pages. It's also a good tool for managing them. Keeping your pages up to date is an important part of having your own Web site. And thanks to Personal Publisher, you have no excuse not to.

Web Publishing Resources on AOL

Personal Publisher already has a lot of resources built right in, thanks to the templates: graphics, suggested layouts, and so on. But as you continue developing your Web site, sooner or later you're likely to come up against a problem you don't know how to solve. Maybe you have a specific image in mind for your page, but you don't know where to find it. Maybe you've been browsing through other Personal Publisher-created pages and you've seen something you'd like to emulate, but you don't know how it was done. That's where America Online's extensive Web publishing-related resources come in. Help is only a few mouse clicks away!

Online Help

The first place to look for answers, of course, is in the help files included with Personal Publisher. Almost every Personal Publisher screen includes a Help button that brings up specific files that relate to the current screen. For example, clicking Help on the Edit screen brings up information on how to edit your Web page, as shown in Figure 7-1.

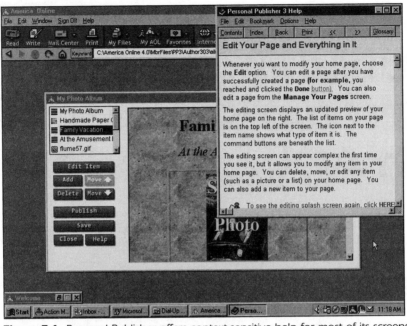

Figure 7-1: Personal Publisher offers context-sensitive help for most of its screens.

For basic information about how to use Personal Publisher 3, you can't beat the online help. It's easy to use, it's succinct, and it's there when you need it. To find answers to more complex Web design problems than simply using the templates, however, you may want to range further afield.

Frequently Asked Questions

Chances are, you aren't the first person to face whatever challenge it is you're facing with Personal Publisher 3, or the first person to have a question about some specific aspect of the program.

Personal Publisher's introductory screen (see Figure 7-2) includes a menu of additional resources you can access, one of which is Frequently Asked Questions (usually abbreviated FAQ).

 The resources that appear in the list box on the Personal Publisher 3 introductory screen, or any other AOL screen, are subject to change without notice. If you can't find one of the resources discussed in this chapter, chances are AOL has moved it, redesigned it, or replaced it with something else.

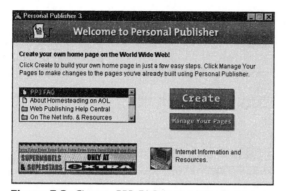

Figure 7-2: Choose PP3 FAQ in the introductory screen to view frequently asked questions and answers about working with Personal Publisher 3.

Double-click the PP3 FAQ menu item to bring up a menu of questions that are often asked about Personal Publisher 3 — and their answers (see Figure 7-3).

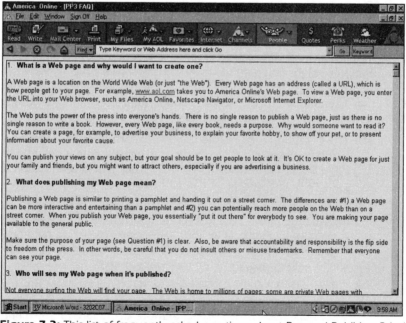

Figure 7-3: This list of frequently asked questions about Personal Publisher 3 is the first place you should go when looking for general information about the program.

Web Publishing Help Central

If you still haven't managed to find an answer to your question, the next place to try is Web Publishing Help Central, also available from the initial Personal Publisher screen. The Web Publishing Help Central opening screen is shown in Figure 7-4.

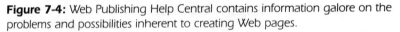

Figure 7-4: Web Publishing Help Central contains information galore on the problems and possibilities inherent to creating Web pages.

Web Publishing Help Central contains several files and links to other sites that you might find helpful. They are as follows:

→ The first two files, "About Personal Publisher" and "About My Place," are simply brief explanations of those two topics.

→ The "Creating a Page" file contains information on creating, naming, uploading, and accessing your Web pages, plus a helpful file on Web Page Do's and Don'ts that outlines what you can and can't do with your AOL Web pages.

→ The "Editing and Adding Features to a Page" file folder contains information about adding everything from text files and graphics to mail links and sounds to your Web page. You'll find help on both using Personal Publisher and using HTML (the programming language with which Web pages are ultimately constructed).

→ Other Web Resources leads you to HTML editors and resources, graphics resources, and sound resources available on AOL and on the Web. I discuss some of these in more detail later in this chapter and in chapters to come.

→ AOL Press Help provides information about AOL Press, a free Web page editor used by many members to create and edit their Web pages on AOL.

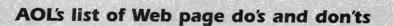
AOL's list of Web page do's and don'ts

Creating and publishing a Web page on America Online means that the whole world can see your work. That means *everyone*—including children.

America Online's Terms of Service (TOS) apply not only to your online conduct, but to information you publish on the Web pages you can create with Personal Publisher or pages stored on AOL servers. Have fun and be creative, but remember these basic guidelines:

- Don't use your Web page to harass, threaten, embarrass, or cause distress, unwanted attention, or discomfort to anyone. If you have a disagreement with someone's point of view, address the subject, not the person.

- Don't display sexually explicit images or other offensive content on your page.

- Don't display unlawful, harmful, threatening, abusive, harassing, defamatory, vulgar, obscene, or hateful content, or racially, ethnically, or otherwise objectionable content.

- Don't impersonate any person on your Web page.

- Do use your page to advertise your business, but don't violate any applicable local, state, national, or international law.

- Don't offer a product or service based on the structure of a pyramid scheme — they are not permitted on AOL.

- Don't copy pictorial images, logos, or blocks of text you find on AOL or the Internet.

- Don't copy excerpts from online news services.

Remember, if the America Online service is notified about a Web page that doesn't conform to the TOS, AOL will investigate. As indicated in the Terms of Service, if it violates TOS, AOL has the right to have the page removed. Following these guidelines makes it easier for everyone to enjoy their America Online membership.

➡ On The Net: Internet Information and Resources is an AOL site devoted to (what else?) Internet Information and Resources — including tricks, tips, and tools for those who create Web sites and those who browse them (see Figure 7-5). You'll find links to FAQs on browsers and Web publishing; links to pages on the World Wide Web chock-full of helpful information, such as CMPNet's TechTools site; and links to AOL forums and regularly scheduled chat sessions about publishing on the World Wide Web.

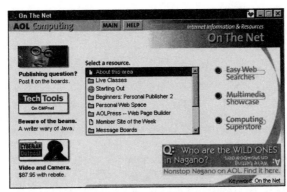

Figure 7-5: Whether you're looking for the best way to add sound and graphics to your Web site or to experience sound and graphics on other people's Web sites, On the Net can point you in the right direction.

➡ Online HTML & Web Publishing Classes are perfect for those who prefer a more structured approach to learning about Web publishing than just picking it up here and there. AOL's Online Classroom offers lessons in everything from using animated GIFs to adding counters, guestbooks, and forms (see Figure 7-6). The classes are free and interactive (they're chat based), and you don't even need to register in advance.

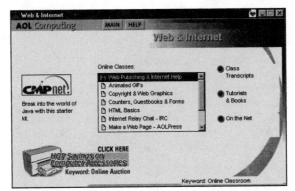

Figure 7-6: Learn more about creating Web pages, and about the Internet in general, in AOL's Online Classroom.

To take an online class, follow these steps:

1. Sign on to AOL and go to the Online Classroom (keyword Online Classroom).

2. Check out the Class Schedule, find the classes you want to attend, and mark your calendar.

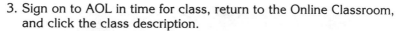
3. Sign on to AOL in time for class, return to the Online Classroom, and click the class description.

4. Click Enter Classroom to join the class.

AOL even offers a free reminder service which sends out an e-mail so you won't forget to come to class — and if you do miss a class you're interested in, you'll find a transcript posted in the Online Classroom afterward, complete with any class material or handouts.

Clicking the Tutorials and Books button points you in the direction of even more online lessons found all over the Web (see Figure 7-7).

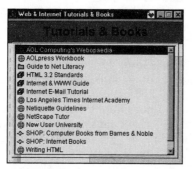

Figure 7-7: Web Publishing Help Central can also point you to some of the many World Wide Web sites devoted to Web-publishing topics.

Picture Resources

One question many first-time Web page designers ask is, "Where do other Web designers get all those cool pictures?"

From the Personal Publisher home page, AOL points you to a number of picture resources in answer to that question. Some of the resources you can link to from here are commercial enterprises (EZ Scan, for instance, will turn your photos into computer files — for a price). If you're interested in purchasing hardware or software to help you create and edit digital pictures, a good place to visit is AOL's Digital Shop. (Although AOL doesn't provide a direct link to it from the Personal Publisher home page, you can reach it by using keyword **Digital Shop**.) Here, there's a great selection of digital cameras, scanners, and image software (see Figure 7-8).

Figure 7-8: The Digital Shop is a one-stop online shop for everything related to creating and editing digital images.

Other picture resources you can access from the Personal Publisher home page provide free help and advice on obtaining or creating photographs and other images for your Web pages. If it's photographs you're interested in, the Photography Forum (keyword **Photography Forum**) has just about all the information about photography you could imagine (see Figure 7-9), plus files full of photographs (make sure you get permission from the photographer before using any of them on your Web page, however!).

Figure 7-9: The Photography Forum can answer questions about putting photographs on the Web, and has libraries full of photographs that you may be able to use, if you make arrangements with the photographers who posted them.

There's a different photography area in AOL's Hobby Central (keyword **Hobby Central**), and it's another good place to learn about the process of putting photographs online and to find photographs you can use. It provides links to oodles of photography-related sites on both AOL and the World Wide Web (see Figure 7-10).

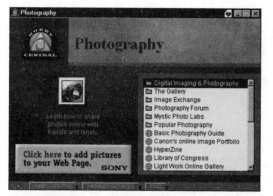

Figure 7-10: Hobby Central's Photography area also contains lots of information — and lots of links to more information — about using photographs online, and can point you to photographs available for your use.

Image Exchange (keyword **Image Exchange**), shown in Figure 7-11, is another good resource for pictures; from here, you can obtain images ranging from historical photographs to classic artworks to contemporary celebrity images. Again, it's important to make sure, if an image is copyrighted, that you have obtained permission to use it.

Figure 7-11: Image Exchange can lead you to just about any kind of image you can imagine.

If you're looking for even more exciting additions to your Web page, check out AOL's Multimedia Showcase (keyword **Multimedia Showcase**). This site, which is also available from the Web (`http://multimedia.aol.com/internal/gallery.htm`), contains tips, tools, and examples of exciting uses of multimedia — everything from adding sound and animations to full-motion video (see Figure 7-12).

Figure 7-12: AOL's Multimedia Showcase is the place to go for those who are ready to move beyond static pictures and static text.

Message Boards

You can dig through AOL and the Web all you like, but sometimes you just can't find the answer to your question. When that happens, what you really want is someone knowledgeable to whom you can talk. You can find people like that on AOL's message boards. AOL's On the Net message boards, which you can access from Personal Publisher's initial screen, are arranged among four main topics: Internet Discussion, Internet Utilities, Your AOL Web Page, and Beyond HTML: Advanced Topics.

Personal Publisher users will be most interested in Your AOL Web Page, where subtopics range from Web Graphics and Sound on My Web Page to HTML Questions and Answers (see Figure 7-13).

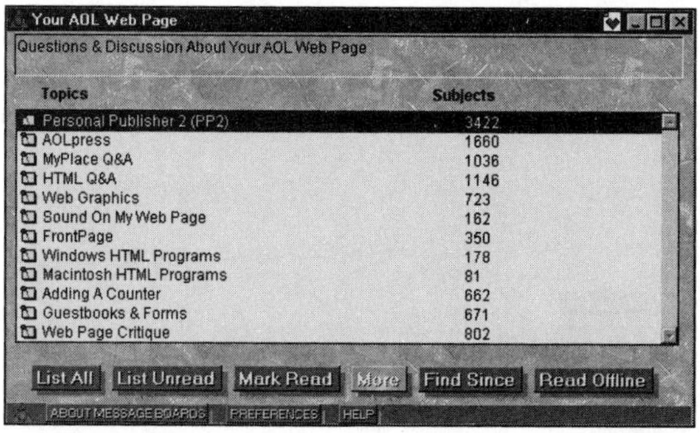

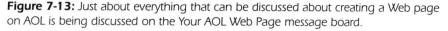

Figure 7-13: Just about everything that can be discussed about creating a Web page on AOL is being discussed on the Your AOL Web Page message board.

If you're ready to move on to such advanced Web design topics as JavaScript and Perl, you'll find them under discussion under Beyond HTML: Advanced Topics. For more suggestions on where to find more advanced information about Web page design, see the Appendix in the back of this book.

Summary

No matter what kind of problem you run into while trying to create Web pages on AOL with Personal Publisher, you're not alone. There's always a Help button, an AOL site, or a message board close at hand, with answers to your questions.

Text and Hypertext

8

When the World Wide Web began, it was primarily text based — it was intended, after all, as a means for scientists to post, exchange, and cross-reference documents. Over time, graphics have become more and more prominent. But text is still the most basic element of almost any Web page, because it's the text that communicates your message to your viewers (that old saw about a picture being worth a thousand words notwithstanding). But it's not enough to just throw any old text onto the Web. To make your page work for you, and to make it a cool place for visitors, you need to give careful thought not only to what you write but how you format it.

Adding Text to Your Web Page

You can add text to your Web page at any time by using the Personal Publisher Editing tools (see Chapter 6, "Managing Your Pages"). To add text, follow these steps:

1. From the Edit screen, click **Add.**

2. Choose **Text** from the Add an Item dialog box, and click **OK.**

3. Enter the text you want to add in the Text dialog box, as shown in Figure 8-1.

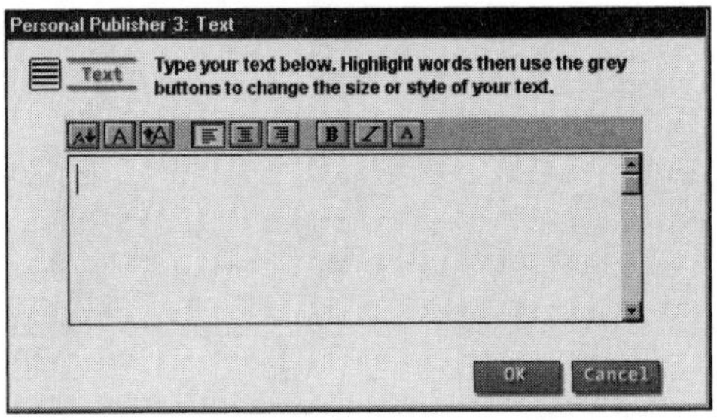

Figure 8-1: Enter text with this dialog box.

You can place text into the Text dialog box in one of two ways:

➡ **Type it in.** Use this method if you're comfortable composing on the fly. But if you want more time to think about what you're writing. . .

➡ **Paste it in.** This allows you to write your text off-line using your favorite word processor.

To paste text into the Text dialog box, follow these steps:

1. **Write and edit the text you want in your word processor.**

2. **Once it's ready to be inserted into your Web page, highlight the text and copy it to the clipboard.**

3. **Log on to AOL.**

4. **Go to the Personal Publisher screen.**

5. **Choose Manage Your Pages.**

6. **From the pages saved on your hard drive, select the page you want to add the text to and click Edit.**

7. **Click Add.**

8. **Choose Text from the Add an Item dialog box, and click OK.**

9. **Press Ctrl+V to paste the text from the clipboard into the text dialog box.**

Once you've entered text into the dialog box, you can format it in various ways, using the buttons across the top. From left to right, they are as follows:

➡ **Decrease font size.** In most Windows programs that use text, you can use any font size you want. The Web, however, limits you to certain specific sizes: a size considered ideal for body text (the default size), then sizes smaller than that (for less-important text), and sizes larger than that (for headlines and subheads). Click this button to make selected text the next smallest size.

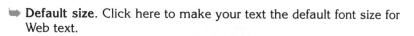
→ **Default size**. Click here to make your text the default font size for Web text.

→ **Increase font size**. Click this button to make selected text the next largest size.

These three options are illustrated in Figure 8-2.

Default font size

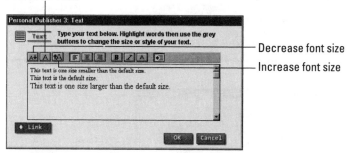

Decrease font size
Increase font size

Figure 8-2: *The first group of three buttons in the Text dialog box controls the size of the text.*

→ **Align left**. This aligns a selected paragraph with the left side of the Web page. It always affects the entire paragraph, even if you've only highlighted a word or two.

→ **Center**. This centers a selected paragraph on the Web page. It, too, affects the entire paragraph.

→ **Align right**. This aligns a selected paragraph with the right side of the Web page. It, too, affects the entire paragraph.

These three options are illustrated in Figure 8-3.

→ **Bold**. This makes selected text bold.

→ **Italic**. This makes selected text italic.

→ **Text color**. This allows you to change the color of selected text.

You can combine these styles.

Text can be bold, italic, *or* a different color.

Text can be bold *or* italic *and* a different color

Text can be bold *and* italic *and* a different color.

These three options are illustrated in Figure 8-4.

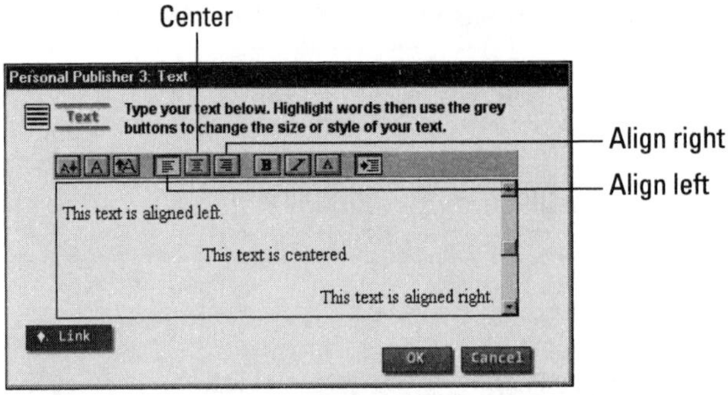

Center

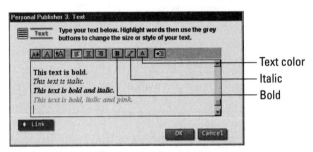

Align right

Align left

Figure 8-3: The second group of three buttons in the Text dialog box control the alignment of text.

Text color

Italic

Bold

Figure 8-4: The third group of three buttons in the Text dialog box controls the text style.

➥ **Increase indent**. This button is only available when you have saved your page and are editing it. It moves a selected paragraph further from the left margin (see Figure 8-5).

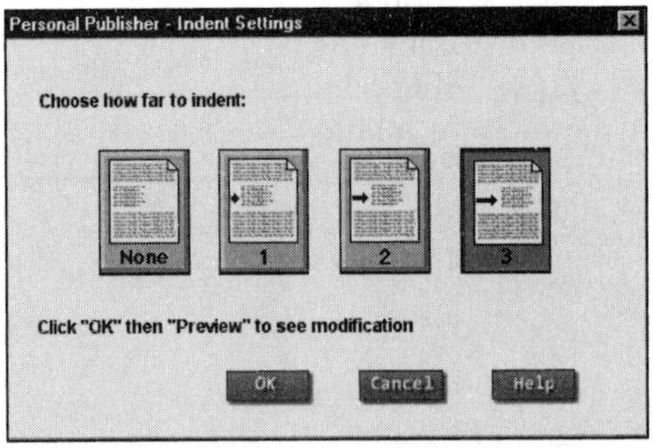

Figure 8-5: You can choose one of three levels of indent to apply to selected text.

Writing for the Web

If you're making the effort to add text to your Web page, then presumably you have something you want to communicate. That means getting viewers not only to visit your site, but to stay there long enough to read your text. Here are three ways to help ensure that visitors take the time to read what you wrote — and take it seriously.

Rule 1: Keep it short

There's a famous story about a writer who apologized to a friend for having sent him a long letter. He just didn't have time to make it shorter, he explained.

Those of us who write for a living know exactly what he meant. It's often easier to ramble on and on than to get to the point, easier to throw a whole bunch of words at a topic and hope some of them stick than to pare them down into a tight, elegant linguistic dart.

In print you can sometimes get away with a certain amount of rambling, especially if you're writing a long piece. Many students who regularly write term papers, in fact, become quite expert at disguising the paucity of their knowledge with the size of their vocabulary. But if you want to attract visitors to your Web page and keep them there, you don't have that luxury. Two basic principles affect everything published on the Web:

➡ **On-screen text is hard to read.** Staring at a computer screen is fatiguing to the eye; clicking the mouse to scroll through page after page of text is fatiguing to the hand. The amount of energy expended isn't great in absolute terms, but it's certainly much higher than that expended in reading an ordinary magazine.

➡ **Something else is always just a mouse click away.** While it may be harder to read text on the Web, it's easier to stop reading it. Once you've settled down in a comfortable chair with a book or magazine, you're willing to let the author take a little time to come to the point. On the Web, though, your text is competing not only with millions of other Web pages just a couple of mouse clicks away but whatever diversions the reader has installed on his or her own computer, from Solitaire to Quake II.

When it comes to writing text for your Web page, the first rule is Shorter is better. A huge mass of text simply isn't going to be read by many visitors to your page (see Figure 8-6).

That doesn't mean you can't offer lots of information. It just means you have to break it up into smaller, more easily digestible chunks. A simple way to do that is shown in Figure 8-7.

"Beam me up, Scotty, there's no intelligent life here!" How often have you wished you could escape unpleasant situations just by flipping open a communicator and asking to be instantaneously whisked away? (Using your cell phone to have yourself paged doesn't count.) Well, teleportation of human beings--causing them to vanish in one location and instantaneously appear in another, a la Star Trek--may still be a pipe dream, but teleportation itself is not: it's been achieved.

A team at the Institute for Experimental Physics in Innsbruck, Austria, has succeeded in transferring the properties of a photon--a single particle of light--to another photon, instantly and without any connection between the two. In their ground-breaking experiment, the first photon disappeared and an exact duplicate appeared three metres away.

To understand how, you need to understand a couple of basic principles.

First, quantum mechanics states that elementary particles such as photons don't have precise properties until they are measured--before that, they exist solely as a set of probabilities. Second, something called the Heisenberg uncertainty principle prevents you from ever measuring the state of an elementary particle with precision: the very act of measuring it disturbs it. The more accurately you measure it, the more disturbed it becomes; before you achieve complete accuracy, you've disrupted the particle.

Since teleportation involves making an exact, particle-by-particle replica of an object, and you can't measure particles that precisely due to the uncertainty principle, teleportation was long assumed to be impossible. But a couple of years ago six scientists figured out how to get around the uncertainty principle.

The method they came up with, and which the Austrian group used, uses an aspect of quantum mechanics so bizarre Einstein refused to believe it was real, even though he first discussed it in a 1930 paper cowritten by Boris Podolsky and Nathan Rosen. Certain pairs of particles have a mysterious linkage called the "Einstein-Podolsky-Rosen (EPR) correlation," or "entanglement." Measuring one particle of an entangled pair instantaneously determines the state of the other particle of the pair.

Figure 8-6: A big page of gray text such as this is going to lose Web page viewers just about as quickly as a major power outage.

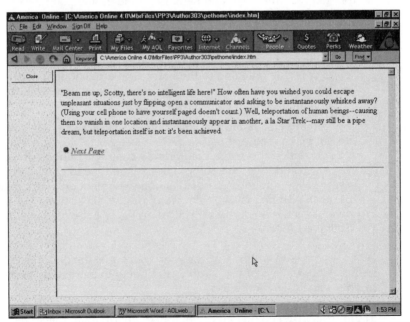

Figure 8-7: One easy way to break up large amounts of text is to spread it over several Web pages, with each page ending in a link that takes you to the next page.

That's kind of awkward, though, and you're still going to lose readers. The best bet remains: pare the text down as much as you can without sacrificing important information.

Rule 2: Keep it sweet

There's more to successful writing on the Web than just keeping text short. *How* you say what you have to say is almost as important as *what* you say.

Writing that works perfectly well in the gray columns of a major metropolitan newspaper comes across as staid and dull within the colorful, ever-changing confines of the Web. As a result, the best Web writing tends to be informal, and fun (and funny) — in short, cool.

A good rule is to imagine that you're writing a chatty letter (or better yet, a chatty e-mail) to a friend. That sense of warm familiarity will make visitors to your Web site feel welcome, and if you can crack a few jokes or say something witty along the way, all the better.

In other words: be hip, be cool, use the words you want to use instead of the words your high-school English teachers made you use in those endless essays they used to assign — be yourself. Let your individual voice come through on your Web page, and you'll make it that much more your own.

Inverted pyramid style a natural for the 'Net

There's another trick you can use to offer a lot of information and keep your readers interested: *inverted pyramid style*. Stories written using this classic journalistic technique have the most important facts in the first paragraph, with more details and less important facts in the subsequent paragraphs. Inverted pyramid style allows editors to cut stories to fit available space simply by chopping paragraphs off the bottom. It also recognizes the fact that many people only skim newspapers, often reading the first paragraph or two of stories at most.

What's true for newspapers is even more true for the Web: people tend to skim the first paragraph of text, then move on. By making sure the most important information you want to impart is in that first paragraph, you stand a better chance of communicating with your viewers.

Rule 3: Spelling counts!

Having just made a snide comment about high-school English teachers, it behooves me to hastily add that they say a great many important things, including, "Spelling counts!" So do grammar and punctuation, and all the other mechanics of writing you may not have paid as much attention to as you should have.

This is one area where thinking of what you're writing as a chatty e-mail to a friend won't work. Your friend may not care that you misspelled every other word—someone coming to your page looking for whatever information it is you want to impart, however, has little reason to trust that information if it appears to have been written by someone for whom spelling is an arcane art (see Figure 8-8).

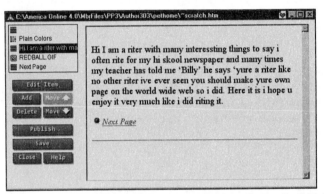

Figure 8-8: Would you believe anything this author writes? Unfortunately, this is hardly even an exaggerated example of some of the bad writing on the Web.

Oh, sure, there's a lot of bad spelling, grammar, and punctuation to be found on the Web, and the people responsible for it probably don't care when they encounter it on other people's Web sites. But if you want to reach as wide an audience as possible, take the time to check for errors before posting your site. Otherwise, you run the risk of half your potential visitors taking one look at your page and immediately discounting it. Remember, every other site on the Internet is only a few mouse clicks away. Don't scare off your audience before it's had the chance to see what you offer.

Text and Hypertext

There's one other important element of writing text for your Web page: the judicious use of *links*. Links are what distinguish ordinary text—the kind you're reading in this book—from *hypertext*.

What is hypertext?

Hypertext sounds like something out of a Star Trek episode. ("Captain! If we don't get dilithium soon, the hypertext generator is gonna be toast!") But hypertext is simply a way of presenting information that's nonlinear: that is, readers don't have to learn things in the order the author of the text wants them to. Instead they can create their own order, which means they may also construct their own meaning — something the author or authors involved never intended or foresaw.

Links are what make this happen. They allow readers to jump from one piece of information to a related (or unrelated, for that matter) one (see Figure 8-9). If that second piece of information also has links embedded in it, the reader quite possibly will never come back to the first piece of information. Instead he'll follow the continuing trail of links across the World Wide Web.

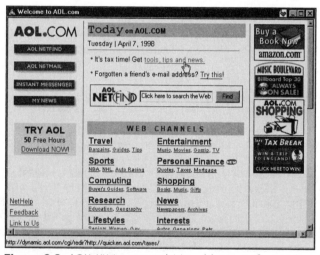

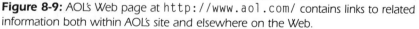

Figure 8-9: AOL's Web page at `http://www.aol.com/` contains links to related information both within AOL's site and elsewhere on the Web.

As a writer, I'd prefer that my reader come back to my original site — and if I've designed it well enough, and stocked it with interesting enough information, they probably will — but there's no guarantee of that. And that's fine, because that's what the World Wide Web is all about.

Hypertext is great because it reflects the way humans learn. In general, we can figure things out better if we move at our pace instead of someone else's, and are able to further explore the things that interest us.

In a sense, if you provide interesting links within your site's text, you're not so much writing a complete document for your readers to peruse and learn something from, but simply writing a single page of a much larger, personalized document readers create for themselves as they surf the Web.

Adding links to text

Using Personal Publisher 3 to add links to your text is easy. Follow these steps:

1. Go to the Edit screen and select the text you want to add links to from the menu in the upper-left corner.

2. Click Edit.

3. In the Text dialog box, highlight the text to which you want to add a Link.

4. Click Link.

5. In the Link Choices dialog box, open the pull-down "Click to see choices" menu, and select the kind of link you want to add (see Chapter 5, "Advanced Options," for details).

6. Click OK.

While adding links is easy; knowing how many to add and where each link should take you isn't.

Here are some suggestions to remember when adding links:

➡ **Anticipate needs.** As you look over your text, ask yourself, "Is my reader going to want more information about that? If so, where can I point him to get it?" It may take some research to find good links to meet the need for more information, but to write good hypertext you need to be prepared to do that research — and if you're writing about a topic that interests you, chances are you've already found some top-notch sites related to it somewhere on the Web.

➡ **Organize your material carefully.** Give prominence to the most relevant and interesting links by placing them in the main body of your text, or giving them special formatting. You may want to group less-important links together in a list at the bottom of the text.

➡ **Make sure those links in your text really are relevant and interesting, because links distract the reader.** Remember, every link is an invitation to go elsewhere. Don't add it unless you're prepared to have your viewers abandon the paragraph you wrote in favor of the new site to which you've pointed them (see Figure 8-10).

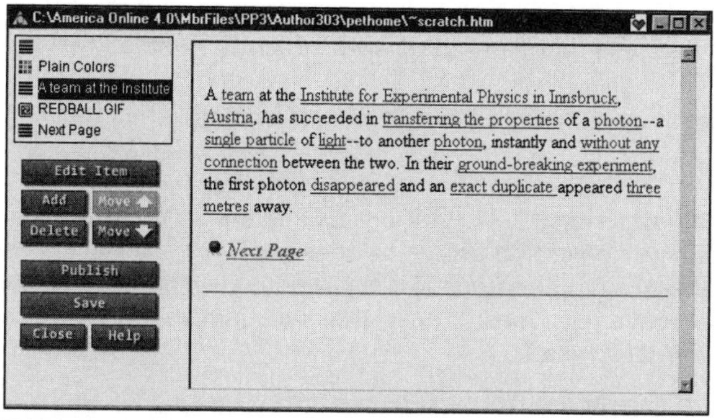

Figure 8-10: Too many links spoil the text. This writer is so eager to send his readers off on side trips that you have to wonder why he wrote the paragraph in the first place.

➡ **Don't use sentences such as "Click here for more information."** It's much less distracting if you write the way you normally would and simply attach the link you want to include to the most appropriate word or words within the sentence.

➡ **Use colors for your links that closely match, but are distinct from, your text color.** As noted earlier, reading from the screen is not something people enjoy for long periods of time; there's no need to make them deal with hideously ugly (and hard to read) links, as well.

The Laws of Legibility

Here's a bulletin for you: for people to understand what you've written on your Web page, they have to be able to read it. You'd think this would be so obvious there'd be no need to tell people, but you don't have to surf the Web long to realize that nothing could be further from the truth. I'm sure the number of unattractive, ugly, or plain illegible color combinations isn't infinite, but sometimes it seems that way.

Color choice is only one element of legibility. The size of type and its layout can also affect this most critical aspect of text on the Web.

If everything's bold, nothing is

As noted earlier, Personal Publisher 3 makes it easy for you to make text bold, italic, or both, and to change the size of type. But both should be done only to highlight or otherwise set off specific sections of text. If you make all your text large in the hope it will stand out, it doesn't, because it's all the same size. You're better off using larger type sizes to set off headlines or other important labels. Similarly, if everything is bold, then nothing is, because there's nothing with which the bolded text contrasts.

Here are some good, general rules to keep in mind while formatting your text:

➡ **Avoid all-uppercase text.** Our brains use the shape of words to speed our reading, so we don't have to necessarily register every letter within the word. A word like *Look* has a shape quite distinct from, say, *Query*. All-uppercase text doesn't have these distinctive shapes, and thus is much harder to read.

➡ **Minimize capitalized words in headlines and subheads.** Similarly, headlines where every word is capitalized are harder to read than headlines where only the first word is capitalized. That's because the shape of the top half of words has more to do with determining legibility than the bottom half. Capitalizing the first letter of every word in a phrase, as in, "If Everything's Bold, Nothing Is," disrupts our perception of the tops of the words, making the phrase harder to read.

➡ **Use indents to keep lines of text short.** Magazines and books, you've probably noticed, have fairly narrow columns; many Web pages don't. Narrow columns are easier to read because, at normal reading distances, the eye's movement only spans about three inches. Wider columns require readers to move their heads slightly, or strain their eye muscles. Most Web pages are almost twice as wide as the viewer's eye span, so it's no wonder they're no fun to read. Keeping columns of text narrow will make it more likely your viewers will actually read your text online.

➡ **Avoid excessive use of bold and italics — especially when mixed with links.** Both make text stand out, but if you use them too much, they lose their impact — and they make your paragraph ugly, and hard to read, especially if they're mixed with links (see Figure 8-11).

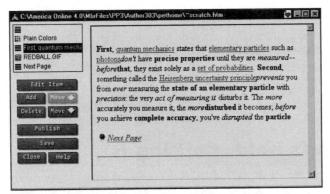

Figure 8-11: Trying too hard to emphasize important words only ensures that everything gets lost in a welter of special effects, like the plot in some movie blockbusters.

➥ **Size isn't everything.** Save extra-large text for extra-important headlines. Making all the text extra-large has an odd effect on viewers; they get the distinct impression you're shouting at them, and most people don't like to be shouted at. On the other hand, don't shrink text so you can get more onto a single screen. It's hard enough to read text on a computer monitor without having to get out a magnifying glass to do it.

Be careful with color

Personal Publisher templates include a number of possible background styles, which have already been designed to be legible. But with the advanced options, you have the opportunity to change background colors and text colors, which means you can easily, if you aren't careful, make reading your text difficult.

Black on white may seem like a boring and old-fashioned, ink-on-paper kind of choice, but studies have shown that black on white is the most legible color combination, both on paper and especially on the computer screen.

The typical computer screen displays text at somewhere between 72 and 80 *dots per inch* (dpi), the equivalent to about 5,200 dots per square inch, which is almost 300 times less sharp than text displayed on the typical magazine page (around 1,440,000 dots per square inch). With that loss of legibility, even white text on a black background is harder to read.

If you really want a colored background, muted tones work best. Bright red or a brilliant blue may look sharp, but they're hard to read.

Sometimes, of course, you may think looking sharp is more important than being as legible as possible, and that's cool. In that case, do your readers a favor and keep text to a minimum. If you do want visitors to read lots of text on your Web page, consider providing it black on white — just like this book.

Summary Text is an important part of almost every Web page, so it's important that it be as carefully designed as all the other elements. Keep it short and to the point, be careful with formatting, choose colors carefully, and you can ensure that visitors to your Web page leave with your message firmly embedded in their cerebral cortex — right where you want it.

Graphics

9

As I note in the introduction to Chapter 8, World Wide Web pages are using more and more pictures. The goal of every Web page is still to communicate something, and text is usually the key to doing that, but if you want impatient, thrill-seeking Web surfers to take the time to read and understand your message, you first have to reach out and grab their attention. Eye-catching pictures are a good way to do that. But as with all elements of Web page design, using pictures poorly can be worse than not using them at all.

Adding Pictures to Your Web Page

You can add pictures to your Web page at any time by using the Personal Publisher Editing tools (see Chapter 6, "Managing Your Pages"). To add a picture, follow these steps:

1. From the Edit screen, click Add.

2. Choose Picture from the Add an Item dialog box, and click OK.

3. In Personal Publisher's Picture dialog box (Figure 9-1), click Get My Picture (Get Clip Art is only available when you are using a template to create a new page).

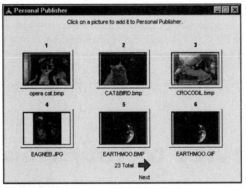

Figure 9-1: Use this dialog box to select a picture from your files to insert into your Web page.

4. A new dialog box will appear that allows you to browse your hard drive, floppy drive, or a CD-ROM for pictures. Select a file folder that contains pictures, and then click Open Gallery. This will display a series of small images of the pictures in that file folder, as shown in Figure 9-2.

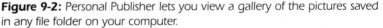

Figure 9-2: Personal Publisher lets you view a gallery of the pictures saved in any file folder on your computer.

5. Click the picture you want to use. This will insert it into Personal Publisher's Picture dialog box, as shown in Figure 9-3.

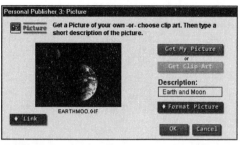

Figure 9-3: Personal Publisher holds your selected picture here so you can edit it.

6. Click Format Picture to call up controls for adjusting the size and placement of the picture (see Figure 9-4). Enter the percentage of full-size you want the picture to be in the Size box, choose how far in from the left you want the picture to be indented, and choose an alignment: None, Left, Center, or Right. You can also click Edit Picture to crop and rotate your picture. (For detailed information on formatting and editing pictures, see Chapter 5, "Advanced Options.") When you're done, click OK to return to the Format Picture dialog box, and then click OK again to return to the Picture dialog box.

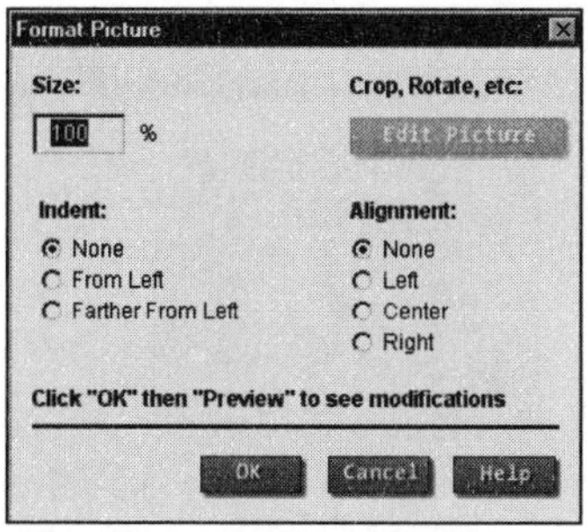

Figure 9-4: Here you can fine-tune the picture to fit just the way you want it to in your Web page.

7. Finally, if you want to add a link to your picture, click Link. You'll be asked if you want the link to cover the whole picture or just sections of it. If you choose the former, you'll be taken directly to the Link dialog box described in Chapter 5, "Advanced Options," where you can choose from several different types of links, including your Favorite Places, any URL, or another page of your Web site. If you choose the latter, you'll see the dialog box shown in Figure 9-5.

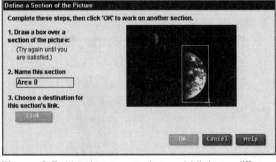

Figure 9-5: Use these controls to add links to different sections of your picture.

8. Draw a box on the picture to mark the area where you want the link to be active, give a name to that area, and then click Link. Once you've chosen the kind of link you want from the Link dialog box, click OK to return to the Define a Section of the Picture dialog box, and click OK again.

9. Now the Linked Sections of Picture dialog box opens (see Figure 9-6). If you want to add another link, click Add New Section. This will take you back to the Define a Section of the Picture dialog box.

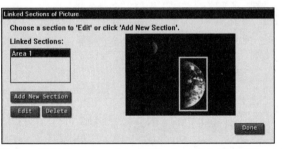

Figure 9-6: You can add, delete, or edit links within pictures from here.

10. If you wish, add a second linked section, give it a name, and click OK to return to the Linked Sections of Picture dialog box again.

11. If you want to change your original linked section, click Edit. This will also take you to the Define a Section of the Picture dialog box, where you can redraw the box defining the section you want linked. Click OK to return to the Linked Section of Picture dialog box.

12. When you're satisfied, click Done to return to the Picture dialog box.

13. Once you're happy with your picture, click OK to insert it into your Web page (see Figure 9-7).

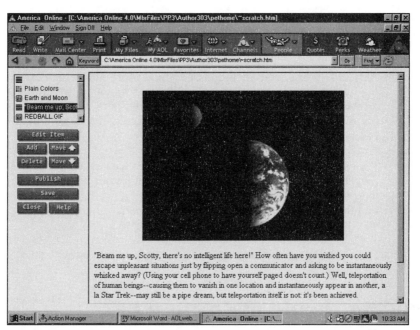

Figure 9-7: Here's our picture, happily ensconced within the cozy confines of our Web page.

Too Many Pictures, Too Little Time

Graphics are wonderful things, but they have one big problem: they can take a long time to load. And the larger (and higher resolution) the graphic, the longer that time is. For that reason, it's important to not just insert graphics for the sake of having graphics. You should only use graphics when there's a good reason to do so.

Graphics can either be purely decorative, or they can illustrate something mentioned in the text. Don't get carried away with purely decorative graphics; you're making your page load slower without really adding anything to your message. A few well-chosen decorative graphics are great, but more isn't better: a truckload of graphics may make your Web page load so slowly that you lose half your viewers before they've even seen it. Web users are only willing to wait a few seconds for a routine graphic to load before they get antsy.

Illustrations — say, a picture of your dog on the page you've devoted to her, or an exploded drawing of the Blunderbuss 4000 leaf-blower your home-hardware business sells — should only be as large as they need to be. If you really must include a high-resolution, poster-sized photograph of Aunt Sue, try putting a small, quick-loading version on one page and linking it to the full-sized, slow-loading version on its own separate page elsewhere on your site.

Although high-speed access is becoming more and more common, many Web surfers are still using 28.8 Kbps modems, which means even a relatively small file, say, 36K in size, could take up to 10 seconds or more to load (because a 28.8 modem typically averages only about 3.6K per second of actual data transfer).

For example, say you have six 36K picture files on your page. This means they'll take a full minute to load. Try holding your breath that long. It's a long time, isn't it? Do you really want your viewers to have to hold their breaths (figuratively) that long, too? If the answer is yes, you'd better make sure the pictures they're waiting for are worth it.

Once high-speed access is commonplace, you can always add more pictures.

How big should my picture be?

The people who will be visiting your site come in all sizes, shapes, and colors, and so do their computer monitors. Maybe you always run your computer at 1024 × 768 resolution, but chances are many of your viewers will be using 640×480. A picture that easily fits on your monitor at 1024× 768 will overflow the edges of the 640×480 user, forcing him or her to scroll both up and down and side to side to see the whole thing — annoying. As well, it won't fit on letter-size paper, should your viewer want to print it — even more annoying.

For that reason, it's a good idea to keep your pictures small enough to fit within a 640×480 display. The best way to make sure you achieve that is to preview your pages at 640×480 (see Figures 9-8 and 9-9). If a picture is too large, call it up again from the Edit screen and reduce it using the Size control in the Format Picture dialog box.

 See Chapter 5, "Advanced Options," for more information about adjusting the size of a picture.

 Many graphics programs will tell you the dimension of pictures in *pixels* (a pixel is a "picture element," or, to put it another way, a colored dot). To ensure the picture fits comfortably in most browsers, make sure it's no more than 595×295 pixels. If you want to ensure it will print well on letter-sized paper, make sure it's no more than 535×295.

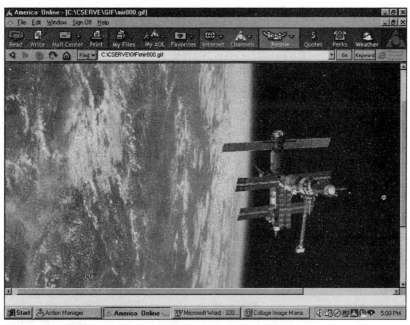

Figure 9-8: A picture that looks fine at 800×600 resolution . . .

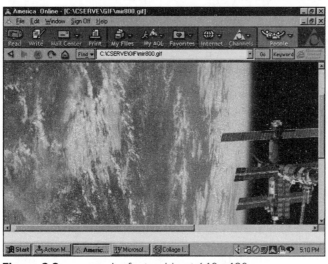

Figure 9-9: . . . may be far too big at 640×480.

What the GIF is a JPEG (and vice versa)?

There are a number of graphic formats that can be viewed by today's browsers, but by far the most common are *GIFs* and *JPEGs*. Each has its own benefits and detriments.

GIF stands for *Graphic Interchange Format*. This format for efficiently transmitting pictures from computer to computer was popularized by CompuServe (now owned by America Online) in the 1980s. Because it was so well known, it was adopted by the designers of the World Wide Web in the early 1990s, and as a result, the majority of pictures on the Web are GIFs.

GIF images are compressed to keep their file size at a minimum, and as a result they're limited to 256-color palettes. That limitation is one reason JPEG (short for *Joint Photographic Experts Group*) format is becoming more popular, especially among photographers, artists, and anyone else who wants as high quality a picture, with color as close to the original, as possible. JPEGs can display millions of colors.

JPEG files are also often smaller than GIF files. The JPEG compression system allows you to decide how much you want to compress a picture file (although, the smaller you make it, the more you degrade the picture). Still, you can often get acceptable results with a file noticeably smaller than a typical GIF file, which means your Web page will load more quickly.

JPEG compression makes photographs look great but can make diagrams and text blurry. As a result, most Web pages use GIF for most graphic elements, while reserving JPEGs for photographs.

Bullets, Icons, and Imagemaps

A *bullet* is a picture or character that sets off text, like so:

➡ This text is bulleted.

➡ As you can see, bullets are good for lists.

They're called bullets because the most commonly used symbol looks like a little bullet hole.

On a Web page, though, a bullet can be more than just a way to set off a line of text: it can be a small picture in its own right, linked to another part of the Web site or to another site entirely. Several Personal Publisher templates use their own unique bullets (see Figure 9-10).

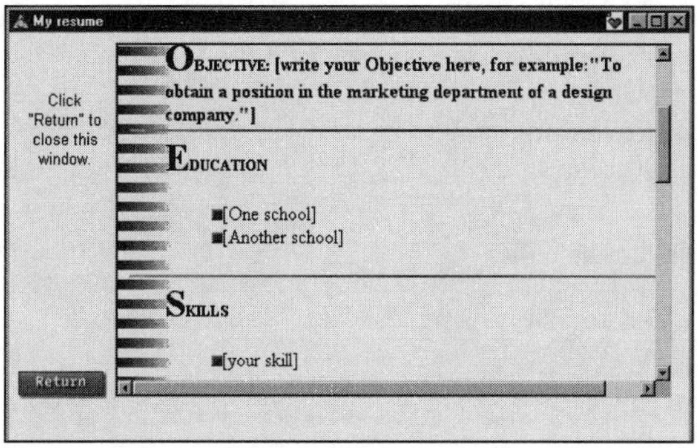

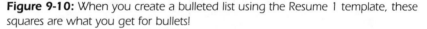

Figure 9-10: When you create a bulleted list using the Resume 1 template, these squares are what you get for bullets!

Internet iconography

Many Web pages use pictures as *icons*, which viewers click to accomplish some task — generally, on a Web page, to link to another site.

The best icons are self-explanatory, carrying simple pictures that indicate to the viewer what will happen if they're clicked: a picture of a house, for instance, to take viewers back to the home page, or a pair of eyeglasses for an icon that launches a search engine. Icons should be simple not only because, as picture files, they slow down the loading of your page but because if they're too complex your visitors will have trouble figuring out their purpose. Also, because icons are usually small, if they're too complicated they may not show up clearly on-screen.

Good examples of icons can be found in the AOL software or just about any other Windows-based software (see Figure 9-11).

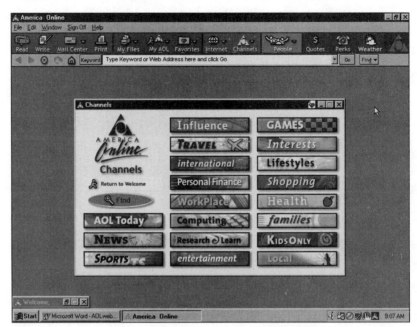

Figure 9-11: The pictures across the top of the AOL Channel screen are good examples of icons. You can add similar icons to your Web page.

To add icons to your own Web page, follow these steps:

1. From Personal Publisher's Edit screen, click Add.

2. Choose Picture from the Add an Item dialog box, and click OK.

3. In Personal Publisher's Picture dialog box, click Get My Picture.

4. Browse your computer for the picture you want to use as an icon by finding the file folder it's located in, selecting it, and clicking Open Gallery.

5. Click the picture you want to use to add it to your Web page.

6. Click Format Picture. Unless the picture you're using is already small, you'll probably have to reduce it to make it icon-size. Enter the percentage of its full size you want in the Size box. Use the other controls to position and edit the picture as necessary.

7. Click OK to return to the Format Picture dialog box, and click OK again to return to the Picture dialog box.

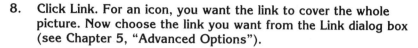

8. Click Link. For an icon, you want the link to cover the whole picture. Now choose the link you want from the Link dialog box (see Chapter 5, "Advanced Options").

9. Click Done to return to the Edit screen.

10. Click OK to insert your icon into your Web page.

Imagemaps

An *imagemap* is a single picture with multiple links built into it (see Figure 9-12). A typical use for an imagemap would be a banner picture for the top of your page with multiple "buttons" inside it. Such imagemaps have become common because they combine good looks with efficient use of space.

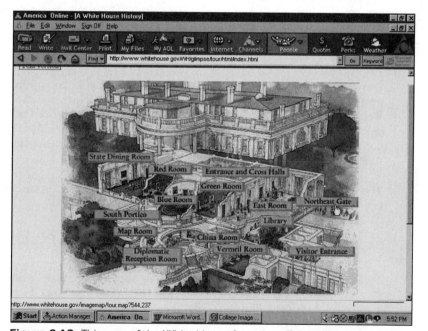

Figure 9-12: This map of the White House from the official White House Web site at http://www.whitehouse.gov is a good example of an imagemap. Clicking one of the various rooms takes you directly to a description and pictures of that room.

Personal Publisher makes it easy to create imagemaps, and they can be a valuable addition to your Web site. For example, you could use an imagemap as a menu for your Web site. You could create a virtual storefront displaying items you want to sell, where clicking any item will take the visitor to a description of it. Or you could take visitors on a tour of your community, combining a road map with an imagemap, so that visitors could get more information about interesting features by pointing and clicking.

See the section on adding pictures to your Web page, earlier in this chapter, or Chapter 5, "Advanced Options," for detailed instructions on creating imagemaps.

Where to Find Pictures

Digital pictures are everywhere, but they're not all freely available for you to use on your Web page. Something too many first-time Web page designers forget is that many pictures belong to someone — and that someone has to give you permission to use them. It's called *copyright*, and using copyrighted material without the permission of the copyright owner is against the law.

Sometimes it's hard to tell if material on the Internet is copyrighted. The best way to be sure is simply to ask. If you see a picture on someone else's Web site you'd like to add to yours, e-mail the Webmaster of that site and ask if the picture is copyrighted; if it is, ask who owns the copyright and (if copyright belongs to the Webmaster or whoever owns the site he or she runs) if you can have permission to reproduce it on your site.

The actual process of saving pictures from the Internet to your computer is easy:

1. From within a Web page, right-click the picture you want to save.

2. Choose Save Picture As.

3. Locate the file folder you want to save the picture in and, in the usual Save As dialog box, type the name you want to give the picture (see Figure 9-13).

You can save any picture file this way, from a photograph to a button, or from an icon to a dividing line. (Generally, you don't have to worry about copyright with buttons and lines; you can borrow them freely from the sites you visit.)

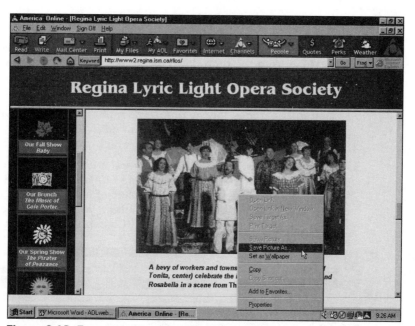

Figure 9-13: To save a picture from the Internet to your computer, just right-click and choose Save Picture As from the pop-up menu.

Finding pictures on AOL

AOL itself offers many sources of pictures for Web page designers, such as the Photography Forum, Hobby Central's Photography area, and Image Exchange. For more details on these picture sources, refer to Chapter 7, "Personal Publisher Resources on AOL."

Finding pictures on the Internet

Of course, as noted earlier, the World Wide Web is full of pictures — although they're not all available for your use because of copyright. Finding the one you want, however, can be a challenge.

Fortunately, several sites offer more-or-less organized collections of clip art, or clip art focused on specific topics. A good way to find these sites is just to search for *"clip art"* with AOL NetFind.

To search for clip art with AOL NetFind, follow these steps:

1. Click the Internet icon in AOL's main toolbar, then choose AOL NetFind from the drop-down menu. (Or simply enter the keyword NetFind.

2. Enter "clip art" in the Search box. (Use quotation marks so NetFind searches for the phrase as a phrase; otherwise it will search for all the Web pages it can find that contain either the word *clip* or the word *art*, most of which won't be applicable.)

3. Click Find. NetFind will then display the first ten of however many links it finds that contain the phrase *clip art* (see Figure 9-14). Make sure to check out the "Try These First" links that appear at the top of the list of results: they'll take you directly to online sources of pictures, including the PC Graphics forum on AOL.

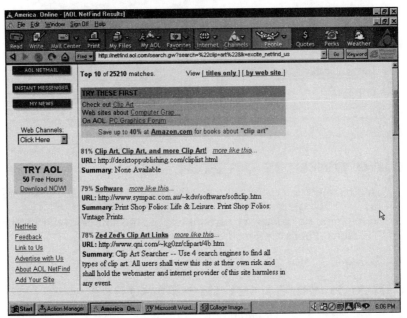

Figure 9-14: These are just some of the many Web sites devoted to clip art turned up by AOL's NetFind.

4. **To go to any of the sites displayed, just click its name.**

Another good way to find pictures related to a specific topic is to search for Web sites related to that topic. Once again, though, remember to ask for permission before copying any pictures you may find to your Web page.

Other sources of pictures

You can obtain pictures for your Web page in several other ways:

➡ **Buy a collection.** Most computer stores sell a variety of CD-ROMs laden with thousands of clip-art pictures for you to use. AOL's own Software Shop (keyword **Software Shop**) is one good source of clip-art collections. As well, AOL's GraphicSuite (see Figure 9-15—keyword **GraphicSuite**), a CD-ROM-based collection of tools for editing and organizing digital pictures, includes 10,000 royalty-free photos and images.

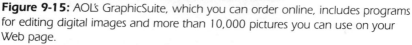

Figure 9-15: AOL's GraphicSuite, which you can order online, includes programs for editing digital images and more than 10,000 pictures you can use on your Web page.

➡ **Use clip art from another program.** Many computer programs, such as Microsoft Office, come with a large collection of clip art which you can also use freely.

➡ **Scan them.** If you have access to a scanner, you can turn anything printed on paper into a digital file, including photographs you've taken yourself or artwork you've created. Again, however, be aware of copyright; scanning in a photo out of a magazine, for example, and then placing it on your Web page, is illegal unless you obtain permission from the copyright holder.

➡ **Create them yourself.** You can create your own icons, banners, lines, buttons, and more by using a graphics program to save them as GIFs or JPEGs for use on your Web page.

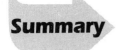

Summary

The World Wide Web is using more and more pictures, which means your Web page needs good pictures if you want people to enjoy viewing it and to come back often. Sources of good pictures are everywhere, from AOL to the Internet to your own artistic talent (if you have any!). But don't use pictures for the sake of using pictures: use them carefully and wisely to heighten the impact of your message. Too many pictures can make your page so slow loading that nobody will sit around long enough to see how beautiful it is!

Multimedia — The Extra Dimension

10

One of the most exciting abilities computers have is to weave a variety of media — text, pictures, sound, video — into a seamless, informative, and entertaining whole. It's called *multimedia*, and it's a brand-new way of presenting information. Suppose you're finding out everything you can about life aboard an eighteenth-century sailing vessel. Through multimedia, you could explore the ship at your own pace, moving from room to room, examining tools and other items in detail, all the while hearing the creaking of the rigging and the rush of water, watching sailors scramble aloft to set the sails, and reading fascinating information related to what you're experiencing. About the only thing multimedia can't deliver yet is the smell of the sea and the taste of salt spray on your lips. So far, CD-ROMs are the best way to deliver this multimedia experience, but the Web is catching up, especially as faster Internet connections become possible (multimedia requires lots of bandwidth). But even with today's relatively slow modems, you can use some forms of multimedia on your Web page, adding sound, video, and animations. You won't be able to create something that rivals the latest CD-ROM encyclopedia, but you can add a few exciting multimedia touches to help intrigue and inform your visitors.

Adding Sound to Your Web Page

The world would be a different place without sound. Stop for a moment and listen. What do you hear? I hear the distant roar of a jet, the whir of my computer's fan, music playing in another room, a car going by on the street outside, the sound of my own breathing. Sound makes the world seem alive.

Sound can bring your Web page alive, too. Are you a singer? You can post a sample of your talent. Do you have a band? Post a demo. Maybe you're a bird watcher who has spent 20 years collecting recordings of bird songs. Post them on the Web and share them with the world. Or maybe you just want to share your newborn baby's cries with Grandma and Grandpa, who live half a world away. The possibilities are endless.

Windows 95 comes with a basic sound-recording program. Open the Programs menu, and look in the Multimedia folder for Sound Recorder. With this simple program and a microphone, or jacks connecting your sound card to another source of sound, such as a stereo, you can create your own sound files for posting on the Web.

There are other methods of creating sound files, too, which we'll look at a little later in the chapter.

Personal Publisher 3 doesn't include the option of adding sound via its templates, but there's an indirect way that works perfectly well. To add sound to your Web page, follow these steps:

1. **Create your sound file and save it on your computer.**

2. **Go to My Place (keyword My Place); at the introductory screen, click Go to My Place. You'll see the dialog box shown in Figure 10-1.**

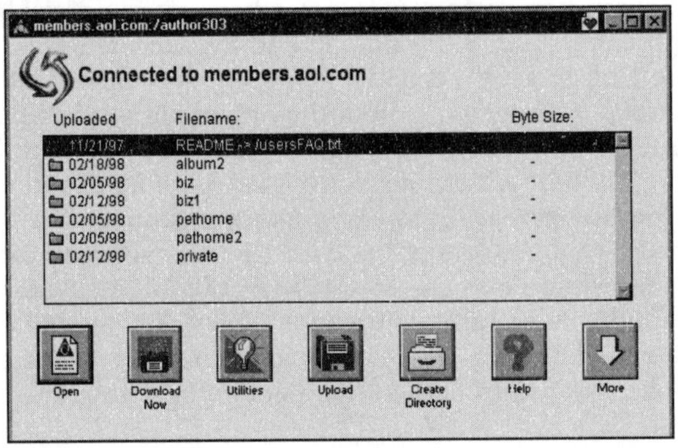

Figure 10-1: These controls allow you to place files such as sound recordings in the data storage space AOL has reserved for you on its computers.

3. **Click Upload. This opens the dialog box shown in Figure 10-2.**

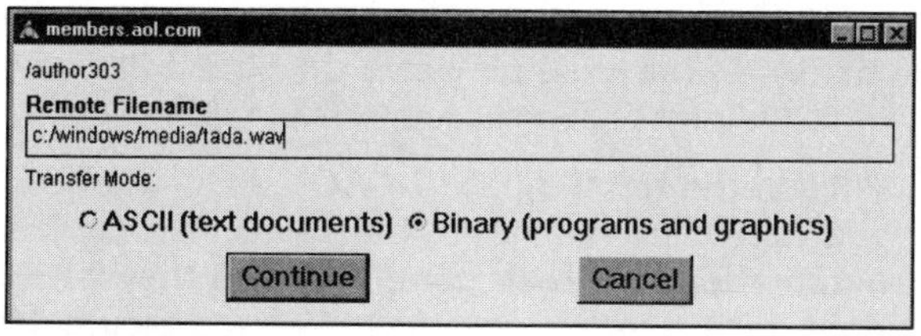

Figure 10-2: Specify the name you want the uploaded file to have in My Place here.

4. Give the file you're about to upload a name for My Place. Make sure the Binary radio button is selected, then click Continue.

5. In the next dialog box (see Figure 10-3), click Select File to browse your computer for the file you want to upload. Once you've selected it, its name will appear in the File box.

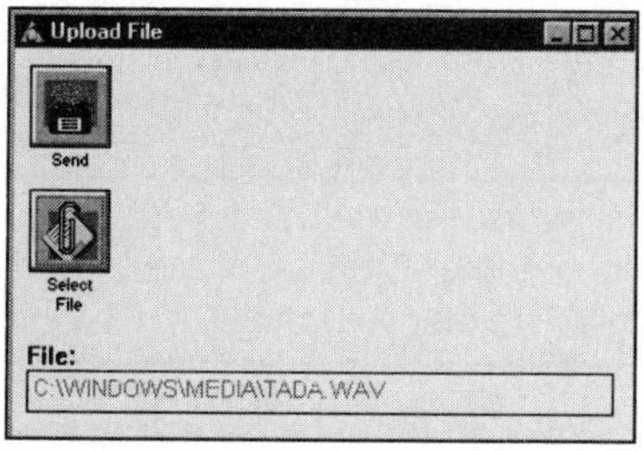

Figure 10-3: From here, locate the file you want to upload.

6. Click Upload Now. You'll see a progress bar showing you how much of the file has been uploaded (see Figure 10-4). AOL will tell you when the upload is finished. If you then go back and take a look at the list of files contained in My Place, the file you just uploaded should be among them.

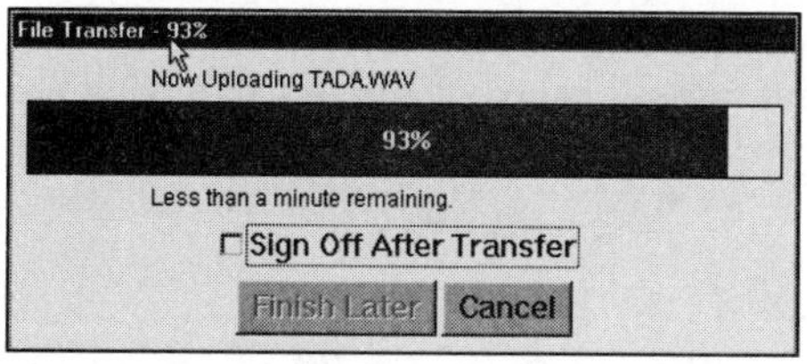

Figure 10-4: AOL keeps you informed as to how much of your file has been uploaded, so you know if you have time to go get a cup of coffee.

7. Now return to Personal Publisher, click Manage Pages, and Edit the page to which you want to add sound. Add a link (either by linking existing text or graphics, or adding new text or graphics

first) to the sound file (choose Type Any URL from the Link menu). In the example here, the sound file would be `http://members.aol.com/Author303/tada.wav`.

8. Publish the revised page to AOL. Now whenever visitors to your site click the link to the sound file, the file will download automatically to their computer, and they'll be able to play it right away or whenever they like (see Figure 10-5).

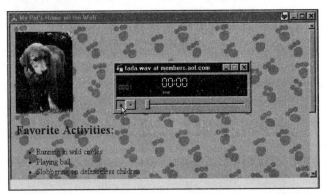

Figure 10-5: When visitors click the link to your sound file, the file will be downloaded to their compute. Then they'll see a little control box like this one, which they can use to play the sound.

MIDI, WAV, and other strange creatures

Sound files come in a number of different formats, with a variety of filename extensions, such as `.aiff`, `.au`, `.wav`, and `.mid`. Internet Explorer, which is built into AOL as your default browser, will automatically play all of these formats, as will Netscape, the other most popular browser.

What's the difference between the different formats? Well, first of all, WAV, AU, and AIFF are all *waveform* formats. They're created much like a tape recording: someone spoke, sang, or played a musical instrument into a microphone attached to a computer, which recorded the sound digitally. WAV, AU, and AIFF were each designed for the following specific types of computers:

➡ **AIFF** stands for *Audio Interchange File Format*. Developed by Apple for storing high-quality sampled audio and musical instrument information, it's also used by various types of professional audio software. Most AIFF files were created on a Macintosh.

➡ **AU** is the format in which UNIX machines save sound. It's common on the Internet because many of the machines on which the Internet is based run UNIX.

➡ **WAV** is the Windows standard for waveform recordings, so when you see a WAV file, you can figure it was created on a PC.

MIDI stands for *Musical Instrument Digital Interface* and is something quite different. While waveform files are really digital recordings of actual sounds, MIDI files are more like digital sheet music: they contain instructions for musical notes, tempo, and instrumentation which a properly equipped computer or synthesizer can use to play sound.

MIDI files have one great advantage over waveform files, and one great disadvantage. The advantage is that they are much, much shorter than most waveform files. A high-quality recording of a complete piece of music in waveform format could take hours to download; a MIDI file of the same piece of music could be downloaded quickly. Even a tiny 5K MIDI file can produce several minutes of music.

The big disadvantage to MIDI files is that they only sound as good as the equipment used to play them. A synthesizer or a high-quality computer sound card, plugged into a good set of speakers, can make a MIDI file of an orchestral work sound like a live recording of the Berlin Philharmonic. An old sound card from just a few years ago, on the other hand, will make that same MIDI file sound like someone batting out a tune on a $20 electronic keyboard. (If you're lumbering along with an outdated sound card, you're missing out on a good chunk of the full Web multimedia experience. A good place to shop for new sound cards is the AOL Store's Hardware Center, keyword **Hardware Center,** where a variety of sound cards are available at competitive prices.)

A variety of software and hardware is available for creating both waveform files and MIDI files. As well, you can find both kinds of sound files all over the Internet. As with graphics, however, make sure you have permission from the copyright owner for any piece of music you post to your Web page. Just like art, music almost always belongs to someone.

Adding Video to Your Web Page

Video files can also add excitement to your Web page, though they require more equipment to create: you need a video camera, obviously, as well as a video card that accepts video signals for recording, and software to do that recording. (Again, a good place to look for this kind of hardware is AOL's Hardware Center.)

You can use video files to give visitors a tour of your home town, a sample of your acting ability, or the amazing footage you shot of the UFO that buzzed your car. You can use video to share exciting moments from your family's life with relatives around the world, or to convince Web surfers to come spend a few days at the bed and breakfast you run. As with audio, the possibilities are tremendous.

Adding video to your Personal Publisher Web page works exactly like adding audio. Just follow these steps:

1. Create your video file and save it on your computer.

2. Go to My Place (keyword My Place). At the introductory screen, click Go to My Place.

3. Click Upload.

4. Name the file, make sure the Binary radio button is selected, and then click Continue.

5. Click Select File to browse your computer for the file you want to upload. Select it; its name will appear in the File area.

6. Click Upload Now.

7. Once the upload is finished, return to Personal Publisher. Click Manage Pages, select the page to which you want to add a video file link, and click Edit.

8. Add a link to the video file to text or graphics. Choose Type Any URL from the Link menu, and enter the location of the video file (`http://members.aol.com/Your Screen Name/video file name`).

9. Publish the page to AOL.

Video, like audio, comes in a variety of formats, including

➡ **AVI**. AVI stands for *audio/video interleave*. It's the file format used by Video for Windows.

➡ **MOV**. MOV (short for *movie*) is the format used by Apple Computer's QuickTime video system. Although QuickTime was originally developed for Macintosh computers, there are players available for PCs. QuickTime can also be used for sound files or graphics.

➡ **MPEG**. MPEG stands for *Moving Pictures Experts Group* — it's the video equivalent of JPEG, discussed in Chapter 9. It compresses sounds and movie files to make them easier to move around the Internet.

The biggest problem with video files in any format is that they tend to be LARGE. In fact, one or two AVI files would be enough to fill the 2MB of storage space AOL allots each screen name. Their size also means they can take a long time to load — so you want to be absolutely certain that they're worth the wait.

 A good way to tempt viewers to view your video clip is to make the link a still image from the clip. It's also a good idea to list the size of the video clip and how long visitors can expect it to take to load; that way they don't get halfway through the download, get fed up, and leave without ever seeing the video.

 Most browsers play AVI files automatically. However, you may need special plug-ins to play MOV and MPEG files, or some of the many other video formats on the Web. If you provide a link to a video file that some visitors may not be able to view without a plug-in, provide a link to a site from which they can download the plug-in.

When viewers call up the video clip, a special window will open in their browser (as shown in Figure 10-6) in which the clip, complete with sound (if any), will play. With most video formats, viewers can immediately "rewind" and watch the clip again.

Figure 10-6: It's not exactly big-screen TV, but it's still pretty cool: video on your computer.

Animation: Getting Your Web Page Moving

There's more than one way to add animation to a Web page. You can link to a video clip (as described earlier); you can create a script using a special programming language such as Java; or you can take the easiest, lowest-tech route, and use an *animated GIF*.

An animated GIF is a series of regular GIFs that appear one after the other in the same spot, creating an illusion of movement. Most recent browsers support animated GIFs. The great thing about them is that once an animated GIF is created, you can insert it into your Web page with Personal Publisher, just like you'd insert any other graphic.

Creating an animated GIF

Creating an animated GIF requires special software. If you already have a graphics program, check to see if it will let you make animated GIFs; if not, there are several shareware programs available on the Internet that will. Two good ones are the GIF Construction Set, available from Alchemy Mindworks Inc. at `http://www.mindworkshop.com/alchemy/alchemy.htm`, and Animagic GIF Animator, available from Right to Left Software at `http://www.rtlsoft.com`.

Animated GIFs work just like Saturday morning cartoons: you create a series of still pictures, each of which advances the action a little bit more. You have to be careful with animated GIFs, because although each individual picture may not take up all that much storage space or bandwidth, they quickly add up. Even a small animated GIF with several frames can take as long to load as a large picture. Since the whole idea of putting animation on your Web page in the first place is to make it come alive, slowing it down until it seems dead is really counterproductive.

Fortunately, you're not attempting to make a feature-length motion picture, so you don't need to create 24 individual illustrations for each second of animation. In fact, you can probably get by with just a handful of illustrations. Figure 10-7 shows the series of four illustrations (really just three, with the second one repeated as the fourth one) I turned into an animated GIF to announce auditions for the Regina Lyric Light Opera Society. On the screen, this little fellow dances up a storm, hopefully soft-shoeing his way into the heart of every visitor.

Figure 10-7: Gotta dance — at least you do when you're an animated GIF and somebody accesses your Web page!

Using animation effectively

A Web page with too much animation looks far, far worse than a Web page with no animation at all. When I see a whole page crawling with animated graphics, I reach for my flyswatter — it reminds me of nothing so much as a swarm of ugly insects. And that's just one of the pitfalls you can run into when adding animation to your Web page. Here are some basic rules to remember:

➥ Only use animation when you really have a need for it, when you really believe it will enhance what you have to say. If it doesn't enhance it, then it's detracting from it, which makes it worse than useless. (Animations that repeat endlessly can be particularly distracting — not to mention annoying.)

➥ Remember that your animated GIF has to load before it starts moving — and if it's too big, it will take so long to load you might as well not have bothered. Try to limit your animated GIFs to 20 – 30K. If they get any bigger, redesign them or get rid of them altogether.

➥ Remember, too, that not everyone has a giant monitor or the latest video card. If you want everyone to feel welcome on your Web page, make sure your GIFs (animated or otherwise) will look almost as good at 640×480 resolution with 256 colors as they do at 800×600 resolution with millions of colors.

➡ Finally, remember there are people surfing the Net with browsers that don't support animated GIFs at all. They're more likely to see either the first or the last image only — so make sure those images can stand alone.

Multimedia Resources

There are lots of online sources of sound clips, animated GIFs, and even movies for your Web page, both on AOL and the Internet.

AOL resources

AOL has a number of places you can turn to for sound, video, and animation for your Web page, including

➡ **PC Music & Sound Forum** (keyword **PC MUSIC**). Here you can learn more about using your computer to create and play music — and the Software Libraries are full of MIDI and WAV files of everything from classical opera to country music to science fiction sound effects (see Figure 10-8).

Figure 10-8: The PC Music & Sound Forum is a great place to go when you're looking for just the right MIDI or WAV file.

➡ **PC Animation & Video Forum** (keyword **A&V Forum**). This area of AOL focuses on (guess what?) animation and video. Its extensive resources include video and animation files, plus useful software for creating, editing, and viewing those files (see Figure 10-9).

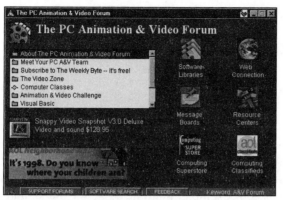

Figure 10-9: Video and animation players and files galore are available from the PC Animation & Video Forum.

➥ **Multimedia Showcase** (http://multimedia.aol.com). The Multimedia Showcase (see Figure 10-10) was created by America Online to provide both AOL members and World Wide Web users an easy way to find the most popular multimedia software for the Web. It includes a gallery of artwork, examples, and links to sites that make good use of multimedia.

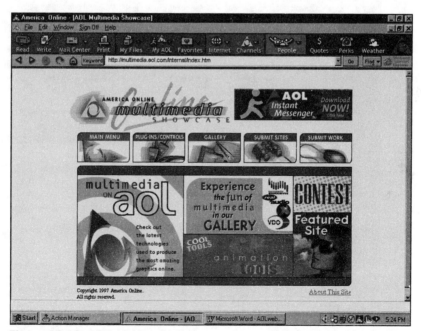

Figure 10-10: AOL's Multimedia Showcase shows off the latest and greatest online multimedia tools and Web sites. Note the link at the bottom to cool GIF animation tools!

Internet resources

As usual, the best way to find Internet sources of sound, video, and animation is to use a good search engine. Hundreds of sites offer MIDI files, WAV files, animated GIFs, and video.

A good place to start, as always, is AOL NetFind. To search for multimedia-related sites with NetFind, follow these steps:

1. Click the Internet icon in AOL's main toolbar, and then choose AOL NetFind from the drop-down menu.

2. Enter the multimedia-related terms you want to search for in the Search box. For example: multimedia sound video animation.

3. Click Find. NetFind will display the first ten of however many pages it finds that contain at least one of your search terms, with the best matches at the top. It will also display a number of links under "TRY THESE FIRST," as shown in Figure 10-11. (Since any search for multimedia topics turns up millions of possibilities, it really is a good idea to try these first. You can always come back later and explore the other links you uncovered.)

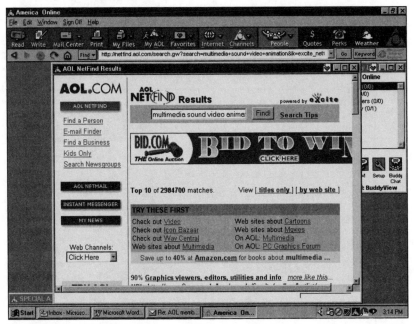

Figure 10-11: These are just some of the many, many sources of sound, video, and animation you can find on the Internet.

4. To go to any of the sites displayed, just click its name.

Here are just a few Internet sites worth checking out:

➡ **The Multimedia Library** (`http://www.hollywood.com/multimedia/`) is a huge collection of production notes, photos, sounds, videos, trailers, interactive press kits, and more from thousands of movies. This is a great place to see some of the many ways multimedia can be used on the Web, but it's not a good place to get material for your own Web page: most of what's here is copyrighted.

➡ **Wav Central** (`http://www.wavcentral.com/`) is an equally huge archive of WAV audio samples from movies, TV, and commercials, plus a collection of special-effects sounds that you can use to make Windows 95 bark like a dog — or add to your Web page.

➡ **The Ultimate MIDI Page** (`http://www.netrunner.net/~jshlackm/`) is a great place to turn to locate MIDI files of everything from ABBA songs to hymns. You'll also find links to software, composer's pages, and more.

Summary

It's easy to link multimedia files such as sound and video to your Personal Publisher page, and, with a little more work, easy to add animation to the page, too. But always remember the limitations of space (you only have 2MB of storage on AOL!) and bandwidth (most people are still using 28.8 or 33.6 Kbps modems). Multimedia can be a tremendous addition to your page — but make sure it serves a useful purpose and isn't there just to show how clever you can be. If it distracts more than it enhances, get rid of it. If it doesn't, go for it!

Creating Cool Personal Web Pages

In This Chapter

Personal Web page checklist

Humor on the Web

Examples of cool personal pages

The personal Web page is an amazing phenomenon. I doubt anyone at CERN in 1989, as they hashed out the details of this new way of putting information on a network, had an inkling that some day ordinary citizens around the world would be posting information about themselves, their families, their pets, their hobbies, even the books on their shelves and the number of shoes in their closet. It seems that almost everyone, upon being exposed to the Web for the first time, gets a sudden hankering to have his or her own presence on it. It's a way of saying "Here I am! Notice me — I'm interesting," a way of standing out from the crowd. One good measure of the popularity of personal Web pages is existence of Personal Publisher itself — and the many different templates it offers for the creation of personal Web pages, including three different "lifestyles" templates, a Generation X template, and templates designed for women and teens: there's something for everyone, in other words.

Unfortunately, too many personal Web pages actually deliver a message more along the lines of "Here I am, but you can ignore me — I'm dull as dishwater." After all, how many people in the online world really care how many shoes are in your closet? If you're going to have a personal home page that anyone other than your closest friends and relatives will ever visit more than once, you have to make it interesting. In this chapter I give you some suggestions on how to do that, and you take a look at a handful of interesting personal pages, drawn from the hundreds of thousands now linked to the Web.

The Personal Web Page Checklist

One key to creating an effective personal Web page is planning ahead. That means knowing what you want to put on the Web page before you fire up Personal Publisher and start tinkering with templates.

Here are ten questions to ask yourself before you begin, to help you focus your thoughts and get a clearer idea of what the content of your Web page should include.

1. **Who is my audience?** You're not really designing your Web page for yourself, you're designing it for visitors to your site. That means you need to give some thought to who those visitors will be. If you're designing a Web page that is intended merely as a bulletin board for posting bits of family news for far-flung relatives and friends, you'll design the page one way. If you're going after a broader audience, you'll need more content than Jimmy's latest report card to keep them interested. And a Web page designed for kids is going to look far different from a Web page designed for World War II veterans.

2. **What is my message?** Web pages are means of communicating with others, which means you need to have something to communicate. What is it? Do you want to tell your visitors all about you and your family? Do you want to tell them about your collection of ancient Roman coins? Do you want to express your strong opinions on U.S.-Canada relations? Get your message clear in your head—then write it, keeping your audience (Question 1) in mind and tailoring the text to fit it (see Figure 11-1).

3. **What kind of tone do I want to project?** To a large extent, this flows out of your audience and your message. Say your audience is kids and your message is "Cooking can be fun!" That tone should carry through both the text and your choice of graphics: red lettering on a black background, embellished with skulls, would not be a good choice. If your message is more serious, you might use a conservative background style and few flashy graphics. And if you happen to be a Stephen King fan, then that red lettering on a black background embellished with skulls might be just the thing.

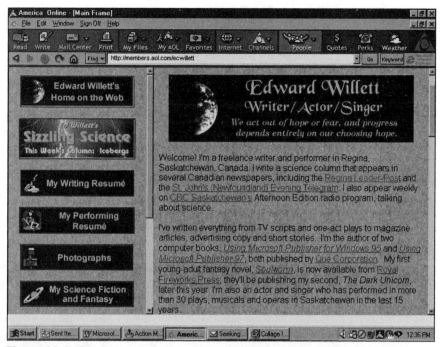

Figure 11-1: On my home page at `http://members.aol.com/ecwillett`, my message is essentially, "I'm a writer and performer—hire me!" I decided my audience is probably adults who might be interested in what I write. This influenced the look of my home page, which is conservative without being boring (I hope!).

4. **Has someone else done something similar?** There's no point in reinventing the wheel, so before you start designing your page, do some surfing to see how other people have designed similar pages. Hometown AOL is a good place to start, because that's where you'll find other pages designed using the same Personal Publisher template. If you register your page with AOL Hometown after you publish it, you'll be joining a community of people with the same interests. By studying other people's pages, you may find valuable information you can bring to your own page. Also, you may get great new design ideas, and most importantly, you'll be better equipped to answer the next question.

5. What can I bring to my message that no one else can? In your research, you probably found that you're not the first person to decide to put up a Web page devoted to his or her cat, or family, or car, or on whatever you've decided to focus. That being the case, you need to find something that's unique to you to add to that message, either in the information presented or in the way in which you present it, to make it stand out from the crowd (see Figure 11-2). (Standing out from the crowd, remember, is what this personal home page business is all about.) Maybe your cat page is unique because it contains photographs of your house taken from a cat's-eye point of view. Maybe your essay on Canada-U.S. relations focuses on your unique experience as someone who moved from Texas to Canada as a young boy, lives in Canada today, but attended university in Arkansas and retains his American citizenship. Make full use of your creativity on your Web page — otherwise, what's the point?

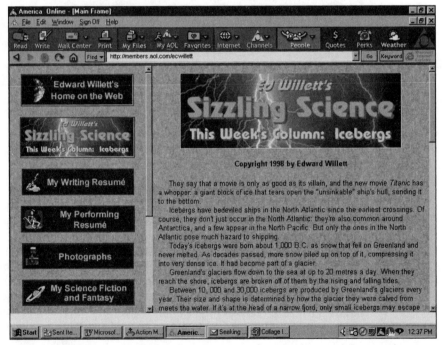

Figure 11-2: I decided the most unique aspect of my writing, and the one that best suited itself to a Web page, is the weekly science column I write for various newspapers.

The first five questions of our personal Web page checklist are the big questions, which determine the broad design choices you'll make concerning your Web page. But once you've answered them, you can start asking yourself the following questions, whose answers will provide you with more specific guidance in the construction of your page:

6. How much storage space do I have available? America Online provides 2MB of storage space to each screen name (10MB per account). Two megabytes may seem like a lot, but if you have lots of other files tucked away in My Place, you may not have as much space as you think.

7. How do I want to balance text and graphics? If you're simply replacing the placeholder content in a Personal Publisher template with your own text and pictures, this question has already been partially answered for you. You can rest assured that a reasonable balance has been built into the template. If, however, you started with the blank template, the choice is entirely up to you. You need both, no question: a text-heavy site can look gray and forbidding, while too many graphics makes a site look cluttered and poorly organized. But there's lots of room to maneuver between those two extremes. Sometimes the answer may be decided for you: you may not have access to that many graphics, or the purpose of your site may be more to show off photographs than to write about them. Other times, though, you have a choice. Write your text and gather your graphics before you begin designing your page, and then sketch out a rough design on a piece of paper. Aim for a clean, uncluttered look. That little bit of extra planning can make the difference between a quick-loading, attractive site and a slow-loading, nerve-jangling mess.

8. What useful links can I provide? Remember, the World Wide Web is based on the hypertext principle — the idea that any piece of information can be linked to any other to become instantly available. A Web page without links is only half a Web page. But links for the sake of links won't do your visitors or your Web page's appearance any good. Before you begin designing your Web page, do some digging on the Internet for good links, related to your message, that you'd like to make available for your visitors (see Figure 11-3). If you're registering your page with Hometown AOL, you can probably find a lot of pages within your own community to which you'll want to provide links. Once you've decided where you want your links to lead, give careful consideration to how you'll insert those links: within the body of your text (remembering that that's an invitation to quit reading your text and go somewhere else), as a standalone list, as icons, or as an imagemap. Don't

forget internal links, as well, for navigating among your various Web pages (if you have more than one), or even from section to section on the same Web page. And be sure to plan for an e-mail link to yourself so your visitors can tell you what they think of your site, or ask for more information.

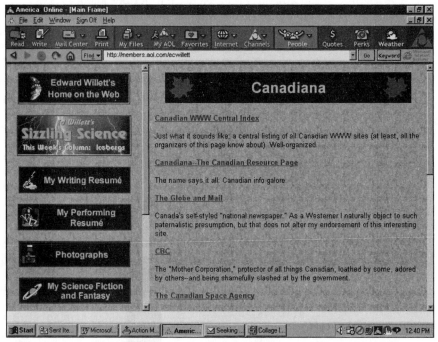

Figure 11-3: I provide lots of links to interesting Web sites and try to make those links more useful to visitors by also providing brief descriptions of them.

9. **Do I want to add multimedia?** As is pointed out in Chapter 10, "Multimedia — The Extra Dimension," multimedia — sound, video, and animation — can be an exciting addition to a Web site, but it can also cause problems. Too many animations on a single page are more annoying than anything else, and they slow down the load time. Sound files are at the mercy of the sound system of the visitor's computer, and video files tend to take up enormous amounts of precious storage space. All of which means that during the planning process, you should decide how (if at all) multimedia could enhance your message, then carefully decide where to use it — and use it sparingly. (You can always add more as high-speed Internet access becomes more widespread and download times decrease.)

10. Can I do all this in one page — or do I need more? A single-page site has an advantage in that all the information is right there — there's no need for visitors to click to get to the rest of the site (which is good, because they might just click to go somewhere else entirely). On the other hand, if you have lots of information you want to communicate, a lot of photographs, or dozens of links, a single page can soon get unwieldy, taking a long time to load and requiring endless scrolling. Multiple-page sites allow you to better organize information. which in turn makes it easier for your visitors to access only that information in which they're interested. Multiple pages can be smaller, which means they load more quickly, too.

If you do decide to go the multiple-page route, then use the same Personal Publisher template for all your pages. Switching backgrounds or text colors from page to page destroys the overall coherence of the site, making it feel like many different sites instead of one that just happens to have several pages (see Figures 11-4 and 11-5).

Figure 11-4: My pages all have a unified look, whether they contain photographs . . .

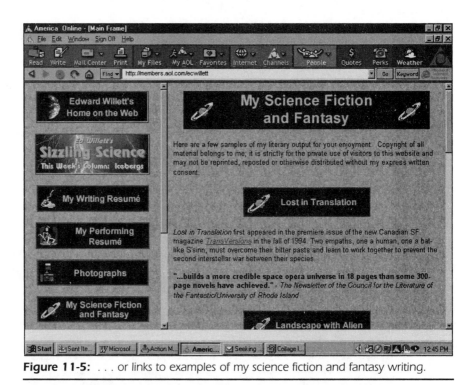

Figure 11-5: . . . or links to examples of my science fiction and fantasy writing.

Are You Trying to Be Funny?

The best personal Web sites generally don't take themselves too seriously. Even if your message and overall tone are quite serious, a little humor can lighten things up and make a visit to your pages more pleasant. And if your message and tone aren't serious at all, then the more humor the better . . . within reason. Some suggestions — and warnings — about the use of humor:

➡ **Not everyone has the same sense of humor.** That joke about the frog in the blender you think is hilarious will offend some visitors, while others just won't get it. Again, it's important to consider your audience, and aim your humor at them. If possible, test it out on some live victims — um, acquaintances — before posting it to your Web page.

➡ **Parody can be an effective form of humor, if you do it well.** What if you made your personal Web page a parody of the oh-so-serious corporate Web pages out there, complete with a "mission statement" and a message from the "CEO" (you). Or a parody of a software manual . . . or the liner notes from a rock album . . . or the menu of a fancy restaurant. The possibilities are endless.

➡ **Don't break any laws.** The latest political joke may be safe enough if told about the president because he's a public figure, but told about, say, your boss, it could be considered libel. If you're aiming for biting satire or commentary, run your biting bytes by a lawyer, first.

➡ **People are most likely to laugh at something to which they can relate.** This explains the preponderance of computer-related jokes on the Web. The more esoteric your humor, the more you limit your audience.

Examples of Personal Home Pages

One of the best ways to get ideas for your personal home page is to look at other personal home pages. There are hundreds of thousands — possibly millions — of these on the Web, though, so knowing where to begin can be a problem.

Again, the best place to start is Hometown AOL, where you'll find communities of people who have built Web pages around specific interests, many of them using particular Personal Publisher templates. You can browse through these communities or search all of the pages on Hometown for words or phrases related to your interests.

Another good place to start is with AOL's NetFind Internet search engine. Just insert a few keywords related to your interests, and you'll soon have dozens of links you can explore in your search for personal pages similar to the one you want to create.

You can also turn to reviews for advice on which pages merit your attention. For example, NetFind lists reviews of pages of all sorts — including personal home pages. They rank them on a scale of one to four, although instead of using the usual stars (as in a four-star hotel), they award magnifying glasses, as shown in Figure 11-6.

Now let's take a look at some actual personal home pages, some by AOL members, others drawn from across the Web, to give you a hint of what's possible and to inspire you to create your own memorable addition to the enormous diversity of the World Wide Web.

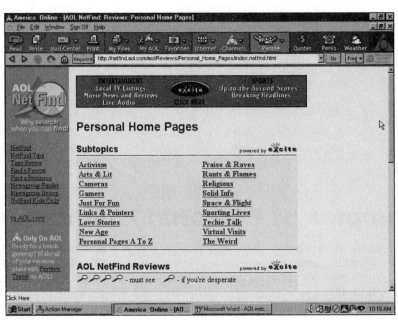

Figure 11-6: *Looking for examples of what other people have done with their personal home pages? AOL's NetFind Reviews rank pages on a scale of one ("if you're desperate") to four ("must-see"), at* `http://netfind.aol.com/aol/Reviews/Personal_Home_Pages/index.netfind.html`.

Lil Place Away From Home

Lil Place Away From Home, at `http://members.aol.com/~cowtowning`, created by Ingrid (no last name given), is one of the most attractive AOL members' home pages I've encountered. The warm welcoming screen, with its soft pink background and beautiful image of wildflowers (see Figure 11-7), tells you something about the personality of the person behind the page at first glance — and also tells you that it's someone you'd like to get to know.

Ingrid has created more than just a single page, though; she's created an extensive site, with pages devoted to her family, her interests, and even her poetry (see Figure 11-8). It's interesting to note that not all of Ingrid's pages are even hosted by AOL; she maintains pages in a number of other locations, too.

However, by creating links to them from her AOL home page, visitors feel like they're visiting a single site, even if the pages that make it up are scattered among several hosts. As I've said before, on the World Wide Web, any other site is always only a mouse click away.

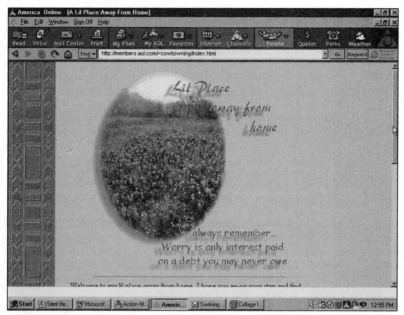

Figure 11-7: Ingrid's Lil Place Away From Home exudes Texas hospitality from the very first page.

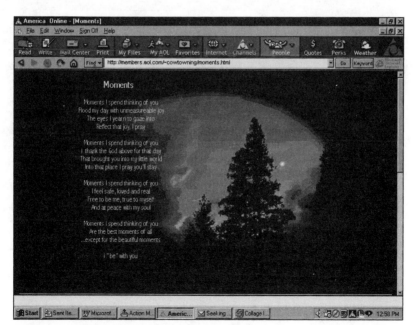

Figure 11-8: Your personal Web pages are a great place to show off your creativity whether it takes the form of artwork, photography, fiction, or, as in Ingrid's case, poetry.

All in all, Ingrid has created a comfortable, interesting site that's full of her own personality and the things she loves — the definition of an excellent personal home page.

Ed Hobbs's Web site

Ed Hobbs's Web site at `http://members.aol.com/edhobbs` has an entirely different, quirky kind of feel. Ed has set up a simple but very effective navigation system that looks like a stack of road signs (see Figure 11-9). They're topped off by a sign that welcomes you to Ed Hobbs's Web site, "Population: 3,000,000 bytes."

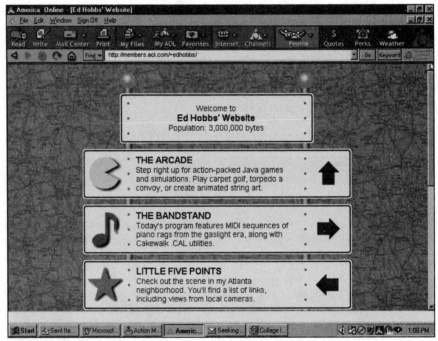

Figure 11-9: Ed Hobbs's Web site is an AOL site that fits in perfectly with Hometown AOL's philosophy of creating a virtual community: Ed's already created one all by himself!

Each sign on the home page links to a different part of the site: Java Games, a collection of MIDI files called The Bandstand, information about Ed's neighborhood in Atlanta, an old B&O Railroad manual included just for nostalgic kicks, and personal information about Ed in "The Mayor's House."

Notice that the background on Ed's home page is that of a road map, again tying in with the site-navigation signpost. Ed Hobbs's Web site is a perfect example of using a simple, unified design theme to create an eye-catching, aesthetically pleasing and, most of all, easy-to-navigate Web site.

John Cartan's Home Page

John Cartan is a writer and programmer who lives on an island in San Francisco Bay. His home page at `http://www.sirius.com/~jcartan/` is simple, but intriguing, from the warm welcome — "Please take off your shoes and pour yourself a drink. Unravel your obligations. Become idle, then curious, then child-like. Relax." — to the interesting images down the left side of the page that link to his essays on topics as diverse as Ireland and a cat named Aristippus (see Figure 11-10).

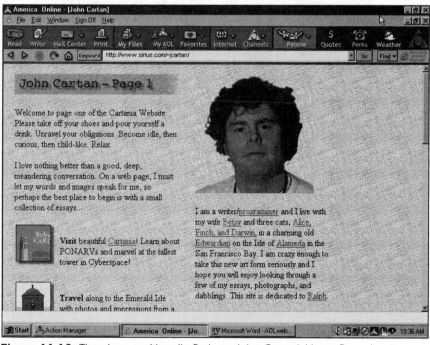

Figure 11-10: There's no multimedia flash on John Cartan's Home Page, but you immediately get a feel for the person who created it and want to follow its links deeper into the site. (Design and text © 1997 by John Cartan)

Within his site, John has balanced text and graphics well to produce lovely pages like the one outlining the trip he and his wife made to Ireland in search of information about his ancestors. Pictures large enough to be entertaining, while small enough to load quickly, march down the left side of the page, while on the right side, text, accompanied by the occasional additional graphic, provides a running commentary. The effect is of an interesting slide show given by a witty and mercifully short-winded host (see Figure 11-11).

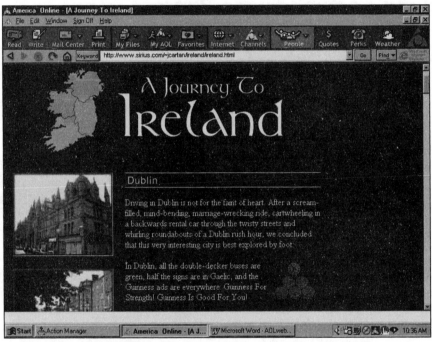

Figure 11-11: Typical of John Cartan's interior pages is this virtual slide show of his trip to Ireland. (Design and text © 1997 by John Cartan)

 Remember that suggestion I made about keeping the same background on each page? John has broken it to good effect here, placing his Irish photos and text on a dark green (what else?) background. Which just goes to show you, rules (especially on the Web) are made to be broken — *if* you have a good reason.

Michael Zyda's Home Page

If there was an award for most audacious use of a graphic, it would have to go to Michael Zyda's Home Page at `http://www.cs.nps.navy.mil/people/faculty/zyda/`, because the first thing you see when you enter his URL is — well, see for yourself in Figure 11-12.

That initial "splash" screen even has its own title, "Look me in the eye and say that . . .", a touch of humor that makes an effective contrast to the more conservatively presented information of the Web site proper (see Figure 11-13).

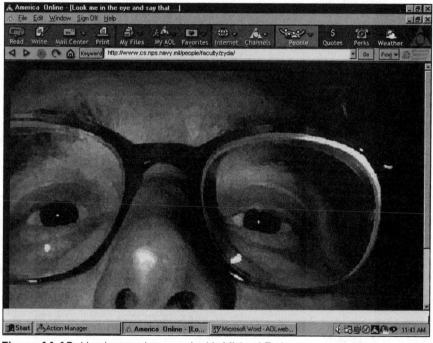

Figure 11-12: Up close and personal with Michael Zyda

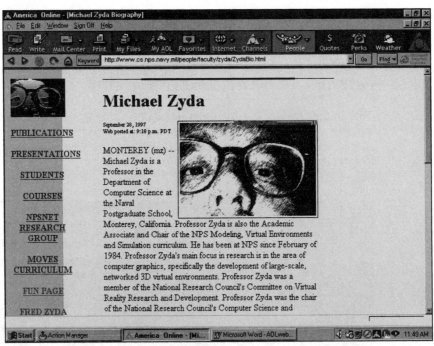

Figure 11-13: Clean, elegantly designed Web pages tell you everything you need to know about Professor Zyda professionally, but that initial screen and a few other touches here and there are what really give you a sense of his personality.

Startling, even shocking, contrasts like this are another effective way to make your Web page stand out. Surprises like Michael Zyda's eyes suddenly filling the screen can make even the most jaded Web surfer sit up and take notice — and more inclined to look at the rest of your site.

Summary

People seem to have an insatiable need to homestead on the digital frontier, to stake their claim to a corner of cyberspace they can call their own. But there are so many personal Web pages out there that most of them get lost in the crowd. To make yours stand out, ask yourself some pointed questions about your audience and your message, and how you can bring the two together in a way that's both effective and unique; add a dash of humor (if appropriate); take a spin around the Net to see what other people have done — and then get busy. The World Wide Web awaits your contribution.

Creating a Cool Small-Business Page

Today's Web surfers are drawn to commercial sites that offer information and shopping opportunities for an enormous range of goods and services. For the small-business owner, the Web offers potential exposure on a scale that would be impossibly expensive to achieve with traditional advertising methods. A candlemaker operating out of her parents' basement in a small North Dakota town can conceivably find herself filling orders from all over the world after she creates a Web page with Personal Publisher and posts it on America Online. But to achieve those kinds of results, you need an effective, interesting site that will draw visitors over and over again. That's what this chapter is about. Again, I offer a checklist for you to consider before beginning your site, some tips for drawing people to your site, and examples of some good small business pages already on the Web, including some by AOL members.

The Internet: What Good Is It?

The Internet is used for as many things as there are businesses, and the type of business you're involved in has a lot to do with how you use the Internet. Here are some examples of how some small businesses are using the Internet:

➡ **Communication.** E-mail has been called the "killer app" of the Internet, meaning it's the single most important ability the Internet provides. (It's importance is illustrated by the fact that e-mail is the single most popular service AOL offers its members.) You don't have to have a Web page in order to have an e-mail address, but a Web page is a great way to make your AOL e-mail address known, and to attract e-mail messages from potential customers, suppliers, or even employees.

➡ **Customer support.** Web sites are a great place to post information that helps customers after the sale is made. If feedback indicates that many customers are having a particular problem, then an explanation of (and hopefully solution for) that problem can be posted on the Web. Also, information about updates, improvements, special offers, and more can be provided via the Web site (see Figure 12-1). By pointing customers to your Web site, you can reduce the time and cost inherent in other methods of communicating with customers, such as mass mail-outs or telephoning.

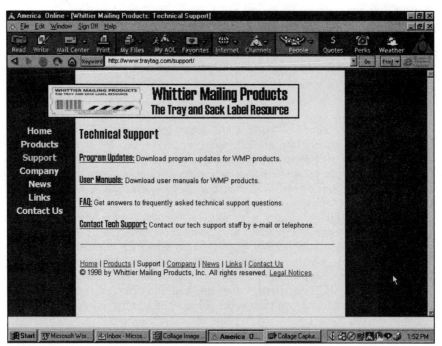

Figure 12-1: This page from Whittier Mailing Products (`http://www.traytag.com/support/`) is typical of customer support pages on business Web sites. (Used with permission of Whittier Mailing Products, Inc.)

➥ **Online catalogs.** Web sites excel at presenting the kind of information traditionally found in print catalogs. The visitor can start on a page that presents a broad overview of the goods and services offered, broken down into categories; clicking each category takes him or her to a list of subcategories, and clicking those to lists of individual items, each of which can then have its own Web page with detailed price and ordering information — even a graphic or video, if appropriate.

➥ **Globalization.** As noted earlier, a home business can become a worldwide business simply by setting up a Web site, because unlike your office in, say, Pierre, South Dakota, your Web site is instantly accessible to anyone with Internet access, anywhere in the world. Of course, it's important to be fully prepared to deal with that first order from Pakistan!

➥ **Competitiveness.** A small business with a well-designed Web site has a more impressive presence on the Web than a huge business with a poorly designed Web site (or no Web site at all). That makes it much easier for small businesses to compete with large ones.

➥ **Public Relations.** By providing information about itself, its employees, and its public activities (supporting Little League teams, donating to the United Way, and so on) on the Web, businesses enhance their reputation as responsible corporate citizens, which in turn makes civic-minded customers feel more kindly toward them.

➥ **Sales.** Personal Publisher 3 doesn't let you set up a business site complete with a secure system of taking credit card numbers online, but that doesn't mean you can't use the Web site to generate immediate sales. All you have to do is provide a phone number (ideally, a toll-free one), an e-mail address or a mailing address — or all three — and clear instructions as to how visitors to the Web site can purchase the goods and services you've advertised there.

The Business Web Page Checklist

If planning ahead is important to your personal home page, it's *vital* to your business home page. If you don't have a clear idea of what you want to do, your Web page will end up in a muddle, and visitors either won't find what they're looking for, or will be so unimpressed by what they do find that they'll write your business off as a place so disorganized and amateurish they wouldn't dare send you any money — bad news, for sure!

Here are ten questions to ask yourself before you begin your business Web page. Any overlap between this and the personal home page checklist is purely intentional: some steps along the way to a cool Web site remain the same, no matter what the final product is intended to be.

1. **Who are my customers?** Are you a supplier trying to communicate with other businesses, or are you reaching out to individual shoppers? The way you'd approach the former would be quite different from how you'd approach the latter. If you are aiming at individuals, who are they? College students? Retirees? Mothers with small children? Teenagers? You have to know to whom you're trying to sell!

2. **What is my message?** Are you trying to sell specific items online or promoting your businesses contributions to the community? Another way of putting this is, "What am I trying to accomplish with this Web site?" If you just want to make a few bucks from Web surfers, you might want a loud, in-your-face, hard-sell approach aimed at generating an impulse to buy on the spot. If you want to build long-term, loyal customers, you might take a more staid approach, focusing on providing excellent information about your products and showing a willingness to listen to customers' needs — and meet them.

3. **What have other businesses done?** There are a lot of businesses already on the Web, some of them similar to yours. Do some browsing via AOL NetFind or one of the other search engines to see what other businesses have done. After all, knowing your competition is the key to business at any level — and on the Web, you're competing not just with similar businesses in your neighborhood, city, or even state but with similar businesses all over the world. Find out what they've done — then do them one better.

4. **What added value can I provide?** How do you improve on what other businesses have done? By taking a close look at your own and seeing what you can do that no one else is doing, or better yet, is capable of doing. If you live in Vermont and you're selling homemade candies, but you're not taking advantage of Vermont maple syrup, then you're missing a bet. Or perhaps you're selling pottery, and your grandfather started the first commercial pottery kiln in your state. Talk to Granddad and get that fascinating history on your Web site. The history alone will draw people there, and they'll be more inclined to buy your pottery thereafter. No matter what your business, there's something unique about the way you do it, the knowledge you bring to it, or your thoughts on it. Share with your visitors, and they'll remember your site — and your business — long after they've forgotten others (see Figure 12-2).

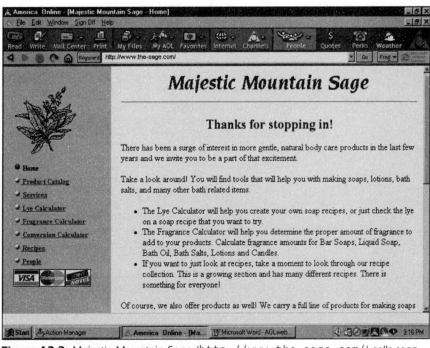

Figure 12-2: Majestic Mountain Sage (`http://www.the-sage.com/`) sells soap-making supplies, like many other businesses on the Web — but they play that down in favor of material of added value, including a lye calculator, a fragrance calculator, and a collection of soap recipes.

5.   **Do I want to take orders from my Web site?** If you're aiming to sell directly from the Web site, then you need to decide how you're going to do that. Will you have a form to fill in, like the cat funhouse people, or will you offer a toll-free number, like the potbellied pig people? Will you take orders by e-mail and ship COD? This needs careful thought, remembering that, once you're on the Web, you could get orders from anywhere in the world. If you're not prepared for that, it's important that you make it clear on your Web site that you can only accept orders from the U.S., North America, or whatever suits your capabilities.

6.   **How much storage space do I have available?** It doesn't matter what kind of Web page you're designing, you've got to keep this in mind. You might love to put a complete catalog of all your products online, but if the graphics are going to take up more space than you have, you're going to have to find some other

way of dealing with it. Storage space and bandwidth are the real determinants of how graphics- and multimedia-intensive a Web site you can create.

7. How do I want to balance text and graphics? This, too, is a question that's exactly the same no matter what kind of Web page you create. Again, write your text and gather your graphics before you begin designing your page, then sketch out a rough design on a piece of paper. Keep in mind the more graphics on a page, the slower it will load. Keep everything as clean and uncluttered looking as possible. And on a business page, pay special attention to how your visitors will navigate the site, if it's more than one page. You don't want them losing their way en route to the Order Here! page, do you?

8. Do I want to add links to related sites? This question is a little different than for a personal home page, and there are two ways of looking at it. On the one hand, on a business page, you want to offer visitors as little opportunity as possible to escape to some other part of the Web, and you may not want to list any links that lead, directly or indirectly, to competing businesses. But resist the temptation to metaphorically lock the doors and windows of your site once visitors arrive. A site with no way out (except the Back button on the browser) feels like a trap. Provide a few external links, but keep them in their own separate area, and vet them carefully. Visitors who access those links from your page are likely to associate your page with those links, and if those links lead only to a waste of good storage space, it will reflect badly on you — and your business.

On the other hand, links add to the general interest of your page. People may come to make use of your collection of links — and stay to browse your page. If you can assemble an impressive enough collection of links, it might be worthwhile to post them all — even if they lead to competitors.

9. Do I want to add multimedia? It bears repeating yet again that while multimedia can add flash, it also eats bandwidth. However, it can be particularly useful on a business site. A short video clip of one of your products in action (assuming it actually does something that can be effectively captured on film) can be a great sales tool. So can an animated GIF diagram. And if you're in the business of selling, say, recordings of your brother's rock band, or yourself as a voice-over performer, audio files are a must. The rule remains the same: if you use multimedia, have a good reason for it. Otherwise, stick mainly to text and graphics.

10. How do I organize my site? Unless your business consists of selling one or two items at the most, you'll probably need more than one page. That means you'll need careful organization. Gather your text and graphics together and decide how best to

categorize it; then create Web pages based on those categories. Try to keep them all a similar size, and fairly small, so they'll load quickly as your visitor moves through your site. Rather than creating your home page first, which is what most people tend to do, you might want to create it last. In a multipage site, it needs to have a lot of impact, and draw people in immediately, so give it extra thought. It's the place for an eye-catching graphic or good animated GIF — provided neither one takes too long to load. Make sure you have a good navigation system worked out which starts from your home page — this is where those automatic links to your other pages that Personal Publisher can add for you will come in handy. Make sure that each link is well labeled so there's no doubt in your visitor's mind what he or she will find on the other end.

More Tips for Business Home Pages

Even after going through the checklist above, you can do additional things to make your business Web site more attractive. Here are some tips:

➡ **Use special promotions.** Seasonal and other promotions are a great way to get people to visit your site in the first place — and come back to visit it often. For example, offer monthly giveaways to people drawn at random from those who e-mail you their name and e-mail address. Not only does this attract visitors, it lets you track where your visitors are coming from.

➡ **Keep it light.** A light-hearted or warm and fuzzy feeling for your site is going to win you a lot more customers than a cold, corporate one. Keep a sense of humor, even a sense of irony, about what you're doing, and you'll appeal to the typical Web-surfer far more than if you come across as a late-night TV infomercial.

➡ **Make connections with people.** Sure, it's a business Web site, not a personal one, but businesses are composed of people. Try to give some sense of the people behind your Web site, so you don't come across as just a faceless company. Put pictures of your employees on the site, and provide links to their home pages if they have them. Include other photographs of people buying things in your store, or using your products. Make it clear that you're just "ordinary folks." A Web site that feels warm and cozy will usually draw — and retain! — more people than one that feels like it's made of chrome and glass.

➡ **Promote your site.** Get your URL out to all the search engines you can. Investigate placing banner ads on related sites. Make sure that every piece of e-mail you send out, as well as every piece of regular mail, every bit of print, radio and TV advertising you may do, and all your business cards have that URL prominently displayed. Don't, unless you want to turn more people against your business than even knew it existed before, send out unsolicited e-mail. This "spam" is considered one of the great banes of the Internet, and you don't want to be associated with it — especially because AOL has been very aggressive in working to protect its members from Spam, having even gone so far as to announce and publicize a "10 Most-Wanted Spammers" list. That's one top-10 list on which you definitely don't want to appear!

Examples of Business Web Sites

Let's take a look at a couple of business Web sites set up by other AOL members, to give you an idea of what's possible — and maybe inspiration for your own business site.

Lorraine's Crafts

When it comes to home businesses, there's nothing more homey than a craft business, and that's what AOL member Lorraine Albert has set up, very simply, at her site at `http://members.aol.com/lor1466`. There's nothing terribly fancy about Lorraine's Crafts, but the judicious use of appropriate graphics, such as the needlepoint-like pattern of hearts across the page and, a little further down, a very cute animated GIF of a kitten that runs, washes, and naps, is very effective (see Figure 12-3).

Lorraine's Crafts is interesting, too, in that it's a true "Information Age" business. Lorraine doesn't sell completed crafts, at least not through her Web site: instead, she sells instructions for crafts, such as a series of cute animal characters made from everyday beverage containers (and which, best of all, still function as containers even after they're turned into animals!). Viewers can print out an order form and send it to her via regular mail; she returns the instructions the same way. It's not high-tech, but it works!

Lorraine's approach may be something you want to consider if you have expertise of some sort that can be taught to others. After all, it's a lot easier to send a few sheets of paper or an e-mail to someone than it is to send a completed product, especially if your expertise is in, say, building grand pianos!

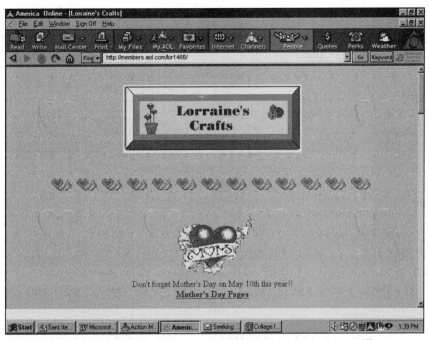

Figure 12-3: Lorraine's Crafts is a very simple Web site, but it's also an effective promotion for Lorraine Albert's small home-based crafts business.

Lorraine also makes use of a good promotional technique by posting a free sample of her expertise, a recipe for Fizzing Bath Oil Balls, on her Web site (see Figure 12-4). Not only do free samples draw people to your Web site, they also serve as a sort of audition piece for you, helping to convince your prospective customers that you know what you're talking about and can really offer them something of value.

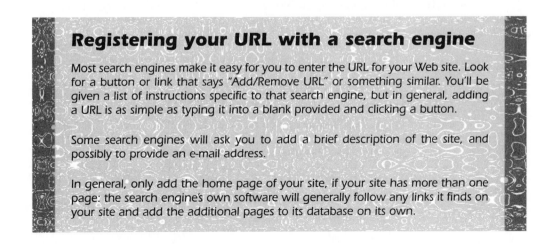

Registering your URL with a search engine

Most search engines make it easy for you to enter the URL for your Web site. Look for a button or link that says "Add/Remove URL" or something similar. You'll be given a list of instructions specific to that search engine, but in general, adding a URL is as simple as typing it into a blank provided and clicking a button.

Some search engines will ask you to add a brief description of the site, and possibly to provide an e-mail address.

In general, only add the home page of your site, if your site has more than one page: the search engine's own software will generally follow any links it finds on your site and add the additional pages to its database on its own.

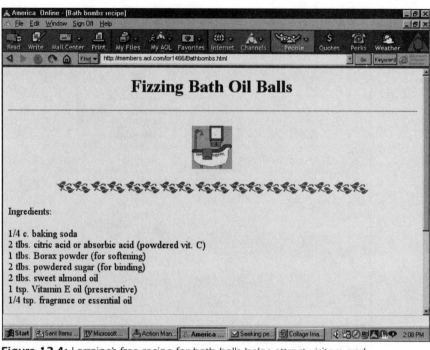

Figure 12-4: Lorraine's free recipe for bath balls helps attract visitors and demonstrates she really does know something about crafts.

Crooked Fence Plaza's Wooden Nickels

Crooked Fence Plaza is a small business specializing in, of all things, wooden nickels, and at their site on AOL at `http://members.aol.com/CFPlaza/woodennickelmessagetokens.html`, customers can find out everything they need to know about what wooden nickels are good for, how much they cost, and how they can use them to promote their own business or event (see Figure 12-5).

This site illustrates something else that should be said about business Web sites in general: there's more than one approach. Lorraine's Crafts was very understated; Crooked Fence Plaza's site is anything but. It comes across like a Web-based version of junk mail, but there's one big advantage to this approach on the Web that junk mail doesn't share: it's unlikely anyone came to this site unless they were already interested in wooden nickels, and that being the case, this approach, which might be abrasive under other circumstances, instead simply comes across as straightforward and informative.

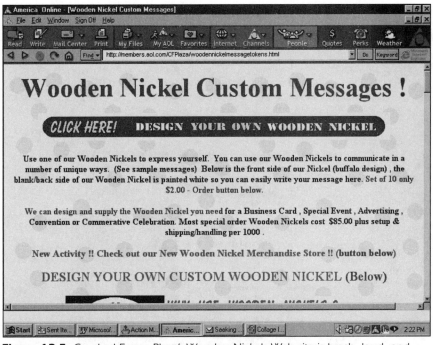

Figure 12-5: Crooked Fence Plaza's Wooden Nickels Web site is brash, loud, and unabashed about what it wants you to do: it wants you to design and buy your own wooden nickels, right now! (CFPlaza@aol.com; http://members.aol.com/ CFPlaza/woodennickelmessagetokens.html)

Another interesting aspect of this site is that it is, in the simplest possible way, interactive: it invites you to print out a copy of a wooden nickel design form and design your own wooden nickel right away. That's the type of interactivity that can add interest to a Web site without requiring you to know anything about Java programming or any of the more complex methods of creating interactive Web features

To order your wooden nickels, again, you simply print out an order form and mail it off.

It can be informative to look at any other small-business page, such as the two mentioned here, but it can be even more informative to examine several pages that offer similar products — especially if they offer products similar to your own.

More AOL support for Web-based businesses

You can certainly create a useful and effective Web site using Personal Publisher 3, but if you feel you're ready to move beyond what you can do with Personal Publisher, or if you need a larger site than you can fit into the amount of disk space available to you in My Place, then you may need to move up to AOL's PrimeHost Service (see Figure 12-8).

Figure 12-6: AOL's PrimeHost offers a plethora of useful services for businesses that need a larger or more complex Web site than is easily constructed using Personal Publisher 3.

PrimeHost offers more space (50 megabytes), more advanced (and hence, more complex!) Web-authoring software, online technical support, marketing advice and guidance and more. It even has its own e-zine, called *PrimeHost PrimeLine*, exclusively for PrimeHost businesses on the web. With PrimeHost you can also create your own domain name (for example, www.mybusiness.com), making it easier for customers to remember your Web site's address and thereby increasing the chance they'll pay it a visit.

PrimeHost is accessible from Personal Publisher 3's opening screen (it's in the menu of other resources), or you can access it directly with keyword **Primehost**.

Another good place to look for information on all aspects of running a business is AOL's Workplace channel. No matter what the size of your business, you'll find a ton of useful resources.

Summary

A Web site for your home or small business is a great way to expand your market, make connections with potential customers and suppliers, and connect with other people in the same business. It can make even the smallest business part of the global economy, on an even keel with competitors that may be many times larger. But its success depends on careful thought, planning, and design; and to really be a success, it's important to move beyond presenting just the facts about your business, and to instead provide added value in as many ways as you can . . . from answering the burning question, "What is a gourd?" to giving away free shareware.

Creating Cool Kids' Pages

In This Chapter

Kids' Web page checklist

What makes a great kids' site?

Examples of cool kids' pages

There's no doubt about it: America Online and the Internet are unbelievable resources for today's children. Fun, games, pen pals from around the world — and the educational possibilities! It's like having an incredible library, not only of books but of images, sounds, and videos, right in your house. But the fact that it's right in your house — and in millions of other houses — also places an awesome responsibility on people who would create Web sites designed for children. Just grabbing kids' interest isn't enough — you want to engage their minds and their imaginations. And if you're a kid yourself creating a Web page for fellow kids, the last thing you want to end up with is something "lame." In this chapter we show you how to avoid lameness, and give you some standards to aim for as you strive to create a site that moves beyond cool all the way into great.

The Kids' Web Page Checklist

If you've been with me for the last two chapters, then you know what's coming: yep, planning ahead. It was important for your personal home page, it's vital for your business home page, and it's absolutely necessary for a page aimed at children. With enough flash and dash — pictures and sounds and videos — you might be able to attract kids to your page, but if you want them to keep coming back (and to tell all their friends about it), you need substance.

Ask yourself the following ten questions, or if you're helping a child create a page of his or her own, discuss these questions with him or her before you set pixel to monitor:

1. **What is my target age group?** Children grow, and as they grow they change. That's just one of the things it means to be a kid. The things that are cool to a seven year old aren't going to be cool to a twelve year old, and definitely won't be cool to a teenager. So don't try to be all things to all ages; narrow your focus. (There's nothing to say that you can't expand it later; after all, Web pages grow and change, too!) There's a big difference between sites intended for preschoolers (see Figure 13-1) and sites intended for older children (see Figure 13-2).

2. **What is my goal?** Are you trying to entertain? To educate? To create a dialog among kids from around the world? They're all legitimate goals, and all possible. You could even attempt to achieve all three. But you need to have a clearly stated goal in mind before you begin building your site, or it will end up confused — and so, likely, will any child who happens to come across it!

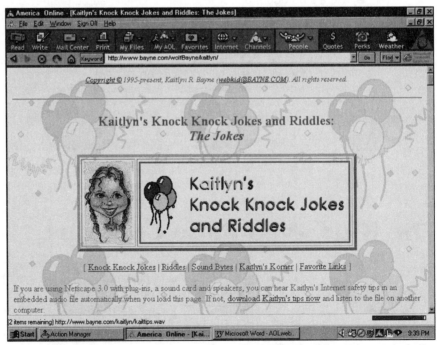

Figure 13-1: Kaitlyn's Knock Knock Jokes and Riddles (`http://www.bayne.com/wolfBayne/kaitlyn/`), is designed for children eight and under . . .

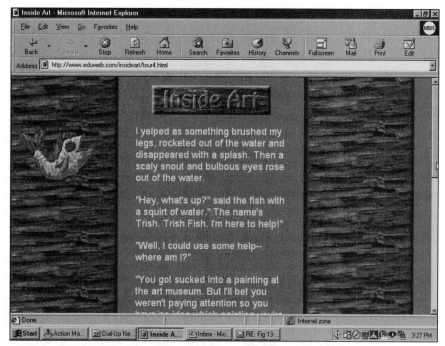

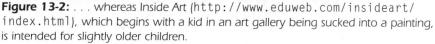

Figure 13-2: . . . whereas Inside Art (`http://www.eduweb.com/insideart/index.html`), which begins with a kid in an art gallery being sucked into a painting, is intended for slightly older children.

3. **What's been done on other children's pages?** There are many not-very-good pages aimed at children, but there are also hundreds of good ones. Study the good ones, especially those that deal with subjects you want to deal with and are aimed at the same ages. Use AOL's NetFind to track down pages on topics similar to yours. If you include keywords such as *kids* and *children*, chances are you'll find pages intended for youngsters or created by them. You say you want to create a children's Web page that's all about bugs? You're probably not the first—but if you look at what others have already done, you may be the best, by providing something they didn't.

4. **What will hold children's interest?** You may need to do some research. If you're not a teacher or parent yourself, talk to some teachers or parents who deal with the children for whom you'd like to create a Web page. Of course, if you happen to be a kid creating a Web page for other kids, you already have a head start—you know what you like, and you know what your friends like. Grown-ups, however, can't rely on their dim memories of what was popular when they were kids. The hottest thing going at my elementary school when I was eight years old was marbles. Marbles are still

played, but they're nowhere near as popular as they were then, when every kid in my town dreamed of winning the big city marble tournament. Things change. So do kids. Get over it and get with it.

5. How can I make my site more interesting? After all the carping I do on too many graphics and too much multimedia slowing things down and taking up valuable space, you may be surprised to hear me say this — but you need something interesting to look at on your page, or you'll never get a kid to stop long enough to see what else is there. Studies of children surfing the Web have shown definitely that graphics, especially animation, catch their eyes. Of course, you have to walk a fine line between making your page eye-catching and making it load so slowly that kids won't stick around anyway. Look for simple, brightly colored graphics that load quickly but still look cool. Rather than a slow-loading photograph, for example, use a quick-loading cartoon. And if there was ever a place for animated GIFs, your kids' page is it!

6. How much storage space do I have available? Just a reminder: don't get so carried away with the eye candy that you run out of room for the meat.

7. Is my content appropriate to the age group? A preschool page probably isn't the right place to go into detail on the birds and the bees, nor is it the right place to attempt to explain black holes. Just a few years later, both topics could be appropriate. This goes back to doing your research. Find out what kids are learning in school; this will give you some idea of the kinds of ideas they're prepared to handle. Even if your site is just, say, a joke page, some jokes are too sophisticated for younger children but may be appreciated by older ones.

8. What can I add to what's already out there? If you're a kid creating a kids' page, ask yourself what's special about you; what do you know how to do that other kids might be interested in? That's a good place to start, and it makes your page unique. If you're a grown-up, ask yourself a similar question: what can you bring to your topic that nobody else can? Again, there's no point in reinventing the wheel. The Web only grows and becomes richer if you add new things to it — not just rehashed versions of things that already exist.

9. Is my information accurate? This is a particularly important question to ask yourself before starting to create an educational site. Adults have a hard time sifting through what's true and what isn't on the Internet; children find it even harder, simply due to a lack of education and experience. That means anyone undertaking to create an educational site expressly aimed at children had better make darn sure that all his or her facts are correct. To fail to make the effort to double-check everything is simply wrong — like lying to a child.

10.   What about links? Links are problematic on kids' pages because there's a lot of stuff on the Web that kids have no business accessing — and one link can easily lead to another that leads directly to those kinds of sites. Don't add a link to a page intended for children unless you have carefully checked it out yourself — and checked the links that branch out from the linked site, too. Children will find things that aren't good for them on the Net — just as in real life — but at least you can do your best to see they don't find them through you.

What Makes a Kids' Web Site Great?

What makes a kids' Web site great? The Children and Technology Committee of the Association for Library Service to Children, a division of the American Library Association (ALA), has developed criteria to answer that question. They need those criteria, because the ALA has a site entitled Great Sites (http://www.ala.org/parentspage/greatsites/) which provides links to more than 700 sites the ALA feels are great for children to visit (see Figure 13-3).

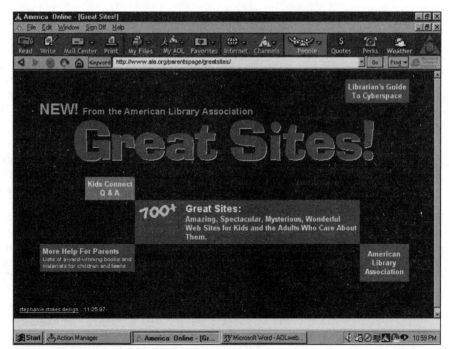

Figure 13-3: You'll know you've really accomplished something if you can land your Web page for kids on the ALA list of Great Sites!

If you want not just a cool site but a great one, consider the ALA's criteria, too (which are posted in their entirety at `http://www.ala.org/parentspage/greatsites/criteria.html`):

➥ **Who put up the site?** You should identify yourself on the site; after all, you're expecting people to entrust you with their kids' brains. For the same reason, you should give a source for any information on the site, where necessary; provide a way for users to make comments or ask questions, and be conscious of copyright and trademark concerns. In other words, if it's not yours to reproduce, either get permission from the copyright holder, or don't reproduce it!

➥ **Every great site has a reason for being there.** And that reason should be clear: to educate, to entertain, to persuade, or to sell. On sites that aren't clearly intended to sell, advertising shouldn't overshadow the content. And most important, the site should enrich the user's experience and expand his or her imagination — free of gender, racial, or religious biases and in accordance with AOL's Terms of Service (see the sidebar, "Internet Safety Tips" later in this chapter).

➥ **A great site has personality and strength of character.** Information should be easy to find and easy to use, site design should appeal to its intended audience, text should be easy to read, and users should be able to get around the site easily. Pages of links should be well organized and appealing to young people, and the links should be well chosen and useful. If the site contains a game, it should have a clear interface and playing instructions. The page should load fairly quickly and should be consistently available and stable. Any extra "plug-ins" required should be clearly identified. Fancy design elements like graphics and animations shouldn't hinder the accessibility and enjoyment of the site. Interactive features should be explained clearly. And finally, the site should be free and users should not be required to provide any personal information to access it.

➥ **A great site shares meaningful and useful content that educates, informs or entertains.** That means the title of a site is clear and appropriate, the content is easily understood by its intended audience, and there's enough information to make visiting the site worthwhile. If there's a large amount of information, some kind of search function, or at least an outline, should be provided, enabling visitors to find information easily. Spelling and grammar should always be correct. Information should be current and accurate — and it's a good idea to include a "last updated" date. Links to more information should be provided. Graphics should be relevant and appropriate to the subject matter, and the subject matter should be relevant and appropriate to the intended audience. The viewpoint of the site should be understandable by the intended audience, and the skills required to use the site should be appropriate for the intended audience. Quality of content is vital; any presentation of mature content (such as might occur at sites dealing with aspects of health and life education) should be appropriate for the intended audience.

Oddly enough — or maybe not so oddly — many of these criteria for a great site are also good criteria for creating a great site for any purpose. Quality of content is always vital, spelling and grammar always count, graphics should always be appropriate and relevant, pages should always load quickly, and so on.

Gee, I think these guys must have been reading over my shoulder!

Examples of Cool Kids' Pages

Now take a look at some of the sites that meet at least most of the criteria laid out earlier, to give you some idea of what can be done in creating a Web page aimed at kids.

Internet safety tips

Many Web sites for children include safety tips designed to keep kids away from some of the darker and danker corners of the Internet, and safe from some of the lowlifes who lurk there. Here are some suggested tips you might like to include on your kids' pages:

- Ask your parents' permission before using your full name, address, telephone number, or school name anywhere on the Internet.

- Always tell your parents or another adult you trust if you see something scary online, or something you don't understand.

- Don't respond to messages that make you feel uncomfortable or uneasy.

- Never give out a credit card number or password online.

- Never arrange to meet anyone you've met online unless you've talked about it with your parents and a grown-up goes with you.

A good resource to point AOL members to is AOL's Terms of Service (keyword **TOS**), especially the section called "Rules of the Road," which explains "netiquette," the rules of civilized behavior on the Internet. It's also worthwhile to remind AOL members about AOL's Parental Controls (keyword **Parental Controls**), which can be used to limit children's access to only child-friendly sites, and can be customized for children of different ages and levels of maturity.

Bats, Bats Everywhere

Bats, Bats Everywhere (`http://members.aol.com/bats4kids`) is a good example of an AOL member's Web site aimed at children: in this case, providing good information about an animal that fascinates kids of all ages, the bat (see Figure 13-4)

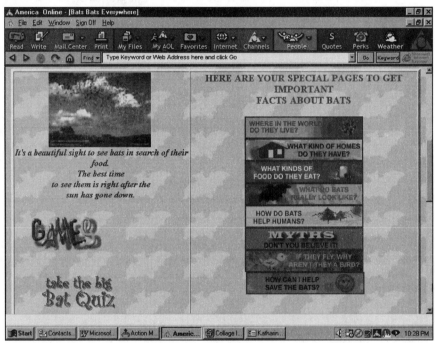

Figure 13-4: Bats, Bats Everywhere answers kids' questions about this fascinating flying mammal.

The creators of Bats, Bats Everywhere have organized their site as a series of pages that answers exactly the kind of questions kids are likely to ask about bats, such as, "If they fly, why aren't they a bird?" (see Figure 13-5). This is a great design for an educational page aimed at children.

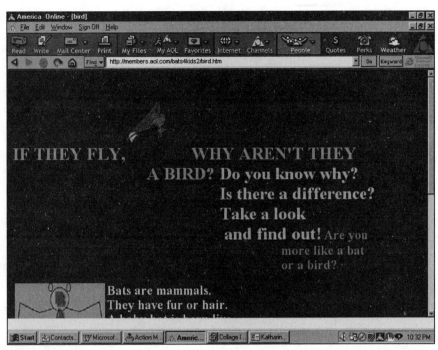

Figure 13-5: Why aren't bats birds? This page answers that question for kids and also includes an excellent example of an animated GIF: that bat between the words *fly* and *why* flaps its wings!

Kids can also find out where bats live, what kind of food bats eat, how bats help humans, and how kids can help save bats, which are endangered in many parts of the world because of the many myths believed about them — myths that are exploded on this site. It's a good example of an effective Web site for children built around a single interesting topic explored in an interesting way.

Animals, Myths & Legends

Animals, Myths & Legends (http://www.ozemail.com.au/~oban/) grabs kids' attention right off with a colorful first page and attractive, fast-loading graphics (see Figure 13-6).

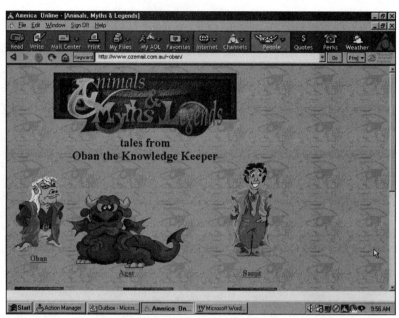

Figure 13-6: Kids will be eager to explore further as soon as they catch a glimpse of the appealing home page of Animals, Myths & Legends. (© WordDesign InterActive; Concept funding provided by AME LTD.)

Animals, Myths & Legends is designed for children ages eight to thirteen. The premise is that Oban the Knowledge Keeper has come to this world to collect legends about animals and to talk to the animals. In addition to a collection of Australian legends like "How the Kangaroo Got Its Pouch," there are "postcards" from animals that provide information about them in a chatty, first-person format (see Figure 13-7).

With its colorful, graphics, chatty style, and computer-game elements, Animals, Myths & Legends is a good example of presenting valuable information in an entertaining way — something you might want to strive for on your kids' page.

Brianna's Name THAT Book!!

Here's a cute, clever site that promotes reading by providing lists of recommended books of all types, from "100 Picture Books Everyone Should Know" to "Best Historical Fiction for Young Adults" (see Figure 13-8).

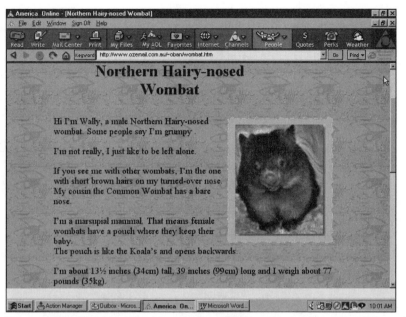

Figure 13-7: Wally the Wombat is just one of the animals with a postcard on the Animals, Myths & Legends site. (© WordDesign InterActive; Concept funding provided by AME LTD.)

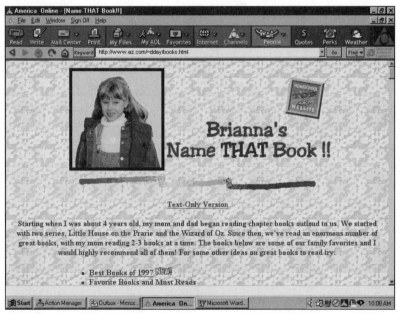

Figure 13-8: Brianna's Name THAT Book!! (`http://www.az.com/~dday/books.html`) is a simple but effective site, with bright graphics and great information.

Brianna's Name THAT Book!! also offers an example of how to create an interactive game that doesn't require Java scripts or any other such bells and whistles. In fact, the site gets its name from this quiz, in which readers are given a list of paragraphs taken from various books, and challenged to name the books from which they came. The answer is provided by a simple link from each paragraph to a description of the book from which they came (see Figure 13-9).

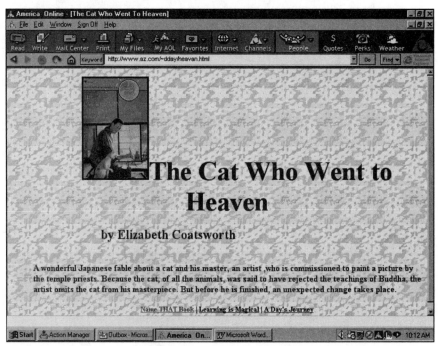

Figure 13-9: When you look for the answer to one of the paragraphs in Brianna's Name THAT Book!! quiz, you're taken to a description of the book, complete with an image of the book's cover.

Brianna's Name THAT Book!! has great content, interactivity, bright, attractive graphics and a clear and worthwhile purpose. It's definitely a cool site for kids!

It's also obvious that it must have been a joint project between Brianna and her parents, because it's unlikely Brianna created it entirely on her own — and that's great! I can't think of a better way to introduce kids to the Internet than helping them create a Web page. If you're a parent, it's a wonderful opportunity to spend time with your child and find out more about his or her interests and abilities. Chances are you'll end up learning as much as your son or daughter does!

The Yuckiest Site on the Internet

Finally, no survey of children's Web sites, however cursory, would be complete without looking at a science-related site. There are a lot of them, but the one that caught my eye was New Jersey Online's Yuckiest Site on the Internet (`http://www.yucky.com`).

This is a perfect example of approaching a topic from a kids' point of view to ensure that kids will be interested. The fact is, kids are interested in yucky topics. When you're ten years old, there's not much distinction between "gross" and "cool." The Yuckiest Site on the Internet has taken that idea and run with it, focusing on everything from bugs to "Your Gross and Cool Body — Burps, spit & more" (see Figure 13-10).

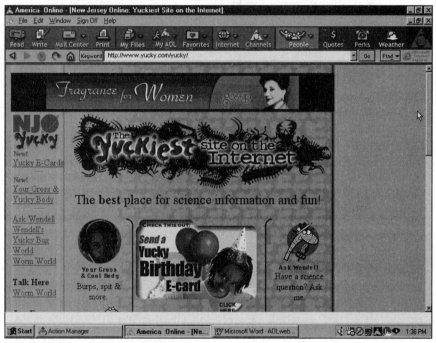

Figure 13-10: The Yuckiest Site on the Internet uses kids' fascination with yucky things to teach science — sneaky, but cool.

The Yuckiest Site on the Internet also contrasts just about as much as is possible with simple sites like Sounds of the World's Animals. It uses lots of graphics, lots of color, and not much text on each page, to catch kids' attention and convince them to click that next link and see what else they can find (see Figure 13-11). It makes looking for information a bit like digging for treasure. Fortunately, the information, once found, is fascinating.

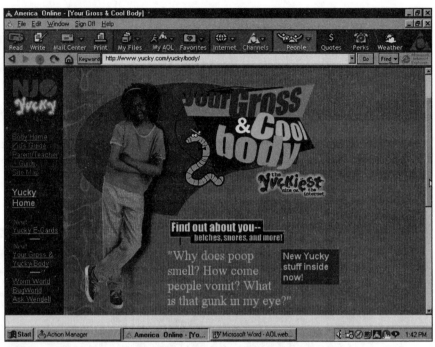

Figure 13-11: Lots of graphics, lots of links to click: the Yuckiest Site on the Internet is a busy place.

There's a place for both approaches among Web pages for kids; the important thing is to remember what they both have in common: excellent content. Children deserve no less.

Summary

Creating Web pages for kids or creating Web pages with kids requires just as much time and attention as creating Web pages for yourself or for your business. It's particularly important to know what age group you're aiming at and what the purpose of your site is. It's also important to find a way to present your site that will capture kids' interest. But most important of all is to put content on the site that's worthwhile and unique. If you can do that, your kids' site may graduate from being merely cool to being great!

A Page for Every Passion

14

In This Chapter

A page for every passion

The final checklist, for any and all pages

Examples of cool pages of all sorts

So far I devote a chapter to the kind of personal home page where you tell people a little bit about yourself and your interests, pages for small business, and pages for kids. But these just scratch the surface of what you can do with Web pages. The fact is, you can do just about anything with them — and that's what this chapter is about. Obviously, because there are countless possibilities, it won't be an exhaustive chapter, but I hope by the time you finish it you'll realize there are no limits when it comes to topics for Web pages — and that you'll be inspired to create new ones that will add rich new threads of color to the ever-growing tapestry of the Web.

A Page for Every Passion

The number of Web sites on the Internet, and the number of topics they cover, is mind-boggling to say the least. Whether you're interested in Argentine drum music or the Transylvanian cuisine, you can probably find a Web site that deals with it. The best way to find those sites is with search engines like AOL's NetFind, which you look at in detail in Chapter 15 (along with some other well-known search engines).

Many search engines provide lists of some of the best sites divided by topic, rather like a library (without the Dewey Decimal System, thank goodness!). Yahoo!, for example, one of the best-known directories, breaks all of the Web pages it lists into 14 broad topics: Arts and Humanities, Business and Economy, Computers and Internet, Education, Entertainment, Government, Health, News and Media, Recreation and Sports, Reference, Regional, Science, Social Science, and Society and Culture.

Just thinking about these topics is enough to get your creative juices flowing when it comes time to create your own Web page. For example:

➡ **Arts and Humanities.** Do you have a passion for Pre-Raphaelite painters? Early American church architecture? The plays of George Bernard Shaw? Or perhaps, like me, you're on the board of a community theater group. The arts are a rich lode of interesting information, fascinating photographs, and amusing anecdotes that make wonderful Web pages. The arts lie at the heart of our culture, and increasingly, so does the World Wide Web; maybe you can help bring the two together.

➡ **Business and Economy.** We've already looked at creating pages for small businesses, but there are other areas to be explored by enterprising Web designers such as yourself. Maybe you have a personal rags-to-riches story you'd like to share. Maybe you have strong opinions on business ethics that you can present in a clear, cogent fashion. Maybe you're a lawyer or accountant with good tax tips for self-employed individuals. Everyone is interested in money — making it, holding on to it, and spending it. Any expertise you may have in any of those activities could be the basis for a fascinating Web page. (But please don't do a mass e-mailing of your latest Get Rich Quick scheme. This will not win you any friends online. Trust me on this.)

➡ **Education.** More and more schools have their own home pages on the World Wide Web — does your child's school? Maybe you could create one. Or perhaps you're a retired teacher with great course material just sitting, collecting dust. Why not put it on the World Wide Web? Is your high-school class holding a reunion? Create a reunion home page, with "Where are they now?" information and yearbook pictures side by side with current photos. Or maybe you feel strongly about the way math is being taught in your school. Create a Web page that lays out your arguments, complete with links to research that supports them. The Web can be used both in education and to educate the public about education!

➡ **Entertainment.** Now here's a broad topic! So narrow it down by asking, "What entertains me?" Do you have a fondness for nineteenth-century operetta? By all means create a site devoted to it! Do you think *Riven* can't hold a candle to *Pong*? Explore your devotion to the original computer game. From marionettes to multimedia, we all have multiple entertainment likes and dislikes — any one of which could be inspiration for a worthwhile Web site. (I just ask one favor: If your favorite TV program is *The X-Files*, please spare us yet another *X-Files* site. We have to draw the line somewhere.

➡ **Government.** The rules of polite conversation — never talk about politics or religion — don't apply to creating a Web page. Politics is, in fact, a sure-fire topic, especially if you have strong opinions on the subject. But not all political Web pages are rants. Are you a proud new American citizen? Create a Web page explaining what your citizenship means to you. Or maybe you're on the student council of your high school. Why not create a student council Web page that provides information about council activities to the student body and gives them an e-mail link to student government? And, of course, don't miss the opportunity for political satire, a fine American tradition and symbol of the right to free speech. (Personally, I'm planning to set up a Web page for my new political party, The Wine and Cheese Party, just as soon as I get my platform together.)

➡ **Health.** Health concerns everyone. So what if you're not a doctor? Have you recovered from a serious illness or disability — or are you still battling one? There are probably many people just like you who would appreciate whatever insights you can offer into dealing with the problem, people with whom you may be able to build a support network through your Web page. Or perhaps you know some great new stretching exercises, low-fat recipes, or relaxation techniques. If you are a doctor, so much the better: sources of reliable, accurate health information on the Web are always in great demand.

➡ **Recreation and Sport.** What do you do for fun? You raise tarantulas? What a great idea for a Web page! You say you're also active in the local field hockey association? Even better! There are a lot fewer field-hockey pages than there are, say, NFL football pages. No matter how esoteric your recreational activities, chances are more than a few people online share an interest in them; creating a Web page based on your personal fun-time passions is a great way to make contact with those people — and maybe recruit new fans to the joys of tarantula-wrangling (see Figure 14-1).

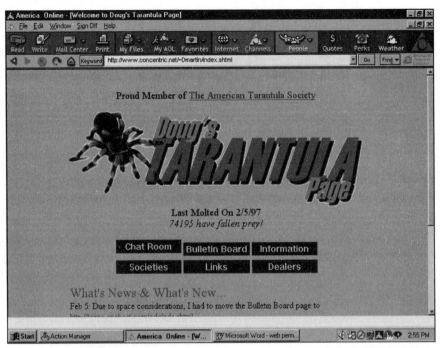

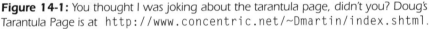

Figure 14-1: You thought I was joking about the tarantula page, didn't you? Doug's Tarantula Page is at `http://www.concentric.net/~Dmartin/index.shtml`.

➥ **Reference.** Solid, factual information is the strongest foundation you can have for a good Web page, and if you can provide information that people can't get elsewhere — or provide it in a new, improved fashion — your Web page may become a place people visit over and over again. Reference pages range from the broad — online dictionaries and encyclopedias (not likely something you're going to try!) to the very specific — the names of the soldiers involved in obscure Civil War battles, for instance. Old photographs . . . clothes patterns . . . even recipes could be valuable reference material for someone. A nice quiet reference Web site — every closet librarian's dream!

➥ **Science.** You don't have to be a scientist to create a Web page about science. I'm not a scientist, but I write a newspaper column on science every week. Pick a topic that interests you — Mars, for example, or dirty snowballs from space (a controversial theory that — well, never mind; I'm sure you can look it up on the Web), research it, provide an overview of it, and provide links to more information. If you do happen to be a scientist, or someone with solid scientific knowledge about a particular topic, then by all means share. You specialize in scorpions? Then why not create a Web site telling the general public all about these misunderstood arachnids? And if you're an inventor, then you definitely belong on the Web, explaining and promoting your invention (make sure you've got that patent lined up first, though!).

➡ **Society and Culture.** Another rather broad category that takes in everything from crime to religion. Create a Web page for your local church, mosque, or synagogue. Celebrate the cultural practices of your ethnic group (English-Scotch-Irish-German-Comanche-American-Canadians, in my case). Rail against the plight of the poor. Retell the tall tales your grandfather told you. Celebrate Christmas . . . Chanukah . . . Halloween . . . Martin Luther King Day . . . 365 days a year. As I think I've already indicated more than once, the possibilities are endless!

Getting some great ideas for a possible Web site (or two or three)? Terrific! Then run through the Web page checklist one more time — ten questions that will help you make any Web page better.

A Checklist for All Pages

In Chapters 11 through 13, I harp on the importance of planning ahead, so why stop now? The checklist that follows is a boiled-down version of the more specific checklists I provide for personal home pages, business pages, and kids' pages.

Before you begin creating your Web site, it is important to ask yourself these questions:

1. **Who is my audience? Are they young or old? Likely knowledgeable about my topic, or coming to it for the first time? Experienced Web surfers, or newbies? You have to know who you're trying to communicate with if you want them to understand and appreciate your message.**

2. **What is my message? As you've seen, a Web page can be created on any topic . . . but eventually, you have to pick one. There's no point in starting if you don't know how you plan to finish.**

3. **What have other people done with my topic? Do your research. Study the Web. Don't just copy what other people have done.**

4. **What can I add that's unique? How do you avoid copying what others have done? By finding something that only you can do. Someone else may have created a great page on growing**

cucumbers, but maybe he doesn't have two dozen pictures of weird-looking cukes like you do. So shift the focus of your page to your "Kooky Cuke Collection" and add a link to his page. He'll probably do the same for you — and together, you strengthen the Web.

5. **What effect do I want to have on visitors?** Do you want them to go away angry? Entertained? Educated? Disgusted? Alarmed? Bemused? Tailor your text and graphics to that end. The one way you don't want them to go away is bored.

6. **How much flash can and should I add?** Graphics are attractive, but too many can slow down your page. Animations are eye-catching, but too many are just annoying. Text conveys your message, but too much is gray and boring. Videos are exciting, but take forever to load. Sound files add interest, but only if they're relevant and extremely well done. Go back and consider your answers to the questions leading up to this one, and that will help you decide how much flair you can afford.

7. **Is my content the best I can make it?** Don't waste space by posting incoherent text, muddy graphics, and fuzzy sound files to the Web. Polish your prose, glitz up your graphics, and adjust your audio until your Web site sparkles and sizzles. When you create a Web page, you're putting part of yourself on display to the world. Shouldn't you look your best? (In the same vein, it's important to keep refining your page, checking for dead links, and so on. Maintenance is as important to a Web site as it is to your car: don't neglect either one. For more discussion of keeping your Web site up to date, see Chapter 16.)

8. **What useful links can I provide?** Links are the heart of the Web — in fact, they're what make the Web a web. But choose carefully: people will judge your site not only by its own merits but by the merits of the sites to which your links send them. Nobody appreciates being sent on a wild-goose chase after a link that proves to be dead — or worse, dull.

9. **How many pages do I need?** A single, well-designed Web page can be as much of a pleasure to visit as a multipage multimedia masterpiece . . . but sometimes a single page just isn't enough. Plan your pages ahead of time. Sketch them out. Decide exactly what will go on each one. And then, finally, ask yourself . . .

10. **How do I organize my site?** By organization, I not only mean making it easy for visitors to move from area to area, or page to page, within your site but also choosing graphics that load as quickly as possible and text fonts and colors that are completely legible. In short, you want a site that's clean, crisp, and professional looking. Personal Publisher's templates can help — but in the end, it's up to you to create the kind of site that you — and I — can really enjoy visiting.

Cool Pages of All Sorts

Now take a look at some sites that demonstrate the incredible variety and vitality of the Web. I've chosen one site (out of thousands) in each of the broad topics from Yahoo! that I described in the first section of the chapter, beginning with . . .

Arts and Humanities: Japanese Garden Database

This is an outstanding site on a topic obviously near and dear to the heart of the creator, Robert Cheetham. It contains a wealth of information, images, and links, all thoughtfully and attractively combined (see Figure 14-2).

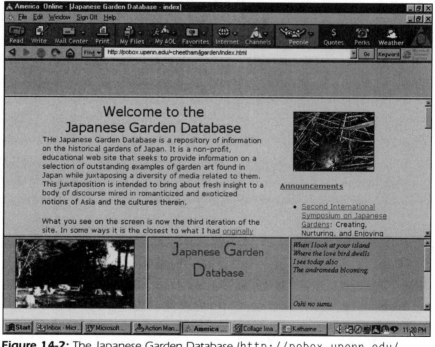

Figure 14-2: The Japanese Garden Database (`http://pobox.upenn.edu/ ~cheetham/jgarden/index.html`) boasts a calm, clear, pleasing design — much like the gardens to which it refers.

The text is highly legible and thoughtfully written, and the subdued color scheme is a delight to run across after some of the more garish pages on the Web. Inside pages are equally delightful and maintain a unity of design with the initial page. There's no mistaking that the page in Figure 14-3 belongs to the same Web site as the one in Figure 14-2.

Also notice in Figure 14-3 that the small photographs are quick-loading images that can be clicked to bring up larger-scale versions — a good way to achieve balance between a page that loads too slowly and an image that's lost all its impact from being too low-resolution.

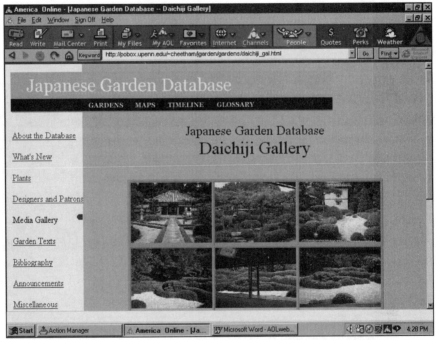

Figure 14-3: Robert Cheetham makes careful use of his images of Japanese galleries, providing quick-loading, small graphics linked to larger graphics for those who want more detail.

Education: Mrs. Silverman's Second Grade Class

Does your school (if you're a student or teacher) or your children's school (if you're a parent) have a Web page? It doesn't? Then maybe you could volunteer to create one — with the students' help. Creating a Web page involves a number of skills (as I hope you've realized by now), including writing, photography, and (of course) computer literacy — all good things.

Your school doesn't have to be large to have a Web site. Even individual classes sometimes have Web sites, like Mrs. Silverman's Second Grade Class from Clinton Avenue Elementary School in Port Jefferson Station, New York (see Figure 14-4).

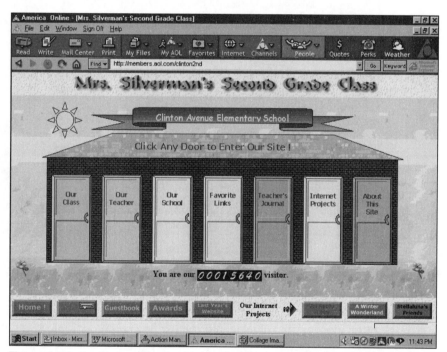

Figure 14-4: Small school, large school — it doesn't matter. A Web site like the one Mrs. Silverman has created for her second-grade class at `http://members.aol. com/clinton2nd` is a worthwhile endeavor..

Mrs. Silverman's Second Grade Class's home page is cleverly designed as a cartoon of a schoolhouse, with each doorway leading to another section of the site: information about the school, about the site itself, about the class, and about Mrs. Silverman is just a mouse click away. There are also links to the school's Internet-related projects such as An Apple a Day (see Figure 14-5), a collection of poetry by second graders not just from Mrs. Silverman's class but from all over the country, gathered via the Internet. And did I mention that music plays as you visit each page?

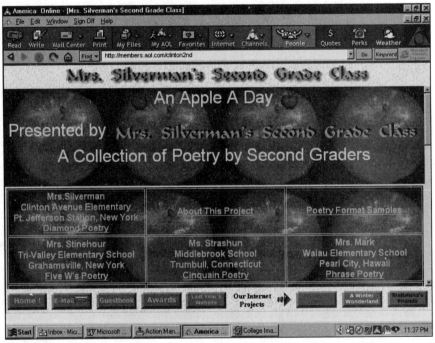

Figure 14-5: An Apple a Day is just one of the Internet-based projects Mrs. Silverman's second-grade class has carried out.

Attractive design, valuable information, logical organization, and innovative use of the power of the Internet make this single-class site the equal of sites by much larger schools all over the world.

Music: The Digital Music Zone

If you're a musician, particularly a guitarist, looking for an unusual effect for your electric guitar, the Digital Music Zone, created by AOL member Jack Orman at `http://members.aol.com/jorman`, is the site to visit. Here you'll find schematics for guitar effects, electronic circuits, and recording tips for amateurs and professional alike (see Figure 14-6).

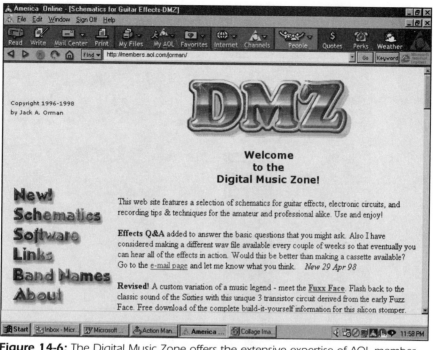

Figure 14-6: The Digital Music Zone offers the extensive expertise of AOL member Jack Orman in electronic music to anyone who can make use of it — a perfect example of how the World Wide Web has revolutionized the spread of information.

Jack Orman is a writer and musician who has been interested in electronic music since the 1970s. Now, thanks to the Web, he can share that interest, and the knowledge and experience he's picked up along the way, with people all over the world. Whatever your area of expertise, you can do the same.

Health: How to Build a Better Body

What's a 19-year-old from Oak Ridge, Tennessee, doing telling people how to build a better body (see Figure 14-7)? Well, he's speaking from personal experience: Eric Williams is one of the top runners in his state. That's why they call him Superman (as he explains on his Web page!)

If you have something to share with people — in this case, tips for training — then by all means, put it on the Web like Eric. Even if nobody has *ever* called you Superman!

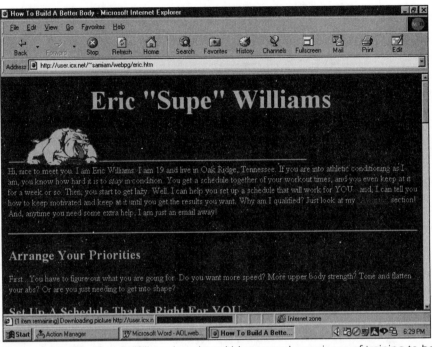

Figure 14-7: Eric "Supe" Williams has shared his personal experience of training to be a champion athlete with the world on his simple Web page (`http://user.icx.net/~samiam/webpg/eric.htm`). (Web page content by Eric Williams; design by Ramona Williams)

Society and Culture: The Werewolf Page

Legends once thought long dead and buried have a way of taking on new life on the World Wide Web, which is rapidly becoming a kind of global attic, where the knickknacks of all humanity's cultures can still be found, if you dig for them.

The Werewolf Page (`http://www.aboutrtown.com/~rs/werewolf/`) is a celebration of one such ancient legend, from its ancient beginnings to its most recent incarnations in books, films, and TV, presenting text, graphics, sound files, and links to other sites against an appropriately blood-red background (see Figure 14-8).

Figure 14-8: There are corners of the Web that are still untamed, where mythical monsters like the werewolf lurk.

The Werewolf Page might seem like an odd choice to end this chapter, but I don't think so. As this page attests, the idea of the werewolf has stirred humanity's collective imagination for hundreds of years . . . and my goal throughout this chapter is to stir your imagination.

Summary

On the Web, werewolves wander, astronomers ponder, and peaceful Japanese gardens grow within hearing distance of lounge, metal, and rap music. New things are always being added, and yet there's always room for more. There's room, in fact, for whatever it is that stirs *your* imagination — for the things you care passionately about, for the ideas you want to share. The Web may be the ultimate medium of self-expression, and it's waiting for you.

Go forth and express!

Your Online Hometown

15

So you've created your Web page! Congratulations! It's a beauty, too. You just have one question: Now what? Well, now it's time to begin integrating your Web page — and yourself — into the online community, and the best way to do that is through Hometown AOL, a place where members are linking with other members to create online neighborhoods made up of people with shared interests. By registering your page with Hometown AOL, linking to similar pages, and corresponding with their creators, you can draw more people to your page and make it more interesting. It doesn't matter where the members of your online community live physically: on the Web, you're all next-door neighbors.

What Is Hometown AOL?

America Online strives to achieve a sense of community among its millions of members: a feeling of belonging, of all being in this online thing together. It has extended that sense of community onto the World Wide Web with Hometown AOL, in conjunction with Personal Publisher 3.

Hometown is simply a collection of AOL-member-created Web pages organized by subject matter. Members can register their pages with AOL Hometown and join the community of their choice. Each community is identified by its specific topic and all Web pages are fully searchable by AOL members and non-members alike. Hometown AOL enables users to browse by neighborhood, or topic, and it also incorporates such familiar AOL tools as Instant Messenger, community message boards, chats, and live events. To create a Web page for Hometown AOL, members can use Personal Publisher 3 or another HTML editor.

While still under development, the organization of Hometown will likely begin with a dozen or so top-level categories: say, Entertainment or Computing. Each top-level category may contain up to 15 second-level categories (under Entertainment, for example, second-level categories might include Music and TV). Finally, each second-level category is subdivided into as many as 15 third-level communities: under Music, categories such as Alternative or Classical.

Important features of Hometown AOL include

➡ **Web page searching.** Pages registered with Hometown AOL are automatically added to a searchable database. Visitors to Hometown can find pages that interest them simply by plugging in related search terms.

➡ **its own Navigational frameset.** All pages appearing in Hometown AOL contain a common set of frames across the top of the page that include navigation tools, making it easy for a visitor to Hometown to move from community to community and page to page.

After creating a Web page, AOL members can become a member of Hometown AOL by registering their page. During this registration process, members can choose which to which community they'd like their page to belong.

Finding Similar Pages

They key to becoming a fully integrated part of the online community is finding Web sites on topics related to your own. Obviously, Hometown AOL makes that easy, both with its organization into communities and by allowing full-text searching of members' pages.

However, finding related Web sites outside of Hometown AOL is a bit harder, because the Web, in case you haven't noticed, is a big place — and getting bigger all the time (thanks to people like you who help it grow by adding new pages). And unfortunately, it has no organization to speak of — no equivalent to the Dewey decimal system of your local library. Just think how hard it would be to find, say, one particular encyclopedia entry if all the pages in all the books in the library had been ripped out and thrown randomly around the building. That's roughly the task you'd face trying to find one page on the World Wide Web if you had to search through it page by page.

Fortunately, there's help available, through what are called *search engines*. Search engines are Web sites that keep constant tabs on what's on the Web, collecting links and adding them to a searchable database. There are several search engines on the Web, but the one you'll probably start with is AOL's own NetFind. I mention this incredibly useful tool from time to time throughout this book, but now let's take a look at it in detail.

AOL's NetFind

You access NetFind by clicking the Internet icon in the main toolbar and then choosing AOL NetFind from the resulting menu, or by using keyword **AOL NetFind**. Your browser window will open, displaying NetFind's introductory page, as shown in Figure 15-1.

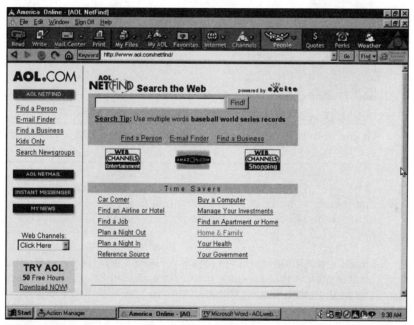

Figure 15-1: AOL's NetFind is the place to start looking for Web pages similar to yours.

You enter words you think might appear in Web pages similar to yours in the blank at the top of the page, and then click Find!

Let me use a concrete example. As I mention earlier in this book, I maintain a Web page for the Regina Lyric Light Opera Society, a community theater organization that produces several musicals and/or operettas each year (see Figure 15-2).

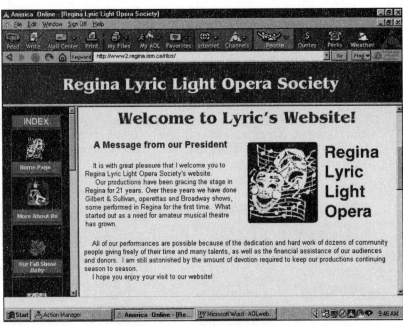

Figure 15-2: Here's the Regina Lyric Light Opera Society Web site I created and maintain at `http://www2.regina.ism.ca/rllos/`.

Although I'm generally pretty happy with this site, one thing I'm well aware that it lacks is links: aside from internal links, the only one to be found is to the Gilbert & Sullivan Archive (`http://diamond.idbsu.edu/gas/GaS.html`).

I think it would be nice to create a page of links to other community theater groups that produce musicals and operettas, and perhaps exchange information with those groups. But first, I have to find them.

For my first attempt, I call up NetFind and type the words *light* and *opera*, the two most important words of my organization's name, into the blank, and then I click Find!

NetFind responds with the results shown in Figure 15-3.

My first search had some promising results, with something called "Light Opera Works" showing up on top. But in the top ten are also such tenuously related Web sites as the American Musicological Society and the New Deal Network Library (which apparently showed up because it contains photographs labeled "Scene from Industrial Opera: Light and Steel").

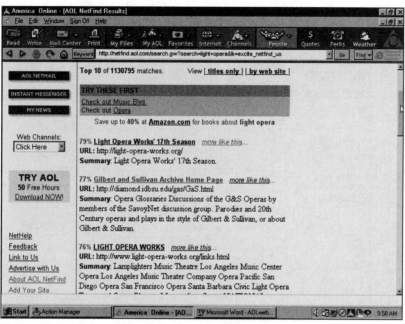

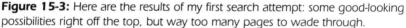

Figure 15-3: Here are the results of my first search attempt: some good-looking possibilities right off the top, but way too many pages to wade through.

NetFind, like most search engines, looks first for pages that contain the words you typed—in any order. NetFind also goes one step further, looking for ideas most closely linked to the words you entered, increasing your chances of finding what you want on the first try. It can actually learn that relationships exist between different words and phrases—that the term "elderly people," for example, is related to the term "senior citizens." Apparently, however, it isn't familiar with the term "light opera."

Notice, too, that NetFind reports finding more than 1.1 million matches to the words I typed. That doesn't mean there are that many Web pages that contain both words, but that there are that many Web pages that contain at least one of my chosen words.

In any event, I obviously need to narrow my search. There are a couple of ways to go about this. One is simply to add more words to be searched for. Light Opera Works, for example, though at least it relates to musical theater, doesn't really fit into my criteria because it's a professional company, and I'm only interested in amateur companies. So I add the words *amateur* and, for good measure, *community* to my list, and I click Find again. Figure 15-4 shows the results of my more narrow search.

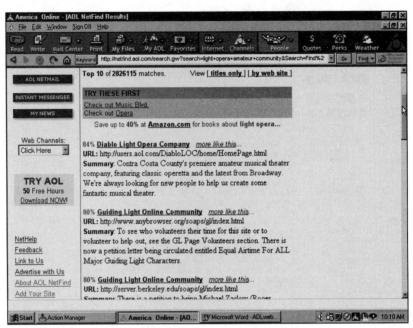

Figure 15-4: I've added extra words to my search request and came up with a better match than before in the top spot.

The number of possible matches has gone up to 2.82 million because of the additional terms — remember, that number tells you the number of Web pages containing any of the words you entered — but adding extra terms has helped me come up with a couple of much better matches in the top 10: The Diablo Light Opera Company, an amateur musical theater company in Walnut Creek, California, and the Richland Light Opera Company, an amateur musical theater company in the Northwest.

On the other hand, I'm also getting the Guiding Light Online Community, which focuses on the soap opera *Guiding Light!*

Another way to try to improve your search is to click the "more like this . . ." link that appears beside the Web page titles. For example, clicking beside the Diablo Light Opera Company title brings sites to near the top of the list that at least seem to be generally theater oriented, although the Ohio Light Opera company turns out to be professional.

The best way to improve the search, though, is to use more advanced methods. NetFind supports several of these:

⟹ **Finding phrases.** To find exact phrases, put quotes around the words. To eliminate the problem of, for example, the New Deal Network Library or the Guiding Light Online Community showing up, I can put quotation marks around *light opera*. Doing this dramatically improves the appropriateness of the top items on the list, as shown by the search results in Figure 15-5.

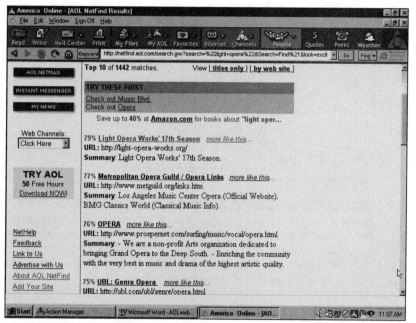

Figure 15-5: All of NetFind's top suggestions now actually contain the term *light opera*, and appear to have something to do with opera in some form or other, unlike before.

⟹ **Using plus (+) and minus (-) signs.** These can help you fine-tune your search by requiring that all Web pages retrieved contain certain words and insuring that they don't contain others. For example, in my search I could insist that all pages contain the word *amateur* and exclude any pages that contain the word *professional* by entering **"light opera" +amateur -professional**. I try that in Figure 15-6, but the results, as you can see, are less than satisfactory.

⟹ **Boolean operators: AND, OR, and AND NOT.** These are the most powerful tools you have for fine-tuning searches. First, they turn off concept-based finding, which is probably a good thing when searching for a term as relatively obscure as *light opera*. Instead, they will search for Web pages that contain exactly the words for which you are looking. You enter these words in all caps, and they must have a space on both sides of them to work.

Figure 15-6: I've actually lost ground with that last request. Although lots of Web sites were retrieved, only the Diablo Light Opera Company site meets all my criteria; instead, since it can't find any more sites containing the term *light opera*, NetFind immediately starts returning sites that only contain the word *amateur* and any others it thinks are appropriate: hence all the astronomy sites.

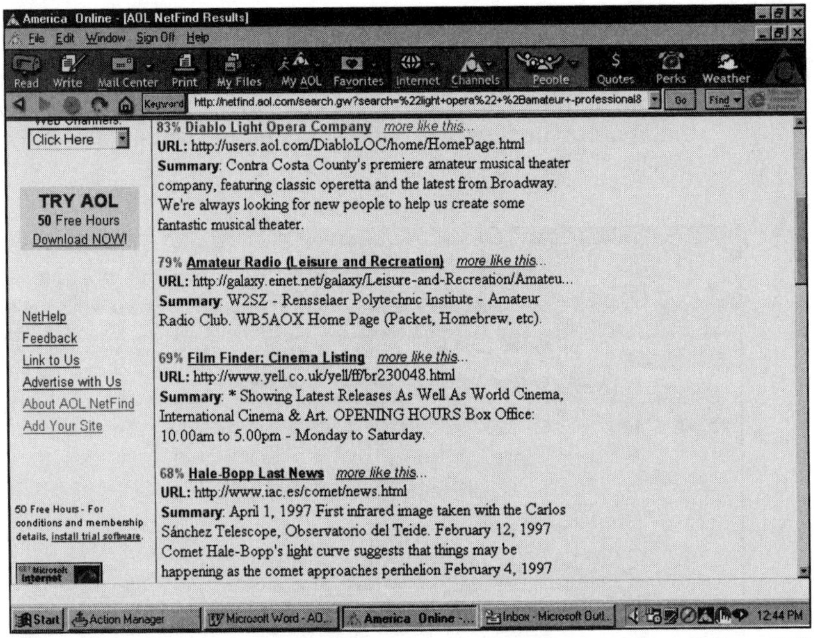

English mathematician George Boole developed Boolean logic. It's sometimes called the "mathematics of logic," because just like addition, subtraction, multiplication, and division are the primary operations of arithmetic, so AND, OR, and AND NOT are the primary operators of Boolean logic — which is why search engines refer to them as "Boolean operators."

- **AND.** Documents found must contain all the words joined by *AND*. The difference between this and the plus sign is that when you use the plus sign, NetFind's concept-based searching is still active. Using *"light opera" AND amateur* reduces the number of Web pages retrieved to a much more manageable 135 sites — and almost all of them appear to have some relevance.

- **OR.** Documents found must contain at least one of the words joined by *OR*. For example, I could search for *"light opera" OR "musical theater"* to widen my net to include sites for companies that, like ours (despite our name), do more than just operettas and Gilbert and Sullivan.

- **AND NOT.** This, like the minus sign (but without concept-based searching), tells NetFind that documents found cannot contain the words that follow. I might enter *"light opera" AND NOT "grand opera"* to try to cut out companies that perform *The Ring Cycle,* as well as *The Merry Widow.*

To make full use of Boolean operators, you need to be able to group them together. For that, you use parentheses. So, for my final fine-tuning of my search, I'm going to enter *("light opera" OR "musicals" OR "musical theater" OR "operetta") AND ("community theater" OR "amateur") AND NOT "professional company".*

Even with such a precise search, I still end up with 101 matches, but now almost all of them offer some promise of being useful (see Figure 15-7).

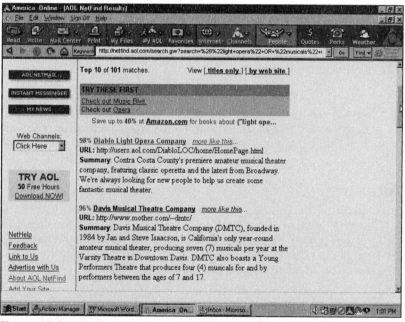

Figure 15-7: With Boolean operators, I've finally been able to make my search precise enough to weed out almost all of the obviously useless sites.

Other Search Engines

NetFind is available right from AOL, and I recommend it, but it certainly isn't the only search engine that's out there. That's all to your advantage, because one thing you'll find as you use different search engines is that they all return different lists. That's because no one search engine can possibly keep up with the ever-changing Web. By using several, however, you increase your chances of finding most, if not quite all, of the pages that interest you.

Yahoo!

I've mentioned Yahoo! (http://www.yahoo.com) several times already in the course of this book. It works on a different principal than true search engines like NetFind, however; rather than send out software into the Web to track down sites, Yahoo! mostly lists sites that have been suggested to it by users.

There are two ways to find things on Yahoo!: moving down through the menu from the top-level directory (as described in Chapter 14) or using the Search function.

When I enter the phrase *light opera* and click Search, I get a list of one related category, and 19 links that have the phrase *light opera* in them — almost every one of them pointing the way to a theater company. I've found sites that are similar to mine, thanks to Yahoo!'s unique organization.

AltaVista

AltaVista (http://www.altavista.digital.com) is another search engine, in the mold of NetFind. If you're not getting satisfaction with Yahoo! (which, remember, lists mostly sites that people have suggested), simply click the AltaVista button to run a ful search of the Web, using the same terms you plugged into Yahoo!

Doing that with the term *light opera* brings up 3,296 possible Web sites, compared to just 19 on Yahoo!, but that's not necessarily a good thing. One reason regular search engines provide so many more hits is that typically every page in a Web site gets retrieved as a separate entry in the list, especially if the phrase you're looking for is in the site's title. So in this case, of my first 20 hits, one third are repeats.

WebCrawler

WebCrawler (`http://www.webcrawler.com`) by default presents you only with the title of the Web pages it has found (you can get more detailed descriptions by clicking "summaries"). It returned 177 pages.

HotBot

HotBot (`http://www.hotbot.com`) is the search engine set up by *Wired* magazine and has the funkiest look of all the search engines. It returned 3,712 pages.

Lycos

Lycos (`http://www.lycos.com`) doesn't tell you how many Web sites it found, but it offers you many different ways to refine your search.

InfoSeek

InfoSeek (`http://www.infoseek.com`) groups together Web pages retrieved from the same site (which makes sense). It returned 1,637 pages.

You'll notice two things as you try each of these search engines. Each returns a wildly different list of sites, with some finding thousands of related pages and some only hundreds. Yet at the same time you'll notice that the same sites keep coming up over and over — in my case, Diablo Light Opera Company is nearly always at the top of the list.

So by all means, in the interest of completeness, use more than one search engine: but at the same time, it's probably not necessary to use them all. AOL's NetFind alone will probably give you an impressive list of pages related to your topic, often all you need. A second search engine (any of them) may give you a few other pages worth checking out; continuing to use different search engines will probably find fewer and fewer sites you haven't already come across. Check out the listed sites, add links to the best ones to your page, and contact the Webmasters to see if they're interested in linking back to yours. In the process, you'll make new online connections with people who share your interests — and begin building an online community.

Attracting People To Your Pages

"If you build it, they will come" only applies to baseball fields, not to Web pages. You can build as many pages as you want, but unless people know they're there, they won't come.

That may not be a bad thing, if you created your Web page mainly as a way to keep family and friends in touch. In that case, you might only want to pass your URL on to a select group. You can't actually stop Web surfers from finding your page — at least, not with Personal Publisher 3, which doesn't allow you to set any access restrictions — but it's highly unlikely they'll stumble there by accident if there are no links to it from anywhere else.

Most of us, though, actually want people to stumble across our page. In fact, we want them to visit it deliberately. In order for that to happen, however, you have to publicize. Here are some ways you can do that:

➡ **Register your site with Hometown AOL.** This is the single most important step you can take to get people to visit your Web pages. AOL's 12 million members are most likely to start here when they're looking for Web pages that interest them, so you definitely want your page to be listed and easy to find. And Hometown AOL is sure to grow into one of the most popular destinations on the Web. Hometown makes it easy for people to find your page!

➡ **Register your site with other online directories and search engines.** Many of the search engines described above let you register your new site with them. If you don't, it could take months before their automated Webcrawlers finally follow a link to your site and add it to the list. Look for a button or link similar to Yahoo!'s Add URL control (see Figure 15-8).

➡ **Use an all-in-one submission site.** Sites such as Submit It! (http://www.submit-it.com) let you submit your Web site to hundreds of directories, magazines, reviews, and awards sites at once, and provide other advice on how to promote your site.

➡ **E-mail everyone you know.** Let all your online friends and acquaintances know that your Web site is up and running. If you're lucky, they'll tell two friends, and they'll tell two friends, and so on.

➡ **Post a message to a Usenet newsgroup.** Newsgroups are online discussion groups where people post messages back and forth on a specific topic. You can access them from AOL by clicking the Internet icon and then choosing Newsgroups (see Figure 15-9). Use the Search All Newsgroups button to see if there is a newsgroup related to the topic of your Web site. If there is, you might want to post a message announcing the Web site's URL to the newsgroup.

Figure 15-8: When you suggest your site be added to Yahoo! or other directories and search engines, you'll be asked to fill out a form similar to this.

Figure 15-9: Access Usenet newsgroups on AOL from this dialog box. There are newsgroups on literally hundreds of topics: chances are, there's one related to the topic of your Web site.

First read the *FAQ* (frequently asked questions) file for any newsgroup you are interested in contacting. Some newsgroups frown on posting news of new Web sites. Make sure such an announcement is welcome before going ahead, or you could get *flamed* (attacked online by newsgroup participants).

➡ **Arrange for mutual links.** This goes back to finding Web sites on topics related to yours. Contact the Webmaster and offer to put a link to his site on your page if he'll do the same for you. If any of your friends or acquaintances have Web sites, offer them the same deal. The more sites that have links to your pages, the more chances there are of Web surfers finding you.

➡ **Join or create a Webring.** *Webrings* are a relatively new innovation on the Web. They're essentially group sites with similar subjects, linked into continuous loops: each member links to the next member until the last member links with the first member, closing the loop. More than 38,000 Webrings are already online, according to Webring.org, the organization which invented them (you can visit them at `http://www.webring.org`). Visitors can either travel the ring by moving consecutively from site to site, or can jump at random to other sites in the ring. By joining a Webring related to the topic of your site, you can make it that much easier for people interested in your topic to find you.

➡ **Use offline publicity.** In other words, don't limit yourself to what you can do online. If you're publicizing a business site, you probably also advertise on radio or in a newspaper; make sure your URL is part of all your ads. You might even consider taking out an ad to announce the Web site's launch. Put your URL on your business cards, your stationery, and your fax cover sheets. You might be surprised by how many people pick up on it and pay you a virtual visit.

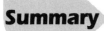

Just having a Web site is cool enough at first, but pretty soon you may find yourself feeling isolated and alone. Nobody seems to be finding your Web site; you've gone to all this work, and nobody cares. That just means your work isn't finished yet. Register with Hometown AOL. Get out there and find similar sites within Hometown and the Web at large and make connections with the people who run them. Build links with both them and their Web sites. Get busy on the Web and off the Web, telling people that your Web site exists. Before you know it, you may find more people visiting than you've ever dreamed . . . and yourself at the bustling center of a thriving online community.

Keeping Your Page Fresh

16

In This Chapter

Keeping your page up to date

The Web theory of evolution

Keeping links alive

It's amazing, really, but some people who wouldn't dream of drinking milk even one day past its best-before date will put up a Web page one day when they have nothing better to do and then forget about it, letting it grow staler and staler until they might as well change the background color to bread-mold green — if they could be bothered to change anything at all. Anyone who's surfed the Web for a while has run into these pages: computer pages extolling the virtues of the latest 14.4 Kbps modem, announcements of events that happened in the spring of 1995, and fearless predictions of who will win the Dole/Clinton presidential race of 1996. Don't let your Web page suffer the fate of that unidentified semiliquid thing in the back of your refrigerator. Creating it is only half the fun; tinkering with it and constantly improving it are part of the game, too.

Keeping Your Page Up to Date

How often you need to update your Web page depends on what kind of page it is, and what you've posted on it. A reference Web page that lists the provinces and territories of Canada and their major industries probably won't have to be changed too often, but a Web page listing events at your high school may need to be changed almost daily, as new things are scheduled and others pass by.

Understanding how much maintenance will be required of your page before you put it up is important. If you're not prepared to keep it up to date, perhaps you should reconsider your page's goals and design.

Boldly or foolishly, for example, I decided to include on my Web page a "Science Column of the Week" (see Figure 16-1).

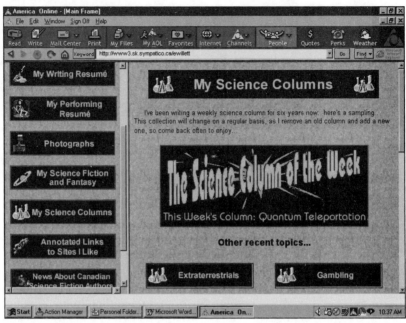

Figure 16-1: By highlighting a "Science Column of the Week" on my Web site, I committed myself to updating my site regularly.

I figured it would be no problem uploading each week's newspaper science column to the page. Because of my design and space limitations, however, I have to take a column off each time I put one on, and shuffle links around. It takes more work than I originally anticipated, and when I get busy with other things — like writing this book — it tends to get shoved to a back burner. As a result, my "Science Column of the Week" has tended to be more like a "Science Column of Some Irregular Period, Generally Not Exceeding a Month," which isn't nearly as catchy a title.

So this is a case of "do as I say, not as I do" — but there's no reason you should make the same mistake I did. If you plan to present any sort of regular feature on your Web page — say, a Hot Link of the Day or a Recipe of the Month, make sure you're prepared to do the work necessary to keep it fresh. Fortunately, Personal Publisher 3 makes updating your pages simple. Just follow these steps:

1. From the Personal Publisher main screen, choose **Manage Your Pages**.

2. After a moment, you'll see a list of all the pages you've published to AOL, on the left side of the screen. Highlight the name of the page you want to update, and click **Unpublish**. This moves the page to your computer, so you can work on it; now it will show up on the right side of the screen.

3. Highlight it again and click Edit.

4. Make whatever changes you need to using the various Edit tools.

5. From the Edit screen, click Save to save the updated Web page to your hard drive, and click Publish to return the updated page to your personal Web space on AOL.

What kind of updating should you do to keep your page fresh? Here are some tips:

➡ **Change or add graphics to suit the season.** Add a sprig of holly at Christmas, or a jack-o'-lantern at Halloween. Wholesale redecoration isn't necessary, but the addition of a graphic or two appropriate to the time of year will make it clear that your site is still under the watchful eye of a caring Webmaster, and not a sad, pitiful orphan like so many other once-proud sites on the Web.

➡ **Date your pages.** The addition of a line somewhere on your page like, "Last modified June 25, 1998," accomplishes two things: it helps your visitors judge how fresh the information on that page is, and it helps you remember when you last updated it (see Figure 16-2).

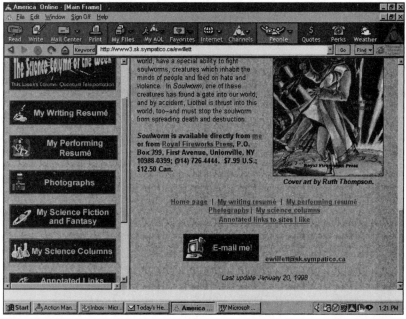

Figure 16-2: By dating this page, I tell both my visitors and myself how recently it was updated.

There are two situations in which dating your page isn't such a good idea: when you know the information on it isn't going to change, and when you know that for some reason you can't commit to regular and frequent updates. In the former case, you may not want a last-modified date on the page because, as it slips further and further into the past, it will make the page appear to be out of date even when it's still perfectly valid. In the latter case, that date will simply notify your visitors that nothing has changed recently, which may spur them to go somewhere else.

➡ **Watch out for dated references in the text.** "As President Bush said in his televised speech last week..." is a blatant example of a reference that is going to quickly seem out of date, but there are subtler ones. Maybe you make reference to a TV show that has since been canceled, or use one of those universal catchphrases that come and go in the space of a few months, or talk about it being winter when outside everyone else's window (in this hemisphere, anyway) it's summer. If you are going to write text tied to a specific time, then, again, you must be prepared to update it regularly, or your site will soon seem as stale as a week-old Danish.

➡ **Keep your links up to date.** Web pages come and go, and as they do so, some of the links on your page may go dead. Over time, these dead links accumulate — and so does the perception that your site is abandoned. Check your links regularly (more on this later in the chapter).

The Web Theory of Evolution

"Change is good" proclaimed the cover of *Wired* magazine not too long ago, which of course is nonsense: things can just as easily change for the worse as for the better.

Nevertheless, there is an element of truth in that statement insofar as your Web site goes. Beyond the simple tips I mentioned in the first section of this chapter, the most important thing you can do to keep your Web site fresh is to continue to play with it.

It's not like Personal Publisher is a chisel that you're using to chip a Web site out of granite. In fact, as I showed you back in Chapter 6, "Managing Your Pages," Personal Publisher makes it easy to add or delete Web page elements or move them around.

That means that if you come across a picture you like better than one you're currently using, nothing is stopping you from replacing the old one with the new one. If your political views suddenly turn around 180 degrees and you're embarrassed by what you previously believed (and posted to your Web site), you can — and should — change your Web site's text. If you suddenly get a great new idea for a navigation system for your site, based on an image map drawn on a photo of your face, then get busy and plaster your face all over the place.

I wanted to promote my aforementioned "Science Column of the Week," so I signed up. As a result, my home page has changed just since I wrote Chapter 11 of this book. Figure 16-3 shows what my home page looked like when I used it as an example in Chapter 11 (and that itself is a fairly new look for the page, since I just added the frames about a month ago); Figure 16-4 shows what it looks like as of last night.

I'm not entirely sure I like that banner ad above my title graphic, so this look may be short-lived. But that, as Martha Stewart likes to say, is a good thing: it means I'm continuing to try to make my Web site all that it can be (which is what the Army likes to say).

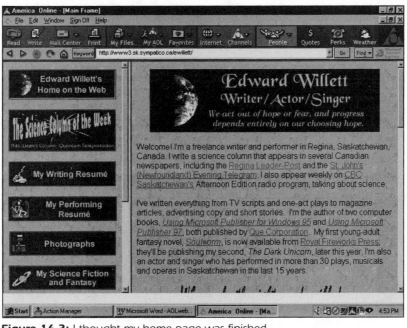

Figure 16-3: I thought my home page was finished. . .

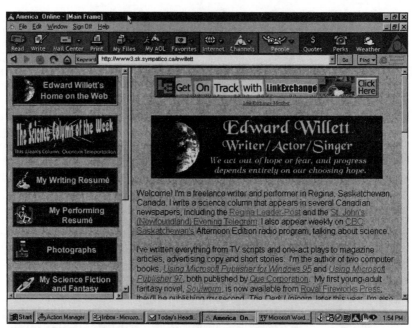

Figure 16-4: . . .until I saw something on the Web (LinkExchange) that I decided I wanted to add to my page, too.

Web pages, like living organisms, adapt and evolve over time (though much more rapidly than your average snail, sturgeon, or salamander). The following factors drive this evolution:

➥ **Changes in the Webmaster.** The reason Web pages change over time isn't that they're really living organisms (not yet, anyway) but because they are created by living organisms — people — and people also change over time. They age, their family situations change, their jobs change, their health changes, their interests change, even their tastes in food, clothes, music, and cars change. This change is most noticeable in young people. If you put up a Web page at age 12 and simply left it, chances are you'd be horribly embarrassed by it before you turned 14. Since personal Web pages in particular (by definition, really) are a reflection of an individual, as that individual changes (unless she changes to the point where she doesn't care about her Web page any more) her Web page will change, too, as shown in Figure 16-5. This applies particularly to resume pages, obviously!

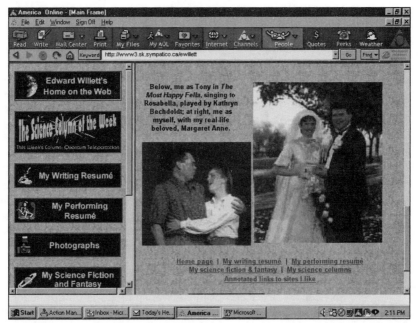

Figure 16-5: My most recent big change? I got married, which required an addition to my Web page.

➡ **Changes in the subject matter.** The world is constantly changing, too, which means there are few topics you can create a Web page about that won't be obsolete sooner or later. Business Web pages have to change as businesses expand, downsize, relocate, or pursue new goals. Organizations change all the time: presidents come and go, programs are altered from year to year, events occur and new ones are planned. Scientific knowledge changes at a bewildering pace: I've been a science writer for less than ten years, and I'm constantly updating old columns with new knowledge. Even a page devoted to Medieval Latin poetry would have to change from time to time to keep up with current scholarship — although not as often as a page devoted to, say, the fortunes of a particular NASCAR driver.

➡ **Changes in technology.** Computers are getting faster and so are connections to AOL and the Internet. That means complex graphics and video will become even more prevalent than they are now. Each new generation of Web browser has more features that pages can take advantage of: frames, forms, background sound, and backgrounds themselves weren't available just a few years ago. And the tools for creating Web pages are changing, too: Personal Publisher 3, after all, is an improvement over Personal Publisher 2, which had more features than Personal Publisher 1. More people have scanners and digital cameras, which makes it easier for them to post photos on the Web.

All of this changing technology finds its way into Web pages as new features.

➟ **Creative contagion.** As new features and fresh approaches to design appear on the Web, they soon find their way to other sites, as Web-creators see them and think, "Hey, that's kind of cool!" Just as I decided to join LinkExchange after seeing their banners all over the Web, so you might decide to copy a particularly clever background graphic or emulate the navigation system of a site you visited last Tuesday. In this way, new ideas prove contagious, spreading through the Web like a virus.

➟ **Survival of the fittest.** Not the fittest Web pages — there aren't any Web predators out there killing ugly and useless sites (alas!) — but the fittest ideas in Web design. To carry on with my contagious disease metaphor, good ideas are as contagious as, say, the Black Death, infecting nearly everyone, while bad ideas infect only a few people's sites (making them deathly ill in the process) before disappearing. In this way, the Web improves over time.

➟ **The imagination explosion.** Thousands of new people add pages to the Web every week. Each of these Webspinners is unique, each has his or her own strengths and weaknesses and passions and philosophy — just like you. As a result, each brings something new to the Web that hasn't been there before, or at least not quite in that fashion. An incredible amount of imagination and creativity has already been poured into the World Wide Web — a never-ending flood of new ideas. Spend even a few minutes browsing through the pages in Hometown AOL, and you'll see this imagination at work. Even Web pages that all started life as the same Personal Publisher template, as many Hometown pages did, become fresh and unique as individuals bring their own knowledge and skills to bear.

There's no need to be frightened of these forces; in fact, we should embrace them. Letting your Web page sit without changing is like stopping the heart of an animal. For a while it looks just fine, but the longer it sits there, the more it decays. Avoid that fate by pumping new blood into your page as often as you can.

Keeping Links Alive

One of the most important things you can do to keep your Web page fresh is to make sure all your links work. Otherwise, your visitors will click something on your site and see the stark words in Figure 16-6 staring back at them.

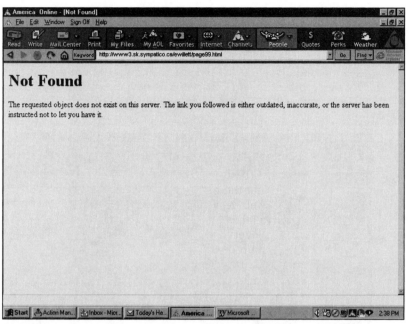

Figure 16-6: "Not found" — the most annoying words on the World Wide Web

Links like this — which go nowhere — are often called *broken links*. They're a nuisance to the viewer, whose time has been wasted (and sometimes you have to wait quite a while before the "Not found" message finally appears), and they reflect badly on you. They're an indication you haven't used that link yourself in some time, which raises the question of why you put it on your Web page — and just how good a Webmaster you are.

Here are some tips for making sure your visitors don't end up lost in file-not-found limbo:

➡ When you first create your page, click every single link to make sure it's active. This includes both internal and external links. If a link doesn't work, check the URL carefully and correct if necessary. If the link still doesn't work, remove it.

➡ Whenever you make changes to your page, check all your links again, especially internal links, to make sure none have been inadvertently broken.

➡ Test e-mail links by sending off a message, to make sure it doesn't bounce back to you as undeliverable.

➡ Test your links at least once a month (see Figure 16-7). If a link to a site you really like seems to have disappeared, see if you can track it down using America Online's NetFind (see Chapter 15, "Your Online Hometown") or another search engine. Often when sites change URLs, a message is left at the old site telling you where the new one is; in that case, replace the old URL with the new one. If the site has simply vanished without a trace, remove the link.

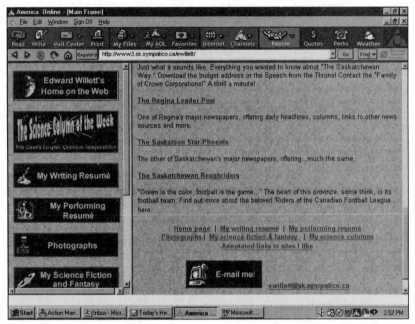

Figure 16-7: This page is nothing but links — internal, external, and e-mail — which means it takes a lot of work to check every one. But it's worth it to keep your visitors from running into an almost-blank white page.

Summary

Don't let your Web page's best-before date go by — a moldy Web page is no good to anyone. Personal Publisher 3 makes it easy to update your page; take advantage of that ability to keep your page fresh. Update it regularly, adding new things to it so that it's constantly evolving and improving, and conduct a regular program of link maintenance. Web pages are like bread and fish: the fresher, the better.

Learning More About Web Page Design

Appendix A

One thing is sure to strike you as you surf the 'Net: a lot of the Web pages out there (even a lot of the ones I use as examples of what's possible on the Web) have features that aren't included in Personal Publisher 3's wizards. There's something called *Java* that makes all kinds of animation and interactive features possible; there are *frames* and *forms*; there are pages where sound starts playing as soon as you arrive, and others where the entire background is one large graphic. Don't get me wrong, you can create a wonderful basic Web page with Personal Publisher 3 — but the day may come when you want to do something a little fancier than Personal Publisher allows. This appendix points you in the direction of sources of additional information on Web page design for when that day arrives.

Books

Some people say that computers will eventually mean the end of books as we know them. Well, it hasn't happened yet. In fact, the computer book industry has exploded over the last few years (a fact that tickles me pink, as you might imagine!). Books are published on every imaginable aspect of computers — including Web page design.

AOL's own Book Shop (keyword **Book Shop**), part of the AOL Store (see Figure A-1), is a great place to find Internet-related books, many of them written from an AOL perspective.

Figure A-1: AOL's Book Shop is a great place to find Internet-related books, many of them written from an AOL perspective.

Click Internet from the stack of books at right to see the latest selection of books on Web publishing and design, or check out the Graphics and Multimedia section for books that can help you make your Web site eye- (and even ear-) catching.

Finally, you can always go browsing for books the old-fashioned way — by actually going to a bookstore and seeing what's on the shelves (a process I highly recommend), or visiting your local library.

Wherever you go looking for books, make sure the book you are considering

➡ **contains the information you need.** If you're interested in learning HTML, there's not much point in buying a book entitled *Creating Web Pages Without Knowing HTML*, is there? Check the table of contents.

➡ **is written at an appropriate level.** People with many different levels of computer knowledge are creating Web sites, and so there are books written at many different levels. If you're a beginner, you'll want something that covers the basics clearly and succinctly. If you've been creating Web sites for a while, you may be ready for something more involved. And if you're an old pro, you might be looking for information about topics that would leave a beginner scratching his head in bewilderment. Buying a book written at too high a level won't do you any good if you can't understand it, and buying one written at too low a level won't do you any good since you already know most of what's in it.

➥ **is current.** The Web is constantly changing, and so is the way Web sites are designed. A book on Web site construction written in 1995 won't even touch on some of the things being done on Web sites today, because some of them were impossible in that long-ago (!) era. Generally, the fresher, the better. You can tell when a book was published by checking the copyright date, usually found on the back side of the title page.

Other Books

IDG Books Worldwide, Inc. is one of the largest, with more than 500 titles in print — including my absolute favorite, the book you're holding right now. IDG Books Worldwide maintains a Web site at http://www.idgbooks.com, which is shown in Figure A-2.

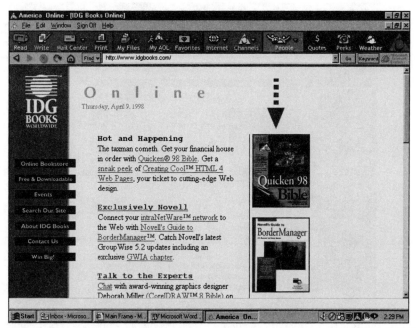

Figure A-2: Looking for a book on any aspect of computers or Web design? IDG Books Worldwide probably has it.

Here are just some of the books related to Web page design that IDG Books Worldwide had available as this was written (there could be more by the time you read it):

Home Page Improvement

Home Page Improvement by Elisabeth A. Parker (published by IDG Books Worldwide, Inc.) shows you how to take your home page to a whole new level of "sophistication, interactivity, and just plain pizzazz." It teaches you how to make your text and graphics more attractive, how to add other types of animation besides animated GIFs, even how to add live video to your site, and comes with a CD-ROM full of useful software and other resources (see Figure A-3).

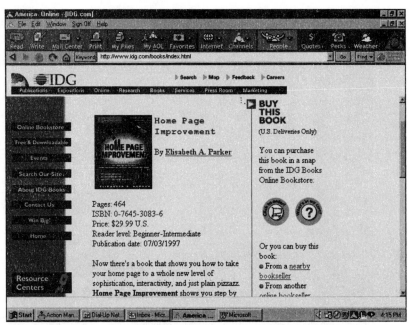

Figure A-3: Books like *Home Page Improvement* can help you guide your home page to the next level of evolution.

HTML & Web Publishing Secrets

Jim Heid, author of *HTML & Web Publishing Secrets* (published by IDG Books Worldwide, Inc.), has experience in writing, design, audio and video production, programming, and publishing — and draws on all of it to provide expert Web-publishing advice in this book. *HTML & Web*

Publishing Secrets is a notch higher on the complexity scale than *Home Page Improvement*, so you wouldn't want to jump into it straight from Personal Publisher 3, but if you're ready to move on to more advanced topics like CGI scripts and the latest HTML enhancements, this book is an excellent guide (see Figure A-4).

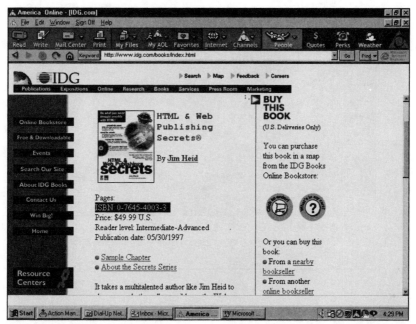

Figure A-4: *HTML & Web Publishing Secrets* and similar books offer more advanced tips, when you're ready for them.

Creating Cool HTML 3.2 & HTML 4 Web Pages

Creating Cool HTML 3.2 Web Pages, Third Edition (published by IDG Books Worldwide, Inc.) and *Creating Cool HTML 4 Web Pages* (also published by IDG Books Worldwide, Inc.), both written by Dave Taylor, are excellent follow-up resources to this book. Tools like Personal Publisher 3 actually generate pages in HTML — you just don't see it, and you don't have to deal with it unless you want to. But to get the most out of your pages, you'll want to.

Creating Cool HTML 3.2 Web Pages (see Figure A-5) and *Creating Cool HTML 4 Web Pages* include step-by-step introductions to HTML, along with real-world examples, important design principles, and helpful marketing tips. Accompanying CD-ROMs feature valuable Web design software tools and sample Web pages.

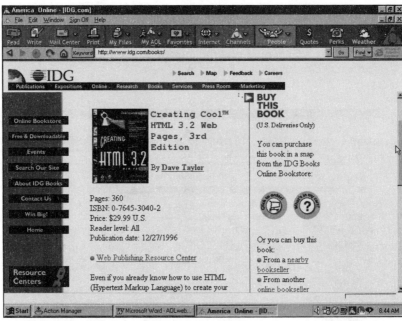

Figure A-5: *Creating Cool HTML 3.2 Web Pages* is a good resource for learning about HTML, the skeleton that underpins all Web pages — so is its sequel, *Creating Cool HTML 4 Web Pages*.

Producing Web Hits

Not satisfied with the number of visitors your site is receiving? Who is? *Producing Web Hits* (published by IDG Books Worldwide, Inc.) by David Elderbrock, Jonathan Ezor, James Nadler, Laura Dalton, and Jed Weissberg delves more fully into how you can convince people to drop by your Web pages than I am able to in Chapter 15. The authors talk about balancing multimedia flash with the need for a fairly quick loading time, tell you how to offer the kind of solid value that draws people to Web sites, show how to measure hits and compile statistics you may be able to use to attract advertisers, and explain how to publicize your site so it shows up near the top of every search engine's results.

Producing Web Hits (see Figure A-6) even comes with a bonus membership to a special Web site containing innovative design elements and sample promotional tools created by the Interactive Telecommunications Program (ITP) at New York University.

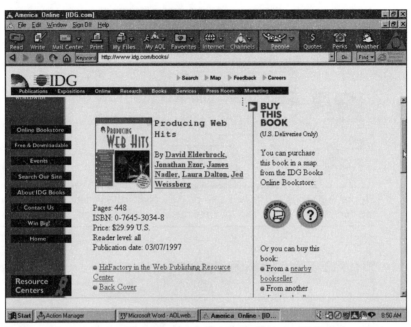

Figure A-6: *Producing Web Hits* can help you make your Web site a popular stop for both surfers and searchers.

AOL Resources

America Online has a number of resources both to help you make the best Personal Publisher page you can, and to move beyond Personal Publisher into more complex Web design efforts. For a detailed description of these resources, see Chapter 7, "Web Publishing Resources on AOL."

In general, the central resource for all things Web-related on AOL is On the Net (keyword **On the Net**). An example of an On The Net screen is shown in Figure A-7.

Among the useful things you can access through On The Net to advance your Web design knowledge are

➡ **live classes.** AOL's Online Classroom (keyword **Online Classroom**) offers courses in everything from HTML basics to counters, guestbooks and forms, animated GIFs, and copyright and Web graphics (see Figure A-8).

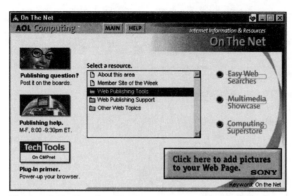

Figure A-7: The On The Net area on AOL contains a variety of information related to the Internet, including help for creating and improving your Web page.

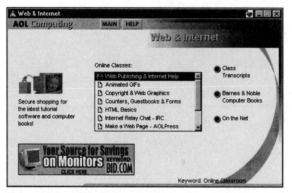

Figure A-8: AOL's Online Classroom is a great place to learn more about creating Web pages.

➡ **AOL Press**. AOL Press (keyword **AOL Press**) is a more advanced Web page creation-and-editing tool than Personal Publisher 3. It uses a WYSIWYG (What You See Is What You Get) interface, so you still don't have to use HTML, and you see exactly what your page will look like on the Web as you work. AOL Press is free, and the Online Classroom even offers courses in how to use it.

➡ **AOL PrimeHost** (keyword **PrimeHost**). PrimeHost is a special Web page hosting service that enables small businesses to create a Web

presence in as little as ten minutes, and maintain it for just $99 a month. Customers can pick a Web site name, choose the layout and design for the Web site from one of the six professionally designed templates, and then customize the Web site with color and style options. Web site owners can also modify Web sites and add to them anytime with AOL Press software, and free technical help is always available. Counters track business to each PrimeHost site. PrimeHost also ensures that each Web site it hosts is listed on Internet search engines such as AOL Netfind and in the AOL Business Directory, where AOL members can search for business Web sites.

➡ **NetHelp.** AOL NetHelp is a World Wide Web page AOL maintains at `http://www.aol.com/nethelp` to answer questions by people who are new to the Internet. It includes a section on Web publishing that contains information about Personal Publisher, My Place, and PrimeHost.

➡ **On The Net Message Boards.** Got a question about Web publishing on AOL to which you just haven't been able to find an answer? You can post your question here and get an answer from an expert (see Figure A-9). Be sure to check out the FAQs first, though; the answer you seek could well be in one of them.

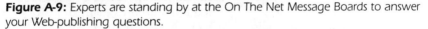

Figure A-9: Experts are standing by at the On The Net Message Boards to answer your Web-publishing questions.

➡ **AOL Multimedia Showcase.** This Web site, easily available by clicking the Multimedia Showcase button on the On The Net main page, is a multimedia extravaganza, built with the latest Web tools. It includes tips and tools for using multimedia and adding it to your Web pages (see Figure A-10).

Figure A-10: If your heart is set on producing a multimedia-laden Web site, you'll want to check out the AOL Multimedia Showcase.

There are a number of AOL areas devoted specifically to graphics, including:

⇒ **The Photography Forum** (keyword **Photography Forum**). Here you can find free advice on obtaining or creating photographs and other images for your Web pages.

⇒ **The Hobby Central** (keyword **Hobby Central**) **Photography Forum.** This is a different site altogether, but it's another good place to learn about the process of putting photographs online. It provides links to oodles of photography-related sites both on AOL and the World Wide Web.

⇒ **Image Exchange** (keyword **Image Exchange**). Here you can obtain images ranging from historical photographs to classic artworks to contemporary celebrity images.

⇒ **PC Graphics Arts Forum** (keyword **PGR**). This is the AOL site devoted to the discussion of using computers to create, manipulate, and store pictures. You can find software, samples, and helpful hints (see Figure A-11).

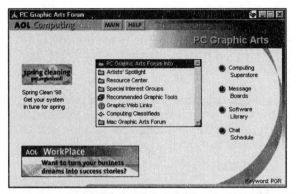

Figure A-11: The PC Graphics Arts Forum is a good place to go if you have questions about adding pictures to your Web page.

Resources on the Web

If there's one thing people who use the World Wide Web like to write about, it's using the World Wide Web, which is why you'll find more information about creating Web pages on the Web than you will anywhere else.

WebReference

The WebReference site (http://www.webreference.com) is loaded with information about all aspects of Web creation and design — and, since it's fully searchable, you can seek out articles on whatever specific topic is of interest to you.

WebMonkey

WebMonkey (http://www.hotwired.com/webmonkey/) is published by HotWired, the online counterpart to print's *Wired* magazine. Subtitled "A How-To Guide for Web Junkies," it features ever-changing articles on Web design and other Web-related topics, such as HTML e-mail, which is e-mail that shows up in the recipient's computer looking like a Web page.

WebMonkey is subdivided into such categories as Web design, HTML, dynamic HTML (used to build interactive Web pages), stylesheets, graphics and fonts, multimedia, browsers (one problem with today's Web pages is that they often look slightly different to different viewers, depending on which browser they're using), Java and JavaScript, Perl, servers, and security. In other words, they cover the Webfront, from A to Z.

TechTools

TechTools is a Web site that you can get to either directly (at `http://www.techweb.com/tools`), or via AOL in the On the Net area. TechTools is part of the enormous CMPNet site.

From the home page, you can access a number of useful areas, including a section devoted to Producers and Designers. Here you can find useful articles ranging from (on the day I visited) "85 Tips for Web Designers" to how to become a multimedia mogul.

Professor Pete's WebMastering 301

Professor Pete's WebMastering 301 (`http://www.professorpete.com/`) is an online course designed to help you create an online business presence. "Professor Pete," a professional Web site designer, promises that after completing the course, you'll have a better understanding of how the Internet can be used by businesses in general and by your business, specifically.

Vincent Flanders's Web Pages That Suck

In this book I've talked a lot about what you should do in the process of developing a Web page or site. Vincent Flanders takes the opposite tactic with his site, Web Pages That Suck (`http://www.webpagesthatsuck.com`), where you "learn good design by looking at bad design."

Flanders puts his money where his mouth is: the page you first see upon entering his site is his first example of bad design. What's wrong with it? Flanders notes that the image is overdone, it doesn't use browser-safe colors, the "ultra-hip" font is overused, there's no way to know what you have to do to get to the next page (it eventually loads automatically, or you can click on the picture — but you can't tell that), there's no information on how to contact the site's owner, and the page has white text on black backgrounds while the rest of the site has white backgrounds — an irritating lack of consistency.

Flanders's site is informative and, even better, funny.

Other Sites

As noted earlier, the Web contains thousands of sites related to Web site design. Just plug the terms you'd like to know more about into any search engine, and you'll see a zillion of 'em. The ones I've listed are good places to start, but there are many more that you might find just as helpful, or even more so. Do some exploring. Fire up AOL NetFind, plug in search terms such as "**Web page design**" or "**Web site creation**," and see what comes up!

Gallery of Cool Web Pages from AOL Members

If one thing's certain, many of America Online's 12 million members have taken advantage of how easy it is to create their own Web pages with Personal Publisher 3 and display them in Hometown AOL. In addition to the AOL members' Web sites already highlighted in the book, on the following pages I've highlighted other creative, entertaining, and otherwise interesting Web pages created by AOL members. Enjoy your gallery tour!

Image of Nepal

This is an interesting use of the "photo album" idea, mainly because it features photos from Nepal that are a lot more interesting that the me-my-wife-and-the-kids photos you find on most photo album Web pages. Notice how small, quick-loading images show you what's in the photos; then, if you want more detail, you can click on the small images to call up a larger, more high-resolution version (http://members.aol.com/mpokhrel).

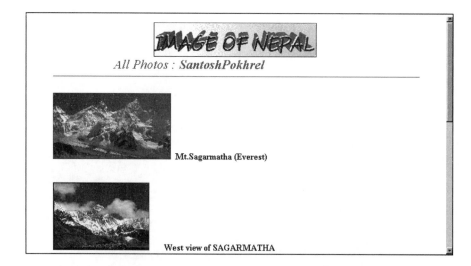

Mt.Sagarmatha (Everest)

West view of SAGARMATHA

The Executable Outlines Series

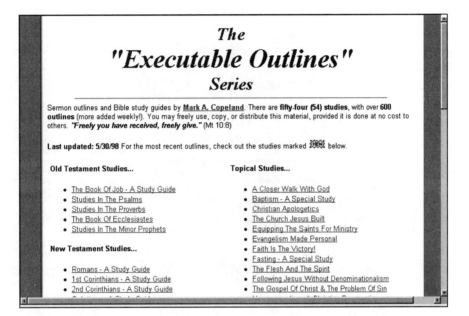

Teachers, preachers, and other public speakers can use the World Wide Web not only to research their presentations, but to share them with others. Florida minister Mark A. Copeland uses this well-done site to share his ready-to-preach sermon outlines (`http://members.aol.com/exeout/index.html`).

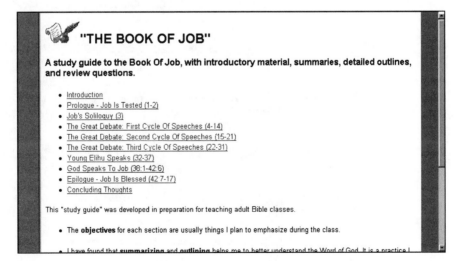

Greyhound Adoption Service

> **Greyhound Adoption Service**
>
> **Who We Are**
>
> Greyhound Adoption Service, Inc. of Salisbury, Massachusetts is a non-profit humane organization dedicated to finding loving, responsible homes for both retired racing greyhounds that can no longer compete and for young greyhounds not placed on the racetrack. Our aim is to let the public know what excellent, loving pets these noble dogs make. Greyhound Adoption Service is operated totally by volunteers and depends on fundraising and donations for its operating expenses. Our small stalwart band of volunteers is responsible for the placement of hundreds of greyhounds. The web site is one of the tools Greyhound Adoption Service uses to educate you, to encourage you to adopt greyhounds and to ask for your support.
>
> **About Our Greyhounds**
>
> Before placement, greyhounds adopted from Greyhound Adoption Service receive a

Have you got a worthy cause you want to promote? You need to be on the World Wide Web like the Greyhound Adoption Service, which finds homes for racing greyhounds who can no longer compete and for young greyhounds that aren't going to be raced (`http://members.aol.com/greycanine`).

> **Greyhounds Available for Adoption**
>
> **Newly Rescued Dogs** - These greyhounds have recently arrived at the kennel, or have lived there for less than one year. Check out the story of newly adopted **Dancer**.
>
> **Hall of Famers** - Hall of famers have been in the kennel for over one year. Are you the right family to finally give these loving dogs a home of their own?
>
> **Special Consideration Dogs** - These dogs have special needs, and require a special family. Can you find a place in your life for one of them?
>
> Look for the ADOPTED ! symbol. These dogs have just been placed in their new homes!

Andy Hoskinson's Home Page

What can you put on your home page? Like Andy Hoskinson, anything you want, from a Gulf War Photo Gallery to articles and essays. Also, as you become more proficient at creating Web pages, you may want to share some of your discoveries. Andy has done that by posting his Java applets (small programs that most browsers run automatically) on his site. He also uses one of his applets to create the scrolling advertisement at left (http://members.aol.com/andyhosk/index.html).

Saxman's Home Page

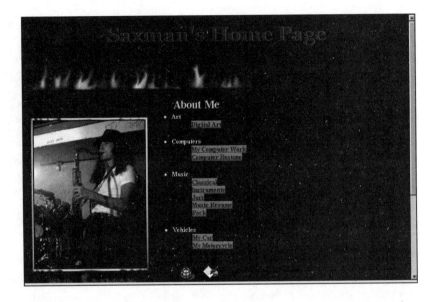

Michael Cooke, (Saxman) is a musician and composer. His Web site includes samples of many of his compositions, which you can listen to while you visit. Michael's site makes excellent use of sound files! (`http://members.aol.com/tfbsaxman/main.html`)

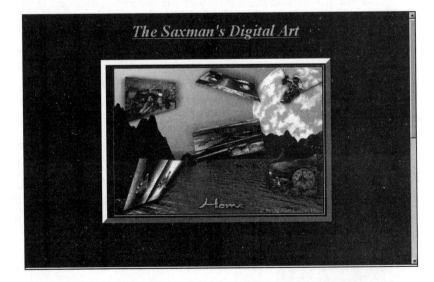

The Vegan Page

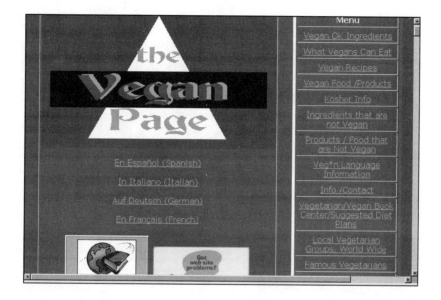

Once upon a time, we were told that one reason we all would have a home computer was to keep our recipes on it. Fortunately, we've found a few more uses for them than that, but recipes and lots of other food topics are still widely available on the World Wide Web. The Vegan Page uses a clear, simple navigation system to guide you to vegan recipes, other vegan foods and products, and information about the vegan lifestyle (http://members.aol.com/docvegan/index.html).

Colin Dalziel's Home Page

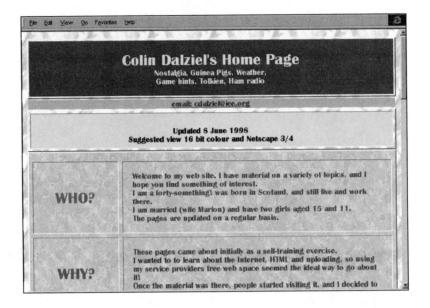

Nostalgia, guinea pigs, weather, game hints, J.R.R. Tolkien, ham radio: Colin Dalziel's home page is a smorgasbord of topics. What's most interesting, however, is his note that he started his Web page just as a learning exercise, to find out more about HTML and Web pages. Once he had his Web page up, though, he found people really enjoyed it — and so did he. You may have the same experience! (http://members.aol.com/cdalziel/homepage.htm)

AirCal

Here's a unique idea for a Web site: the AirCal site is dedicated to the employees of all the airlines that have gone out of business, beginning with Air California but including Braniff, Eastern, and others. The site is full of photos from those airlines' heydays, plus more aviation information and a few links to unrelated (but interesting) topics such as NASCAR. It's an excellent example of how the topic of your Web-site is limited only by your imagination (http://members.aol.com/aircal737/aircal.htm).

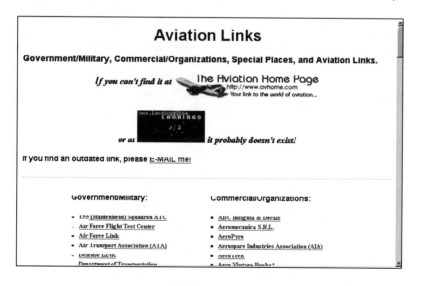

Tux the Portuguese Water Dog

A pet home page is one of the templates available for Personal Publisher 3. Here's an example of an existing pet home page, whose creator (apparently Tux, a Portuguese Water Dog, with help from owner Brendan Gotch) has also used to provide more information about Portuguese Water Dogs and the people who raise them, breed them, and love them (`http://members.aol.com/s500sedan/index.htm`).

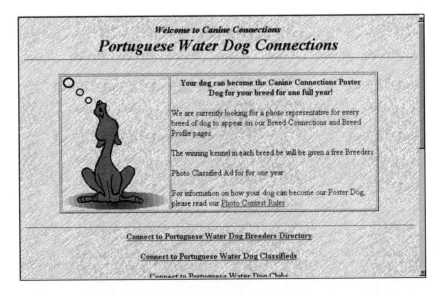

Image-O-Rama

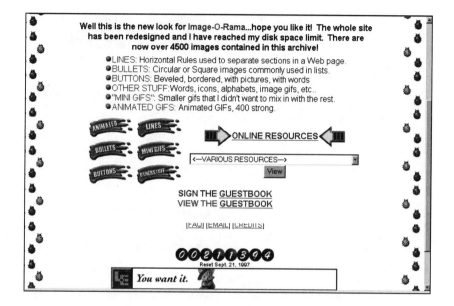

This is not only a cool AOL member's site, it's also a good place to find cool images for your own Web site. People on the World Wide Web love to share, which is what gives us sites like this one (http://members. aol.com/dcreelma/imagesite/image.htm).

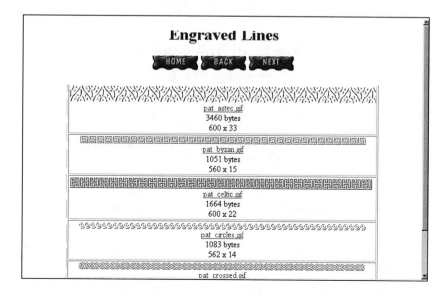

The First Internet Gallery of GIF Animation

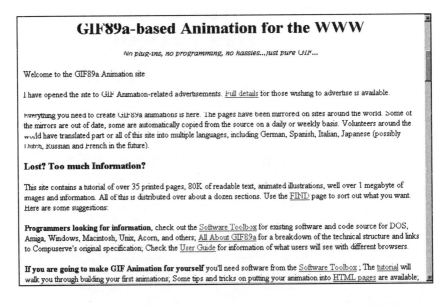

If you're interested in adding animation to your AOL Web site, you should visit the First Internet Gallery of GIF Animation, which also happens to be an AOL Web site. You can find free, ready-to-use GIF animations or learn more about creating your own (`http://members.aol.com/royalef1/galframe.htm`).

GIF89a-based Animation for the WWW

No plug-ins, no programming, no hassles...just pure GIF...

Welcome to the GIF89a Animation site

I have opened the site to GIF Animation-related advertisements. Full details for those wishing to advertise is available.

Everything you need to create GIF89a animations is here. The pages have been mirrored on sites around the world. Some of the mirrors are out of date, some are automatically copied from the source on a daily or weekly basis. Volunteers around the world have translated part or all of this site into multiple languages, including German, Spanish, Italian, Japanese (possibly Dutch, Russian and French in the future).

Lost? Too much Information?

This site contains a tutorial of over 35 printed pages, 80K of readable text, animated illustrations, well over 1 megabyte of images and information. All of this is distributed over about a dozen sections. Use the FIND page to sort out what you want. Here are some suggestions:

Programmers looking for information, check out the Software Toolbox for existing software and code source for DOS, Amiga, Windows, Macintosh, Unix, Acorn, and others; All About GIF89a for a breakdown of the technical structure and links to Compuserve's original specification; Check the User Guide for information of what users will see with different browsers.

If you are going to make GIF Animation for yourself you'll need software from the Software Toolbox ; The tutorial will walk you through building your first animations; Some tips and tricks on putting your animation into HTML pages are available;

Trillogy's Theme Gallery

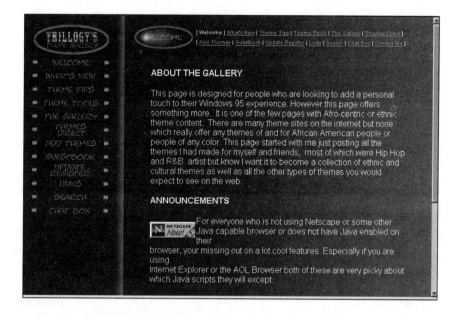

Many Web pages are inspired by a feeling that the Web as it is lacks something. That's what led to Trillogy's Theme Gallery. Here you'll find Windows 95 themes with an Afro-American or ethnic flavor (`http://members.aol.com/~trillogy3`).

Glossary

This glossary contains words used in *America Online's Creating Cool Web Pages* that you may not already be familiar with, and other terms commonly used in the discussion of Web page design that you might encounter elsewhere.

address

The string of characters that identifies the location of a file on the World Wide Web. Also known as the *URL*.

AIFF

Audio Interchange File Format. A digital audio file format used on Macintosh computers.

alignment

The horizontal positioning of an element on a Web page. Left alignment places it against the left side of the page, right alignment places it against the right side, and center alignment places it in the middle.

AltaVista

A popular Internet search engine, located at http://www.altavista.com.

America Online (AOL)

Founded in 1985, AOL is the world's largest online service with more than 12 million subscribers. It was one of the first online services to offer members easy access to the Internet.

animated GIF

A series of GIF graphics that automatically appear one after the other, each one replacing the next, creating the illusion of movement.

animation

Any Web element that appears to move on the screen is said to be animated.

AOL

Short for America Online.

AOL NetFind

AOL's default Internet search engine.

AOLPress

A free Web design software package offered by America Online. It is more complicated, but it also includes more features than Personal Publisher 3.

ARPANET

Advanced Research Projects Agency Network. The research computer network, launched in 1969, that led to the creation of other computer networks and eventually to the creation of the Internet.

ASCII

American Standard Code for Information Interchange. A binary code for text that is built into all personal computers.

AU

The format in which UNIX machines save sound. It's common on the Internet because many of the machines on which the Internet is based are UNIX computers.

AVI

Audio/Video Interleave. The file format used by Video for Windows.

background

The image or color that appears behind the text and graphics in a Web page.

background style

The term Personal Publisher uses for the various combinations of background, text, and link colors it provides with each template.

bandwidth

How much information an electronic line (such as a telephone line) can transmit, usually expressed in bits per second (bps).

banner

A graphic, wider than it is tall, that stretches across a Web page. Often used for advertising.

binary file

Computer files such as programs, word-processing files, and graphics (almost every computer file, in fact, except straight text (ASCII) files).

bit

A binary digit — either a *1* or a *0*. The smallest element of information.

bold text

Text whose characters are thicker than ordinary text. This has the effect of making the text look darker. **This is bold text.**

Boolean operators

Terms used to tell Internet search engines and other databases which words to look for and which to ignore. *AND, OR,* and *AND NOT* are the Boolean operators understood by most search engines.

brightness

The balance of light and dark in an image.

broken link

A hyperlink that goes to a URL that no longer has a Web page associated with it.

browser

Software, such as Netscape Navigator or Microsoft Internet Explorer, that lets users access the World Wide Web and view HTML pages and other content.

bulleted list

A list in which each element is set off by a small graphic image of some sort; often a round dot that looks like a bullet hole, hence the name.

button

A small graphic which, when clicked, causes some action to be performed.

byte

Eight bits, which can represent any number ranging from zero to 255, and through the use of ASCII, a variety of letters and symbols.

caption

Text that provides more information about the contents of a nearby image.

CD-ROM

Compact Disc Read-Only Memory. A compact disc used to store computer data — up to 650 megabytes worth.

CERN

Centre European Researche Nucleare, aka the Center for High-Energy Physics in Geneva, Switzerland. CERN is the birthplace of the World Wide Web.

CGI

Common Gateway Interface. A way in which software that makes use of the Web can pass input to Web servers and on to other software that supports CGI.

channels

AOL's way of categorizing the information available on the online service. Channels have broad names such as Lifestyles or Internet.

clickable image

A graphic that can be clicked to perform some action, usually transferring the viewer to another page.

clip art

Artwork that is purchased or otherwise available for use in Web pages or desktop publishing with few copyright restrictions.

color palette

A Personal Publisher menu from which you may choose the colors to use in your Web Page.

color scheme

The combination of background color, text color, link color, and followed link color used in a Web page.

compression

Saving a file in a more efficient form so it takes up less data storage space.

CompuServe

An online service, owned by AOL, that specializes in services for the business and professional markets.

concept-based finding

A method used by AOL NetFind to increase the number of valuable responses to a search. AOL NetFind looks not only for Web pages that contain the words entered in the search engine but also for other Web pages it judges to be related to the concepts implied by those words.

content

The elements of a Web page — text, photographs, sound, or video — that communicate something to the viewer.

contrast

The range between the lightest and darkest tones in an image.

cool

An indefinable term — but we know it when we see it!

copyright

The exclusive right granted by law to an author, artist, or other creator to sell, print, publish, or reproduce his work in any way.

counter

A piece of software which keeps track of the number of times a Web page is accessed.

crop

To trim an image by adjusting its boundaries.

cyberspace

A term originally coined by William Gibson in his novel *Neuromancer* to describe a futuristic computer network into which people could plug their minds; currently used to describe the online world in general.

data

Information.

database

A collection of related files.

dead link

See *broken link*.

default

A preset option or value that is used unless you specify otherwise.

desktop publishing

The creation of documents using a personal computer. Web page design is closely related to desktop publishing design.

digital

Information which has been converted into a series of numbers so a computer can make use of it.

digital camera

A device like a regular camera, except it stores images as computer-readable digital files instead of on film.

digital imaging

The process of turning a picture, such as a drawing or photograph, into a binary file that a computer can use to display that picture on the screen. A variety of digital image formats are used to store pictures on the World Wide Web; the two most common are GIF and JPEG.

domain

On the Internet, a registration category that helps specify URLs.

download

To receive a file from another computer.

e-mail

Electronic mail. A message sent via a computer network.

emoticons

Emoticons (EMOTional ICONS) are pictures, created with standard keyboard characters, that express emotion. Most are viewed sideways; for example, this :) is a "smiley," which indicates what you've just written is meant to be humorous.

external link

A hyperlink on one Web site that takes visitors to another Web site.

FAQ

Frequently Asked Questions. FAQ files are often created to provide information about Web sites, Usenet newsgroups, software, and other Internet-related topics.

Favorite Places

A list of sites both on AOL and on the Web that you like to visit often, maintained by your AOL software in an easy-to-access list, which can be organized into folders and subfolders.

file

A collection of data — in other words, a word-processing document or a program — that has been given a name and saved in a computer-readable format.

file format

The particular method used to save information on a disk. Programs that use the same file format are able to read each others files.

flaming

To verbally attack someone via e-mail or in a newsgroup or message board.

font

A group of letters, numbers, and symbols in one size or typeface. Arial is a *typeface*; 10-point Arial Bold is a *font*.

form

An interactive screen on a Web browser that allows the viewer to enter information.

frame

A separate, scrollable window within the display of a Web browser.

FTP

File Transfer Protocol. The standard Internet method of transferring files from one machine to another.

GIF

Graphic Interchange Format. A format for efficiently transmitting images from computer to computer popularized by CompuServe in the 1980s and adopted by the designers of the World Wide Web.

graphic

Any visual image used on a Web page, such as clip art, photographs, icons, and bullets.

guestbook

A form that accepts information about visitors and records it.

hardware

Computer equipment, such as the central processing unit, the scanner, the monitor, or the printer.

helper application

An application called by a Web browser that runs in a separate window and displays information the browser cannot handle directly.

hit

The accessing of a Web page. A page that gets a lot of hits has been visited many times.

home page

The page that displays first when a Web site is visited.

Hometown

A Web-based community of people with shared interests.

host

A computer that provides information or signals to a user, other computers, or other devices.

hot spot

Any spot on a Web page that activates a link when clicked.

HotBot

A search engine set up and maintained by the publishers of *Wired* magazine and located at `http://www.hotbot.com`.

HTML

Hypertext Markup Language. The programming language that tells a Web browser what to place on a page and where to place it.

HTTP

Hypertext Transfer Protocol. The method by which Web browsers communicate with host computers.

hyperlink

A link between objects on the Web so that one can be accessed from the other. On Web pages, hyperlinks in text appear in a different color and may be underlined. Hyperlinks can also be attached to graphics.

hypertext

A nonlinear method of organizing data that lets individual elements of the data, especially text, be linked to one another.

icon

A clickable graphic that causes an action to be performed, and whose appearance usually attempts to communicate what that action will be.

imagemap

A graphic in which several hyperlinks are embedded, so that different actions are performed depending on which portions of the graphic are clicked.

indent

To move an object farther from either the left or right margin of a page.

InfoSeek

An Internet search engine located at http://www.infoseek.com.

interactive

An adjective applied to any Web page or computer program that allows and responds to user input.

internal link

A hyperlink that leads to information within the same Web site that contains the link.

Internet

The worldwide network of millions of computers linked together by the TCP/IP protocol. The World Wide Web is one portion of the Internet.

intranet

A TCP/IP-based computer network within an organization, and which may or may not be connected to the Internet.

inverted pyramid style

A style of writing invented for newspapers in which the most important information appears in the first paragraph of a story, with less important information appearing in each subsequent paragraph.

italic text

A way to format text in which all the letters slant to the right. *This is italic text.*

Java

A programming language designed for use on the Internet which is independent of the type of machine running it; in other words, as long as the machine has a Java interpreter, it doesn't matter if it's a PC, a Macintosh, or a UNIX computer.

JavaScript

A simplified version of Java, developed by Netscape, that uses a Web page as its user interface.

JPEG

Joint Photographic Experts Group. An alternative form of compressing graphic files that is most often used to display photographs on the Web, because it can display millions of colors (unlike GIF, which can only display 256 colors).

K

Kilobyte. 1K equals 1,024 bytes, 16K equals 16,384 bites, 64K equals 65,536 bytes, and so on.

keyword

A word assigned to a particular area of America Online. By entering a keyword, you can go directly to that area.

killer app

Killer application. An application so exciting that it causes a new technology to gain wide acceptance.

link

See *hyperlink*.

Lycos

Another popular Internet search engine, located at http://www.lycos.com.

megabyte

One million bytes. Also abbreviated *MB* or *meg*.

menu

A list of possible actions or choices presented to a user by the computer.

message board

An area on America Online where users can post questions and exchange messages about a particular topic.

MIDI

Musical Instrument Digital Interface. A method for encoding the pitches, tempo, and instrumentation of a musical piece so that computers and synthesizers can recreate it.

modem

Modulator-Demodulator. A device which converts the digital signals from a computer into analog signals that can be sent along an ordinary phone line, and converts analog signals from the phone line into digital ones a computer can understand.

MOV

The file format used by Apple Computer's QuickTime video system to store video clips.

MPEG

Moving Pictures Experts Group. A method of compressing sound and video files so they don't take up so much data storage space.

multimedia

The use of more than one medium to communicate, especially media other than text or graphics, such as sound, video, or animation.

My Place

The name AOL gives to the two megabytes of data storage space provided to each AOL screen name (10MB per account), where Web pages and other files can be placed.

newsgroup

A discussion group on the Internet involving an ongoing series of messages about a particular topic.

online service

A computer network similar to the Internet that people pay to join, and which may or may not be connected to the Internet. America Online is an online service; so is CompuServe.

Perl

Practical Extraction Report Language. A programming language designed specifically for system administration and widely used on Web servers.

pixel

A picture element. One dot on the computer screen of all the dots that make up an image.

placeholders

Elements, such as text and graphics, within Personal Publisher 3 templates that you can replace with your own elements.

plug-in

An auxiliary program that works with another program, especially a Web browser, to enhance its capabilities.

PrimeHost

A Web-hosting service from AOL designed specifically for businesses. PrimeHost offers more space for Web site storage, Web-authoring software with more features than Personal Publisher, online technical support, marketing advice, and more.

publish

To place Web pages on a server and give them URLs, so they can be accessed from the World Wide Web.

resize

To change the size of a graphic.

resolution

The number of pixels or dots per inch (ppi or dpi, respectively) in an image, either on the screen or on paper.

scale

To change the size of a graphic without changing its proportions.

scanner

A device that captures a photographic image and converts it into a digital form a computer can handle.

search engine

Software that searches the Internet for information that contains key words provided by a user.

server

A computer in a network that will respond to requests for information from other computers.

software

Instructions for a computer that tell it how to process data; a computer program.

sound file

A collection of data that contains the information necessary for a computer to recreate a recorded sound.

source code

The statements and instructions written by a computer programmer.

spam

Unsolicited copies of the same message sent to large numbers of people on Internet newsgroups or via e-mail.

surf

Slang for exploring the World Wide Web, following hyperlinks from site to site.

TCP/IP

Transmission Control Protocol/Internet Protocol. The set of rules that govern the way computers on the Internet communicate.

template

A blueprint for a Web page in which the various elements can be replaced, using Personal Publisher, with elements of the Personal Publisher user's own choosing.

thumbnail

A miniature copy of an image, which on Web pages is often linked to a larger copy of the same image.

TOS

Terms of Service. The terms that all members of America Online have agreed to abide by as a condition of service.

unlink

To remove a hyperlink.

unpublish

To remove Web pages from a server so they are no longer accessible from the World Wide Web.

upload

To transmit information from your computer to another computer.

uppercase text

Text in all capital letters. THIS IS UPPERCASE TEXT.

URL

Uniform Resource Locator. The complete address of information stores somewhere on the Internet.

Usenet

User Network. A network within the Internet that provides user news and e-mail. About 10,000 newsgroups (online discussion groups) are active on Usenet.

utility

A program that performs a useful system or maintenance function.

vexillography

The art of designing flags. This has nothing to do with Web pages, but it's a cool word.

video file

A file that contains the information necessary for a computer to play back moving images.

virtual reality

Computer-generated graphics and sound that create the illusion of a fully functional three-dimensional world through which a user can move at will and interact with objects.

WAV

The standard Windows format for waveform recording.

waveform

A form of sound recording in which an analog signal created by the sound has been turned into a digital file which a computer can play back.

Web site

A particular Web page or group of pages stored at the same location, and usually linked to one another.

WebCrawler

An Internet search engine located at `http://www.webcrawler.com`.

Webmaster

The person responsible for managing a particular Web site.

wizard

Computer-generated help that guides a user through a series of steps to accomplish a task.

World Wide Web

A collection of electronic documents, accessible through the Internet, that are linked to each other. Each document is called a *Web page*. Links in one Web page let users jump to other pages, whether those pages are on the same computer or stored on another computer halfway around the world. Web pages are viewed with software called *browsers*, such as Netscape Navigator or AOL's version of Internet Explorer.

Yahoo!

An online directory that categorizes Web sites by subject matter, located at `http://www.yahoo.com`.

(continued)

(continued)

The Official AOL BOOK COLLECTION

America Online Tour Guide, Version 4.0

The definitive guide for AOL members since its first edition in 1992. This all-new edition covers all the exciting, new, timesaving, fun features of AOL's latest release, AOL 4.0! Your personal tourguide to AOL, it takes you through the basics, then helps you advance, by explaining some of more powerful features that are built into the service. The original AOL guide, author Tom Lichty has helped more than 1 million AOL members get started. You'll appreciate his engaging and humorous style. Over 600 pages - everything you need to know to enhance your online experience with AOL. For both Windows and Macintosh users.

Item # 5053 $24.95

The Official America Online Yellow Pages

Want to find a particular area on AOL but don't have much time to search? Then let the all new Official America Online Yellow Pages help you find what you are looking for instantly! This complete guide covers thousands of AOL sites, providing full descriptions and keywords. It makes accessing news, stock quotes, sports stats, and even the latest entertainment scoop, as easy as typing in one word. Organized in Yellow Pages style, it will save you time & money by helping you find what you want on AOL fast!

Item # 5468 $24.95

The Insider's Guide to America Online

AOL's own Meg has written the first true Insider's guide to America Online. Experienced AOLers know Meg as the author of all the cool Inside tips at Keyword: Insider. In this book, Meg has compiled and organized those great tips to give you the inside scoop on AOL: the BEST areas and the most USEFUL tools. Learn how to manage your personal finances and investments online, find bargains on everything from flowers to automobiles, locate the best areas for kids and families, find the lowest airfares and best travel deals…and much more.

Item # 5461 $24.95

Upgrade & Repair Your PC
on a Shoestring - AOL Members Edition

Suffering from new computer envy? Well don't throw that old computer away just yet! This book provides the solid advice and information you need to make your computer run faster and do the things you want without a Ph.D. in Computer Technology and a boatload of money! Four sections talk you through upgrading your PC with lots of friendly advice and encouragement. From determining what you need, to explaining components and what they do, to the Nuts & Bolts with complete illustrations and instructions, to resources on AOL to help you through the process. This book also features the information you need to troubleshoot and make simple repairs yourself. Written in simple, easy to understand language for all computer users .

Item # 5055 $24.95

TO ORDER CALL: 1-800-844-3372 EXT. 1027

Power Up AOL AND YOUR PC

AOL Member Exclusive!

An AOL Exclusive!
America Online's
Power Suite

Turbo-charge your AOL and Internet experience!

See your computer *work harder*, *run smarter* and do *more* for you!

Detect and Fix modem problems!

America Online's PowerSuite

Turbo-charge your computer and make it work harder and run smarter! An AOL exclusive, the new PowerSuite CD-ROM is the only software that gives you 14 power-packed programs, utilities and games to make the most of your computing and AOL experience!

✔ Search the Web faster and easier than ever before!

✔ Add full motion video and audio to your e-mail!

✔ Update your software with Oil Change!

✔ Uninstall files easily and create archives!

✔ Easily organize and manage business and personal contacts!

✔ Deluxe Casino Games Pak! BONUS

Item # 6550 $29.95

TO ORDER CALL: 1-800-844-3372 EXT. 1027

Order your **Books and AOL Planner Collections Today**

To order by phone: **1-800-884-3372**, ext. 1027
To order by fax: 1-800-827-4595

Item #	Title	Quantity	Unit Price	Total Price
5532	AOL Official Guide the Internet, 2nd Edition		$24.95	
5517	World Wide Web Yellow Pages AOL Edition		$34.99	
5469	AOL Insider's Guide to Finding Information Online		$24.95	
5053	America Online Tour Guide, Version 4.0		$24.95	
5468	The Official America Online Yellow Pages		$24.95	
5461	The Insider's Guide to America Online		$24.95	
5055	Upgrade & Repair Your PC on a Shoestring		$24.95	
6550	America Online's PowerSuite		$29.95	
6708	America Online's GraphicSuite		$29.95	
6748	AOL's Internet AcceleratorSuite		$39.95	
2817	The AOL Mouse Netbook		$29.95	
2807	Watermen Pen for AOL Members		$29.95	
2809	AOL Pocket Netbook		$15.95	

Prices subject to change without notice.

Shipping and Handling:
Under $20.00 = $4.00
$21.00 - $30.00 = $4.25
$31.00 - 40.00 = $4.75
Over $50.00 = $5.00

Subtotal $ _____

Shipping & Handling $ _____

Sales Tax may be applicable $ _____

Total $ _____

ORDERED BY:

Name _____

Address _____

City/State/Zip Code _____

Daytime Phone Number (_____) _____-_____

SHIP TO: (if different from above)

Name _____

Address _____

City/State/Zip Code _____

Daytime Phone Number (_____) _____-_____

METHOD OF PAYMENT
☐ VISA
☐ MasterCard
☐ Discover
☐ American Express

☐☐☐☐☐☐☐☐☐☐☐☐☐☐☐☐
Account Number

Expiration Date: ☐☐ - ☐☐

_____
Signature
(Required for all credit card orders)

Send order form and payment to:
America Online, Inc.
Department 1024
P.O. Box 2530
Kearneysville, WV 25430-9935

BB27